THE
CRIMINAL LAW
OF
SCOTLAND

Second Cumulative Supplement

to the

SECOND EDITION

THE CRIMINAL LAW
OF SCOTLAND

by

GERALD H. GORDON
Q.C., LL.D.

Sheriff of Glasgow and Strathkelvin, sometime
Professor of Scots Law in the University of Edinburgh

SECOND CUMULATIVE SUPPLEMENT
TO THE SECOND EDITION
Up to date to October 1, 1991

Published under the auspices of
THE SCOTTISH UNIVERSITIES LAW INSTITUTE

EDINBURGH
W. GREEN/SWEET & MAXWELL
1992

First published in 1992
Reprinted in 1993

ISBN Main work 0 414 00618 6
ISBN Second cumulative supplement 0 414 00996 7

A catalogue record for this book
is available from the British Library

Typeset by LBJ Enterprises Limited, Alderrmaston and Chilcompton
Printed in Great Britain by BPCC Hazell Books Ltd., Aylesbury, Bucks.

PREFACE

This supplement is intended to bring the law up to date as at October 1, 1991, except that I have treated statutes passed before that date as if they were in force.

GERALD H. GORDON

Glasgow
October 1991

TABLE OF CASES

TABLE OF STATUTES

(References to repealed provisions are omitted except where the old law is discussed. References in **bold** type indicate that all or most of the statutory text is quoted.)

PUBLIC ACTS

STATUTORY INSTRUMENTS

1989 Draft Code
A Criminal Code for England and Wales, Vol. 1: *Draft Criminal Code Bill.* Law Commission No. 177. H.C. Papers 1989, No. 299.

TEXT

Note—The numbers in bold type in the left hand margin refer to paragraphs of the main work.

INTRODUCTION

PARA. NO.

0–09 Add new section:
A note on maximum penalties

0–10 Certain changes have been made in the maximum penalties available on summary conviction of statutory offences as a result of the Criminal Justice Act 1982 which inserted new sections 289B, 289F and 289G into the 1975 Act. These complicated provisions are discussed in Renton and Brown, 5th edition, paras. 1–05a, 17–03a and b, and 17–22a–d. Statements of penalties in the main work and this supplement must be read subject to these provisions, of which the most important are as follows.

0–11 (1) *Indictable offences*
(i) The maximum penalties available on 10th April 1983 on summary conviction of an indictable statutory offence created by an enactment passed not later than the session in which the Criminal Law Act 1977 was passed are to be amended according to the following table, unless provision is expressly made by any enactment for a larger penalty: s.289B(1). For a discussion of the meaning, if any, of that exception, see Renton and Brown (5th edition), para. 17–03a.

1

Column 1	*Column 2*
Penalty or maximum penalty at commencement of section 55 of Criminal Justice Act 1982	*New maximum penalty*
1. Fine (other than a fine specified in paragraph 3 below, or a fine in respect of each period of a specified length during which a continuing offence is committed).	1. Fine not exceeding the prescribed sum.
2. Imprisonment for a period exceeding 3 months.	2. Imprisonment for a period not exceeding 3 months.
3. Fine in respect of a specified quantity or number of things.	3. Fine not exceeding the prescribed sum in respect of each such quantity or number.
4. Fine exceeding £100 in respect of each period of a specified length during which a continuing offence is committed.	4. Fine not exceeding £100 in respect of each such period.

The prescribed sum was originally £1,000, but was increased to £5,000 by the Criminal Justice Act 1991, section 17. The maximum fine available on summary conviction of any indictable offence mentioned in the principal work or in this supplement is therefore £5,000, unless a larger amount is stated.

(ii) Where different fines are provided on a first and on subsequent summary convictions, the largest fine is now available on any summary conviction: s.298B(2).

0–12
(2) *Summary offences* (see Renton and Brown, para. 1–05a)

(i) Where any Act passed on or before 29th July 1977 (the date of the passing of the Criminal Law Act 1977) provides a maximum fine of less than £1,000 for a summary offence, and that fine has not been altered by the Criminal Law Act 1977, or by Schedule 7D to the 1975 Act, as inserted by Schedule 6 to the Criminal Justice Act 1982 with effect from 11th April 1983, or by any legislation between those dates, then, except for fines for each period of a specified length during which a continuing offence is committed, the fine was increased with effect from 11th April 1983 in accordance with the following table: s.289F(8).

Column 1 *Fine or* *maximum fine*	*Column 2* *Increased amount*
Under £25	£25
Under £50 but not less than £25	£50
Under £200 but not less than £50	£200
Under £400 but not less than £200	£500
Under £1,000 but not less than £400	£1,000

(ii) Almost all fines for summary offences are now expressed in terms of levels on a standard scale and not in monetary amounts. The original standard scale was as follows: s.289G(2).

Standard Scale	
Level	*Amount*
1	£25
2	£50
3	£200
4	£500
5	£1,000

The levels, as set by section 17 of the Criminal Justice Act 1991 are as follows:

Level	*Amount*
1	£200
2	£500
3	£1,000
4	£2,500
5	£5,000

The result of all this is that where, for example, the maximum fine for a summary offence had not been increased by the Criminal Law Act 1977, or between the passing of that Act and 11th April 1983, and was more than £400 at that date, it was increased to £1,000 then by the table in s.289F(8) of the 1975 Act. At the same time it was translated into a fine of level 5 in accordance with the table in s.289G(2) of that Act. It is now increased to £5,000, while remaining a fine of level 5.

The scale does not apply to fines for each period of a specified length of time during which a continuing offence is committed.

0–13 (iii) Where different penalties are provided for a first and for subsequent convictions, the largest penalty is now available on any conviction: s.289E.

0–14 References in this work to fines of a given level are references to fines for summary offences, the level being the level on the standard scale.

Where the reference to the maximum penalty on conviction on indictment, for any offence triable on indictment or summarily, includes a fine, the reference to the maximum penalty on summary conviction should be read as including a fine of the prescribed sum, unless a specific sum is mentioned.

CHAPTER 1

CRIMES, OFFENCES AND THE DECLARATORY POWER

1–04 In *R.* v. *Hull Visitors, ex p. Germain* [1979] Q.B. 425, 452A, Shaw, L.J. spoke of "the essential characteristic of a criminal cause or matter, namely, that it is a penal proceeding for the infraction of a requirement relating to the enforcement and preservation of public law and order."

Footnote 6. *McGregor* v. *T.* is now reported at 1975 S.C. 14.
Footnote 8. *Cordiner, Petr.* is now reported at 1973 J.C. 16.

1–06 Footnote 9. See now Renton and Brown, 5th ed., paras. 12–02 to 12–07.
Footnote 11. See now Renton and Brown, 5th ed., paras. 13–10 to 13–18.

1–10 The Incest Act 1567 was repealed by the Incest and Related Offences (Scotland) Act 1986, thus leaving the corroboration rule as the only remaining link between Scots criminal law and the Old Testament, but intercourse between uncle and niece is still criminal.

1–13 In *Marcel Beller Ltd.* v. *Hayden* [1978] Q.B. 694, which concerned the interpretation of a clause in a life insurance policy which excluded death caused by "a criminal act," it was held that the offences of driving dangerously and driving while unfit through drink were "criminal acts," and would be included as such even if the exclusion were limited to crimes of moral culpability or turpitude.

Footnote 42. See now Road Traffic Act 1988, s.1.

1–26 It is now accepted that to have intercourse with a woman too drunk to give or refuse consent, where she has not been made drunk by the accused, is to commit indecent assault, and the same would apply to intercourse with a sleeping woman: *Sweeney and Anr.* v. *X.*, 1982 S.C.C.R. 509. See *infra*, para. 33–21.

1–29 Footnote 17. See now Road Traffic Act 1988, s.28, which, as amended by s.7 of the Road Traffic Act 1991, applies only to dangerous cycling as therein defined.

1–30 Footnote 24. Now s.178 of the Road Traffic Act 1988.

5

Parliament has now declared that private sexual activity between consenting adult males is not criminal: Criminal Justice (Scotland) Act 1980, s.80.

Shameless indecency was long thought of as a description of certain forms of behaviour between two or more persons, present together in one place, with at least one of them indulging in some kind of sexual behaviour directed towards the other or others. Lord Maxwell said in *Dean* v. *John Menzies (Holdings) Ltd.*, 1981 J.C. 23 at 38, that he supposed "that in the past the crime usually concerned actual physical conduct of the human body"; and, on the supposition that shameless indecency is *a* crime, it did concern itself with that. The crime has, however, been extended to cover quite different situations. This process began in *Watt* v. *Annan*, 1978 J.C. 84, where what the accused had done was to exhibit an obscene film to a number of adult males, *i.e.* run a stag movie night, and he was charged with conducting himself in a shamelessly indecent manner and exhibiting "a film of an obscene or indecent nature which was liable to create depraved, inordinate and lustful desires in those watching it and to corrupt the morals of the lieges." Macdonald's dictum was approved, and it was said that it was for Parliament and not the courts to set limits to it. The converse argument, that any application of the dictum (which technically could have no authority other than as a generalisation of common law decisions) to behaviour of a kind so different from that envisaged by Macdonald could be made only by Parliament, clearly did not find favour with the court. Lord Cameron said at page 89:

> "Whether or not conduct which is admittedly indecent or obscene is to be held criminal will depend on proof of the necessary *mens rea* and upon the facts and circumstances of the particular case. It would be impracticable as well as undesirable to attempt to define precisely the limits and ambit of this particular offence, far less to decide that the nature of the premises or place in which the conduct charged has occurred should alone be decisive in transforming conduct which would otherwise be proper subject of prosecution into conduct which may do no more than offend the canons of personal propriety or standards of contemporary morals. If it were considered desirable or necessary that this was a chapter of the criminal law in which precise boundaries or limits were to be set then the task is one which is more appropriate for the hand of the legislator."

The only limitation on the crime of shameless indecency is, as Lord Cameron put it, at pages 88–89, that:

> "It was accepted, and rightly so, in the submission for the Crown that the conduct to be criminal, in such circumstances as the facts in the present case disclose, must be directed towards some person or persons with an intention or knowledge that it should corrupt or be calculated or liable to corrupt or deprave those towards whom the indecent or obscene conduct was directed."

The offence was further extended in a series of cases (especially *Robertson* v. *Smith*, 1980 J.C. 1) so as to apply to circumstances virtually indistinguishable from those of the statutory offence of selling or exposing for sale obscene material, the purpose of the Crown in seeking such an extension being apparently to circumvent the smallness of the penalty then provided by Parliament for that statutory offence. The crime in such a case is described as selling, exposing for sale and having for sale, indecent and obscene books likely to deprave and corrupt the morals of the lieges and to create in their minds inordinate and lustful desires. The view of the court was that simply to expose for sale material known to be obscene, *i.e.* corrupting, constituted shameless indecency.

Despite its rapid and apparently successful development (on which see Gerald H. Gordon, "Shameless Indecency and Obscenity" (1980) 25 J.L.S. 262; G. Maher, "The Enforcement of Morals Continued," 1978 S.L.T. (News) 281; J.B. Stewart, "Obscenity Prosecutions," 1982 S.L.T. (News) 93; I.D. Willock, "Shameless Indecency—How Far has the Crown Office Reached?" (1981) 52 SCOLAG Bul. 199) it may be that this offence does not have much of a future. Its practical use is much limited by the decision in *Dean* v. *John Menzies (Holdings) Ltd.*, *supra*, that it cannot be committed by a corporation, and the need to resort to it has been much reduced by the provision of substantial penalties for the statutory offence of dealing in obscene materials contrary to section 51 of the Civic Government (Scotland) Act 1982. The *John Menzies* case also disturbed the theoretical basis of the whole development. Lord Cameron, who gave the opinions of the court in *Watt* v. *Annan, supra*, and *Robertson* v. *Smith, supra*, said in *John Menzies* that the shamelessness libelled in an obscenity case was objective, consisting of conduct known to be corrupting, and so was something with which the moral obliquity of the actor had nothing to do: 1981 J.C. at 32. The majority, however, while accepting *Robertson* v. *Smith*, held that all forms of shameless indecency did indeed require shamelessness and indecency in a subjective sense. The accused must, said Lord Stott, be "so lost to any sense of shame" as to authorise the sale of the material: at 36; and Lord Maxwell said that a finding of guilt implied that the accused had used his judgment and discretion in deciding to sell the material "in an indecent and shameless fashion": at 38. If these are requirements of shameless indecency it becomes very difficult to support *Robertson* v. *Smith*, and perhaps only a little less difficult to support *Watt* v. *Annan*—certainly they make the crime more difficult to prove than would the approach of Lord Cameron which requires no more than is needed to prove that the accused knowingly sold articles held by the court to be obscene.

The result of *John Menzies (Holdings) Ltd.* may be, therefore, to introduce some common sense into what was described by Lord Stott in that case as "an area of law in which (as is perhaps indicated by the archaic and faintly ludicrous wording of the complaint) commonsense is not noticeably at a premium": 1981 J.C. at 37. Lord Maxwell in that case expressed sympathy with the view that "in the realm of what is in substance censorship of certain types of magazines, literature, films etc. on the grounds that they are socially unacceptable, it would perhaps be preferable that the matter be dealt with by statute rather than the existing common law, which was I think designed to meet rather different problems": 1981 J.C. at 38. It may be that the strange eruption of shameless indecency into the already peculiar field of obscenity will come to be seen as merely a temporary crop which withered and died under the attack of *Dean* v. *John Menzies (Holdings) Ltd.*

1–32   In *Sommerville* v. *Tudhope*, 1981 J.C. 58 the High Court declined to hold that it was a crime for a wholesaler to possess obscene material for distribution to retailers, on the ground that the public did not resort to wholesale premises so that no affront to public decency or morals was involved. It was said that the penalisation of the mere possession of pornography, as distinct from its exposure for sale, involved "issues of public and social policy which . . . are for the legislature to resolve, but not to be resolved by an unwarranted extension of the common law.": at 64.

In *R.* v. *H.M. Advocate*, 1988 S.L.T. 623 the High Court held that any sexual relationship between parent and child constitutes the crime of shameless indecency as being behaviour which is repugnant to society, even where it does not involve sexual intercourse.

Footnote 36. See Lillian Faderman, *Scotch Verdict* (London, 1985) for an account of this case.

1–34   *Dalton* was followed in *Dean* v. *Stewart*, 1980 S.L.T. (Notes) 85 where it was held to be an attempt to pervert the course of justice to give the police false information as to the identity of the driver of a car which had failed to stop after an accident.

See also *Fletcher* v. *Tudhope*, 1984 S.C.C.R. 267: assisting person to evade police search; *Waddell* v. *MacPhail*, 1986 S.C.C.R. 593 is similar to *Dean* v. *Stewart*.

1–37   Footnote 53. See now Prisons (Scotland) Act 1989, s.13.

1–39   *Kerr* v. *Hill* was approved by the Court of Appeal in *R.* v. *Thomas (Derek)* [1979] Q.B. 326 where it was held to be an attempt to pervert the course of justice to make a false accusation. Wasting the time of the police by falsely reporting an offence or giving rise to apprehension for the safety of person or property, or that one has information material to a police inquiry is a summary offence in England under section 5(2) of the Criminal Law Act 1967. The offence extends in Scotland to any false report to the police, whether or not it involves an accusation of any kind: *Bowers* v. *Tudhope*, 1987 S.L.T. 748; *Robertson* v. *Hamilton*, 1988 S.L.T. 70. See *infra*, para. 48–39.

Footnote 73. See now Road Traffic Act 1988, ss.171, 172; Telecommunications Act 1984, s.43(1)(*b*).

1–40   It is not, however, a breach of the peace merely to sniff glue while in such a state of intoxication as to be oblivious of one's surroundings: *Fisher* v. *Keane*, 1981 J.C. 50; but see *infra*, para. 41–04.

Add new paragraphs **1–40a** to **1–40c**:

1–40a   *Malicious mischief.* In *H.M. Advocate* v. *Wilson*, 1984 S.L.T. 117 it was held that the crime of malicious mischief was not limited to causing physical damage to corporeal property, but extended to cases where loss was caused without any such damage. In that case a generator had been stopped by the pressing of a switch, causing a loss of electricity which cost well over £100,000 to replace: see commentary at 1983 S.C.C.R. 420.

1–40b *Supplying solvents for sniffing.* Although the crimes in *Khaliq* v. *H.M. Advocate*, 1984 J.C. 23 and *Ulhaq* v. *H.M. Advocate*, 1990 S.C.C.R. 593, in which the accused were charged with supplying other persons with solvents, knowing they were to be used for inhalation to the danger of their health and lives, are examples of administering drugs and/or culpably and recklessly endangering life and health, they might be seen from a pragmatic point of view as an extension of the law in order to control the undesirable but not illegal practice of glue-sniffing. *Cf.* Timothy H. Jones, "Common Law and Criminal Law; the Scottish Example" [1990] Crim. L.R. 292.

1–40c *Dishonest exploitation of confidential information.* In *Grant* v. *Allan*, 1988 S.L.T. 11 the High Court held that to copy confidential information obtained as a result of one's employment and offer to sell it was not so obviously criminal in nature as to justify the invocation of the declaratory power.

CHAPTER 2

THE CONCEPT OF RESPONSIBILITY

2–09 See Andrew Ashworth, *Sentencing and Penal Policy* (London, 1983) for a general review of recent sentencing theory and practice. For two recent interesting treatments of the problem of punishment, see R.A. Duff, *Trials and Punishments* (C.U.P., 1986) and Nicola Lacey, *State Punishment* (London and New York, 1988).

2–11 See D.J. Galligan, "The Return to Retribution in Penal Theory," in *Crime, Proof and Punishment*, ed. Tapper (London, 1981), 144.

2–14 See also N.D. Walker, "The Efficiency and Morality of Deterrents" [1979] Crim. L.R. 129; "Punishing, Denouncing or Reducing Crime," in *Reshaping the Criminal Law*, ed. Glazebrook (London, 1978), 391; "The Ultimate Justification," in *Crime, Proof and Punishment*, ed. Tapper (London, 1981), 109.

Footnote 40. For an interesting variation on this approach, see Nicola Lacey, *op. cit.*

2–17 See also *Kiely* v. *Lunn*, 1983 J.C. 4. *Brennan* v. *H.M. Advocate* is now reported at 1977 J.C. 38.

THE CRIMINAL ACT

3–02   In *Niven* v. *Tudhope*, 1982 S.C.C.R. 365 a conviction for indecent exposure was quashed because of the absence of any finding of "wilful conduct."

3–10   See also *The Queen* v. *O'Connor* (1980) 54 A.L.J.R. 349.

3–13   *Cf.* 1989 Draft Code, section 33(1), which treats as automatic actions which are reflexes, spasms or convulsions, or which occur while the actor is in a condition of sleep, unconsciousness, impaired consciousness or otherwise which deprives him of effective control of the act, and are not the result of intoxication. Automatism is not relevant under this subsection where it is the result of conduct of the accused which exhibited the degree of fault required for the offence in question.

3–14   For an example of a reaction to a sudden and unexpected attack which does not count as a reflex action, see *Jessop* v. *Johnstone*, 1991 S.C.C.R. 238.

3–15   See *H.M. Advocate* v. *Raiker*, 1989 S.C.C.R. 149, 154, *infra*, para. 12–16.

3–16   To be classed as automatic, behaviour must be wholly unconscious, and a person who acts when his consciousness is merely clouded, is not acting automatically: *Roberts* v. *Ramsbottom* [1980] 1 W.L.R. 823. Behaviour which is purposive cannot count as automatic behaviour: *R.* v. *Isitt* [1977] 67 Cr.App.R. 44, where the accused drove off after an accident and engaged in manoeuvres designed to escape from pursuing police officers while he was in a fugue and his mind was shut to moral inhibitions. See also *Broome* v. *Perkins* [1987] R.T.R. 321.

3–18 to 3–22   *Cunningham* was overruled by *Ross* v. *H.M. Advocate*, 1991 S.L.T. 564, and it is no longer the law that *any* mental or pathological condition short of insanity goes only to mitigation. *Ross* in effect gives the authority of a full bench to *H.M. Advocate* v. *Ritchie*, 1926 J.C. 45. The accused in *Ritchie* was charged with culpable homicide by killing a pedestrian by reckless driving, and he lodged a special defence that "by the incidence of temporary mental dissociation due to toxic exhaustive factors he was unaware of the presence of the deceased . . . and was incapable of appreciating his . . . actions." He was acquitted. *Ritchie* was specifically overruled in *Cunningham*, but was approved in *Ross*, except that *Ross* holds that while the evidential burden of raising the issue of automatism rests on the accused, the persuasive burden of establishing *mens rea* remains on the Crown. It seems also that the defence of non-insane automatism is not technically a special defence requiring notice, although that point was left undecided.

The law accordingly is that where an accused is incapable of forming the necessary *mens rea* by reason of some external factor which was not self-induced but was outwith his control, and was not a situation which he was bound to foresee, and which resulted in a total alienation of reason amounting to a complete absence of self-control, he is entitled to a simple acquittal. Where, however, the automatism is the result of some internal factor which is likely to recur, then it is either irrelevant, or leads to an acquittal by reason of insanity and a hospital order. It will be seen that the requirements of *Ross* are quite stringent, but it does recognise the existence of the defence of non-insane automatism. In *Ross* itself the accused had committed a number of serious assaults under the influence of drugs, these drugs having been put without his knowledge into the beer he was drinking; it was held that the trial judge should not have directed the jury in terms of *Cunningham*, and his convictions were quashed. The result of *Cunningham* itself, however, would not have been different had the law been as laid down in *Ross*, since the condition of the accused in *Cunningham* was the result of epilepsy.

Ross goes far to equate Scots Law with that of England as laid down in *R. v. Sullivan* [1984] A.C. 156 where it was held that automatism could be classed as non-insane where there was temporary impairment not self-induced by drink or drugs but resulting from an external physical factor such as a blow on the head or a medical anaesthetic.

It can be taken from *Ross* that in Scotland as in England, epileptic behaviour counts as insanity: see *R. v. Sullivan, supra; R. v. Bailey* [1983] 1 W.L.R. 760; *infra*, para. 3–26.

Ross also appears to treat somnambulism and hypoglycaemia as insanity. It remains to be seen whether the Crown will continue to exercise a discretion of the kind they exercised in two pre-*Ross* cases.

In one case involving a 14-year-old boy charged with assaulting his five-year-old cousin in which the accused had pled guilty, the Crown agreed to the plea being withdrawn and deserted the diet on receipt of two psychiatric reports expressing the opinion that the boy had been sleepwalking at the relevant time: *H.M.A. v. X*, Edinburgh High Court, December 1983, unreported; see *The Scotsman* newspaper, 17th December 1983. In *Stirling v. Annan*, 1984 S.L.T. 88 the Crown conceded that a conviction for shoplifting where the accused was apparently suffering from spontaneous hypoglycaemia might have involved a miscarriage of justice, and the conviction was quashed; but see *infra*, para. 3–27.

In *R. v. Hennessy* [1989] 1 W.L.R. 287, however, where the condition in question was hyperglycaemia, brought on by a failure to take food or insulin, it was held to have been caused by diabetes and not by an external factor, and so could not support a defence of automatism. It was held in the same case that stress, anxiety and depression, although caused by external factors, could not support a defence of automatism, since they were states of mind likely to recur, and lacked the features of novelty or accident required by *R. v. Sullivan* [1984] A.C. 156. See also *R. v. Burgess* [1991] 2 Q.B. 92; sleepwalking treated as insanity.

Ross approaches the problem as one of *mens rea* and not as one of *actus reus*, which means that, strictly speaking, it will not be

3–18 applicable in any situation where *mens rea* is not required. It may
to be, however, that in strict liability driving offences, the court will
3–22 concentrate on whether the driving was proved to have been
intentional. *Ross* also requires not merely an absence of the *mens
rea* of the crime charged, but a total alienation of reason or loss of
capacity to control one's actions, comparable to insanity.

3–23 *Ross* v. *H.M. Advocate,* 1991 S.L.T. 564 clearly excludes voluntary intoxication as a factor in automatism.

See also *R.* v. *Bailey* [1983] 1 W.L.R. 760; R.D. Mackay,
"Intoxication as a Factor in Automatism" [1982] Crim. L.R. 146.
Brennan v. *H.M.A.* is now reported at 1977 J.C. 38.

It has been held in England that the effects of taking valium by
someone who believed it to be harmless can negative recklessness:
R. v. *Hardie* [1985] 1 W.L.R. 64, but that no mental illness short of
insanity can displace the inference of recklessness to be drawn from
objectively bad driving in a prosecution for reckless driving: *R.* v.
Bell [1984] 3 All E.R. 842.

3–27 See now *Ross* v. *H.M. Advocate,* 1991 S.L.T. 564; *supra,* paras.
3–18 to 3–22.

In *Carmichael* v. *Boyle,* 1985 S.L.T. 399 the sheriff acquitted the
accused on charges of assault and breach of the peace on the ground
that he was suffering from hypoglycaemia at the time and therefore
lacked *mens rea,* but his decision was overturned by the High Court
who reaffirmed the law as stated in *H.M. Advocate* v. *Cunningham,*
1963 J.C. 80.

That case was overruled in *Ross* v. *H.M. Advocate,* 1991 S.L.T.
564, but only in so far as it reaffirmed *Cunningham.* On its facts it
would probably still not be a case where the defence of non-insane
automatism would be available, diabetes being a continuing disorder
of the body: see *Ross, supra,* L.J.G. at 567B.

3–32 *Cf. Fishmongers' Company* v. *Bruce,* 1980 S.L.T. (Notes) 35, 36:
"[N]o one can be held guilty of contravening a bye-law which
requires that a certain result shall be secured unless he is a person
who is charged by the bye-law or by statute with a duty to secure
that result."

3–33 In *R.* v. *Miller* [1983] 2 A.C. 161 A was a vagrant who fell asleep
smoking a cigarette: the cigarette fell and started a fire. When A
woke up the fire was smouldering, but he went away without putting
it out. The fire spread and destroyed a building and caused a death.
A was convicted of manslaughter and arson. It was said by Lord
Diplock that even if one is initially unaware of a train of events
which by the time one becomes aware of it obviously creates a risk,
one is liable for the consequences if one does not try to prevent or
reduce them.

See also *Jas. Paterson Duff,* Criminal Appeal Court, May 1979,
unreported: a charge of culpable homicide by assaulting V to her
severe injury and thereafter failing to obtain medical assistance for
her, whereby she died as a result of her injuries and the lack of
medical attention.

See also *MacPhail* v. *Clark*, 1983 S.L.T. (Sh.Ct.) 37 where a farmer allowed a fire which he had set to burn straw to spread so that its smoke obscured the roadway and caused a traffic accident in which travellers were injured. The farmer, however, was charged only with culpably and recklessly endangering the travellers and not with culpably and recklessly injuring them.

3–37   Footnote 73. For arguments for and against extending the scope of criminal omissions, see Andrew Ashworth, "The Scope of Criminal Liability for Omissions" (1989) 105 L.Q.R. 424; Glanville Williams, "Criminal Omissions—The Conventional View" (1991) 107 L.Q.R. 56.

3–38   On the elements needed to prove possession, see *Black* v. *H.M. Advocate*, 1974 J.C. 43.

Possession requires both knowledge and control, so that mere knowledge on the part of an occupant of a house in multiple occupation that prohibited articles are in the communal living room does not necessarily amount to possession of them by him: *Mingay* v. *Mackinnon*, 1980 J.C. 33; *cf. Bellerby* v. *Carle* [1983] 2 A.C. 101; *infra*, para. 8–61.

Whether articles found in a house jointly occupied by two people are in the possession of both of them is a question of fact: *Hughes* v. *Guild*, 1990 J.C. 359; *cf. Feeney* v. *Jessop*, 1990 S.C.C.R. 565; *Crowe* v. *MacPhail*, 1987 S.L.T. 316.

Once a person is knowingly in possession of an article he continues to be knowingly in possession of it even during periods of time in which he has forgotten that he has it: *Gill* v. *Lockhart*, 1988 S.L.T. 189; *R.* v. *Martindale* [1986] 1 W.L.R. 1042.

If A gives B permission to leave drugs, say, in his, A's, room while he is on holiday and B does so, then A is in possession of the drugs, even though he did not know these particular drugs were there or that B had taken advantage of the permission granted to him, and even perhaps if he expected B to have removed the drugs before his return from holiday: *Murray* v. *MacPhail*, 1991 S.C.C.R. 245.

Footnote 75. *McKenzie* v. *Skeen* is now reported at 1983 S.L.T. 121.

3–39   See Michael Hirst, "Jurisdiction over Cross Border Offences" (1981) 97 L.Q.R. 80.

Footnote 81. See now Renton & Brown, paras. 1–08 *et seq.*

Footnote 90. *D.P.P.* v. *Stonehouse* is now reported at [1978] A.C. 55.

3–48   A failure to lodge documents is committed at the place where they should have been lodged: *Smith* v. *Inglis and Ors.*, 1982 S.C.C.R. 403.

3–49   There is now authority supporting Macdonald's approach. In *Laird* v. *H.M. Advocate*, 1985 J.C. 37 the accused formed a scheme to obtain money from an English company by selling them steel

3-49 which was not of the quality it was pretended to be. The scheme was formed in Scotland and the steel was delivered to a site in Scotland, but the money was handed over in England following on the uttering there of forged certificates of the quality of the steel. The High Court held that it had jurisdiction since the totality of the events in Scotland played a material part in the fulfilment of the scheme.

Cf. section 4(5) of the Computer Misuse Act 1990 which provides that the requirement of "at least one significant link with domestic jurisdiction" before certain offences can be committed is without prejudice to any jurisdiction exercisable by a court in Scotland apart from the provisions of the section.

3-51 It was held in *Attorney-General's Reference (No. 1 of 1982)* [1983] Q.B. 751 that a conspiracy in England to cause harm to an English company abroad was not indictable in England.

Special provision is made in section 6 of the Aviation Security Act 1982 for it to be an offence for anyone in the United Kingdom to induce or assist the commission abroad of certain offences under that Act in which the United Kingdom courts have extraterritorial jurisdiction.

The approach suggested in the text gains some support from *Clements* v. *H.M. Advocate*, 1991 S.C.C.R. 266, although that case is somewhat special since it deals with the peculiar statutory offence of being concerned in the supply of drugs, contrary to section 4(3)(*b*) of the Misuse of Drugs Act 1971. The drugs were sent from England to Scotland and were intercepted there before they reached the ultimate consumer. The appellants remained in England throughout and one of them did not even know the drugs were destined for Scotland. It was held that the Scots courts had jurisdiction, and although the Lord Justice-General laid great stress on the fact that what was in issue was the breach of a United Kingdom statute occurring within the United Kingdom, reliance was placed on the fact that the crime was directed at a result in Scotland. *Cf. R.* v. *Sansom* [1991] 2 Q.B. 130.

3-52 Footnote 30. *D.P.P.* v. *Stonehouse* is now reported at [1978] A.C. 55.

CHAPTER 4

THE PROBLEM OF CAUSATION

4-06 The High Court have recently held that where A sells to B substances capable of being used in a way which endangers or harms B, in the knowledge that B intends to use them in such a way, and B does use them in this way, A is to be treated as if he had administered the substances to B and so caused the resultant harm or danger: *Ulhaq* v. *H.M. Advocate*, 1991 S.L.T. 614—supplying glue to adults in the knowledge that they intended to inhale the vapours. This suggests that a foreseeable voluntary action by an adult does not count as a *novus actus*, a view which seems to be shared by the English Law Commission—see 1989 Draft Code, s.17(2)—but is contrary to what might be called the "classical" or "traditional" idea of the *novus actus*. For a criticism of the Draft Code provision, see Glanville Williams, "Finis for *Novus Actus*" [1989] C.L.J. 391.

4–25   See also *Gizzi and Anr.* v. *Tudhope*, 1982 S.C.C.R. 442.

4–30   See also *Attorney-General's Reference (No. 4 of 1980)* [1981] 1 W.L.R. 705.

4–31   In *The Oropesa* [1943] P. 32, at 39, Lord Wright said, "To break the chain of causation it must be shown that there is something which I will call ultroneous, something unwarrantable, a new cause which disturbs the sequence of events, something which can be described as either unreasonable or extraneous or extrinsic," and this passage was applied in *Finlayson* v. *H.M. Advocate*, 1979 J.C. 33; *infra*, para. 4–33a.

4–33   Add new paragraph **4–33a**:

4–33a   *Life support machines.* In *Finlayson* v. *H.M. Advocate*, 1979 J.C. 33 an injection of a controlled drug caused brain death, but the victim's heart was kept going on a life-support machine. Thereafter it was decided that because there had been brain death the machine should be turned off. At the subsequent trial for culpable homicide of the person who had administered the drug it was argued that death had been caused by the stopping of the machine. It was held that the effects of the drug were the substantial and continuing cause of death which was not affected by the decision to turn off the machine which was in the circumstances a reasonable one. "It follows accordingly that the act of disconnecting the machine can hardly be described as an extraneous or extrinsic act [in terms of Lord Wright's speech in *The Oropesa* [1943] P. 32] . . . Far less can it be said that [it] was either unforeseeable or unforeseen": L.J.G. at 36. No special point was made of the fact that the victim was, in one sense at least, already dead before he was put on the machine, although it was said that the machine was used only to obtain time to ascertain if there was any chance of restoring brain function: See also *R.* v. *Malcherek* [1981] 1 W.L.R. 690; Watson, Harland and MacLean, "Brain Stem Death" (1978) 23 J.L.S. 433; P.D.G. Skegg, "Termination of Life Support and the Law of Murder etc." (1978) 41 M.L.R. 423.

4–42   Footnote 92. It has been held in England that neither an act of self-defence nor an act done in the execution of a public duty is a *novus actus interveniens*. Where, therefore, A tries to prevent his arrest by holding B in front of him as a shield and firing at approaching police officers as a result of which they fire back and kill B, B's death is caused by A's acts, and the action of the police does not break the causal chain: *R.* v. *Pagett* (1983) 76 Cr.App.R.

4-42 279. The court's view was that the position would have been the same if A had done no more than use B as a shield and had not himself shot at the police, assuming that the conduct of the latter was within the reasonable execution of their duty.

4-52 It was said in *Ex p. Minister of Justice, Re S. v. Grotjohn*, 1970 (2) S.A. 355 (A.D.) that whether or not there is homicide is a question of fact. The court declined to approve a general doctrine that a final voluntary act by the victim would always lead to the acquittal of the accused "without some reservation in regard to the independence of the act." Where the two acts were not totally unconnected, and especially where the result was an eventuality which the perpetrator foresaw as a possibility which he wanted to employ to attain his object (the death of the suicide), or as something on which he could depend to bring about the desired result, "it would be contrary to accepted principles of law and to all sense of justice to allow him to take shelter behind the act as a *novus actus interveniens*." In *Grotjohn* the accused had had a row with his wife who threatened to shoot herself, whereupon he had loaded a rifle and given it to her, saying, "Shoot yourself if you want to, because you're a nuisance," and had been acquitted. The Minister of Justice then referred the case to the court.

In *S. v. Hibbert*, 1979 (4) S.A. 717 (D. and C.L.D.) the facts were much the same, and the accused was convicted on the ground that he must have appreciated the possibility of serious injury and death, and therefore had the necessary intention to murder, and so was reckless as to the consequences of his conduct. Shearer J. said, " . . . the act of pulling the trigger to which all the other conduct conduced, cannot in any sense be described as independent of the course of conduct," so that there was no *novus actus*.

See also D.J. Lanham, "Murder by Instigating Suicide" [1980] Crim. L.R. 215.

4-53 In *Khaliq v. H.M. Advocate*, 1984 J.C. 23 the accused were charged with supplying children with glue and with containers from which the glue could be sniffed, a combination known as a "glue-sniffing kit," in the knowledge that the children intended to sniff the glue to the danger of their lives and health, and with endangering their lives and health. It was held that the supply of the kits to, and the glue-sniffing by, the children were so closely connected as to be equivalent to the administration of the glue to the children, even in the absence of any averment of instigation, and that the charge was relevant. It was observed that although the age of the sniffers was relevant in considering whether the facts amounted to administration, it was not essential to the relevancy of the charge, and *Khaliq* was applied in *Ulhaq v. H.M. Advocate*, 1991 S.L.T. 614, where the accused merely supplied solvents to adults without any accompanying kit, or any advice or persuasion, but in the knowledge that they were to be inhaled.

ART AND PART

5–01   Art and part guilt requires involvement in a specific crime, of which each plotter is guilty. It may be, however, that where A is a member of a gang and is sent out to do "a job" without being told specifically what that job involves, he will be guilty of whatever crime is actually committed, provided it is within the range of activities which could reasonably be expected to be carried out by the gang in the circumstances. So, where a terrorist assists in an attack on a target without knowing whether guns or explosives are to be used and in fact explosives are used, he may be guilty art and part of possessing and using explosives, although his own involvement was only to guide the bombers to the scene of the crime and he drove off without seeing any explosives: *R.* v. *Maxwell* [1978] 1 W.L.R. 1350.

5–02   A person who is not himself related to the parties may be art and part guilty of incest: *Vaughan* v. *H.M.A.*, 1979 S.L.T. 49.

    A man can now be guilty of raping his wife: *S.* v. *H.M.A.*, 1989 S.L.T. 469; *infra*, para. 33–12.

5–05   Section 9 of the Sexual Offences (Scotland) Act 1956 was repealed by the Criminal Justice (Scotland) Act 1980: see *infra*, para. 36–17.

5–06   Footnote 22. *R.* v. *Whitehouse* is now reported at [1977] Q.B. 868.

5–10   Incest can be committed by a person not related to the persons participating in the unlawful intercourse: *Vaughan* v. *H.M.A.*, 1979 S.L.T. 49. See also *Skinner* v. *Patience and Cowe*, 1982 S.L.T. (Sh.Ct.) 81.

    Robertsons v. *Caird* is unlikely to be followed. In *Templeton* v. *H.M. Advocate*, 1987 S.L.T. 171 it was held that a bank manager and his wife (who was not an employee of the bank) could both be charged with contraventions of the Prevention of Corruption Act 1906 in that they corruptly accepted payments in respect of repayments on a loan arranged by them both, as inducements for the manager showing favour to the payer in relation to the bank's business. *Robertsons* v. *Caird* was said to depend on the particular provisions of the Debtors (Scotland) Act 1880, and to have in any event preceded section 31 of the Criminal Justice (Scotland) Act 1949, and the court preferred to follow *Vaughan* v. *H.M. Advocate*.

Footnote 37. Now Bankruptcy (Scotland) Act 1985, s.67.

5–11   In *Fishmongers Company* v. *Bruce*, 1980 S.L.T. (Notes) 35 it was held that the person locally in charge of a fishery could not be convicted of breach of a statutory duty in failing to remove the

5–11   leaders of nets during the weekly close season because the duty of removal was placed only on the proprietor or occupier of the fishery by s.24 of the Salmon Fisheries (Scotland) Act 1868. The decision proceeded on the basis that the offence was one of omission and could therefore be committed only by someone specifically charged with the relevant duty: see *supra*, para. 3–32; the sheriff thought that an act of commission in breach of the statutory bye-law could be committed by anyone.

5–12   In *Valentine* v. *Mackie*, 1980 S.L.T. (Sh.Ct.) 122 a passenger was convicted of aiding and abetting the driver to drive with an excess of alcohol in his blood: see *infra*, para. 8–37.

5–13   Footnotes 47 and 48. Section 176 of the Road Traffic Act was repealed and not re-enacted by the Road Traffic Acts of 1988.

5–15   See also *Vaughan* v. *H.M. Advocate*, 1979 S.L.T. 49.

5–17   In *Capuano* v. *H.M. Advocate*, 1985 S.L.T. 196 A and two other men were charged with assaulting the victims by throwing stones at their car. There was insufficient evidence to show that A had himself thrown stones but the three accused were said to have acted as a group. The other two were acquitted and A was convicted. His conviction was upheld on appeal, on the ground that the Crown case was that there had been a group attack, and the Crown's failure to show that the co-accused were members of the group did not prevent the conviction of A who was proved to have been one of the group.

5–21   A solicitor who advises his client to adopt a criminal course of action may be guilty art and part in the offence committed by the client: *cf. Martin* v. *Hamilton*, 1989 S.L.T. 860, a charge under the now repealed section 176 of the Road Traffic Act 1972 which created a specific statutory offence of counselling another person to contravene the Act. The complaint was dismissed as irrelevant because the course advised was not criminal in the circumstances libelled.

5–22   For a modern example of art and part by instigation, see *Little* v. *H.M. Advocate*, 1983 J.C. 16.

5–25   Add new paragraph **5–25a**:

5–25a   *Dissociation.* There is no defence of dissociation in Scots law. The fact that one conspirator withdraws from the enterprise at some stage after the perpetration of the crime has begun does not relieve him of responsibility for the completed offence, unless, perhaps, he takes steps to prevent its completion: *Socratous* v. *H.M. Advocate*, 1987 S.L.T. 244.

5–26   Footnote 28. In *McLaughlan* v. *H.M.A.*, 1991 S.C.C.R. 733, it was held that a person who intervened in an ongoing fight was responsible only for what occurred after her intervention.

5–27   See also *R.* v. *Maxwell* [1978] 1 W.L.R. 1350; *supra* para. 5–01.

Footnote 80. *Cf. People* v. *Egan* [1989] I.R. 681 where an agreement to assist in hiding the proceeds of what the accused thought was going to be a theft led to his conviction for armed robbery.

5–31   Footnote 91. See also *Quinn* v. *H.M.A.*, 1990 S.L.T. 877; *Stillie* v. *H.M.A.*, 1990 S.C.C.R. 719.

5–35   Where the accused's presence was wholly passive and the Crown are therefore forced to rely on prior concert the jury must be specifically and forcefully directed on the point: *Spiers* v. *H.M.A.*, 1980 J.C. 36.

A senior police officer who fails to interfere when a junior officer assaults a prisoner whom they are both escorting may be art and part guilty of the assault: *Bonar* v. *McLeod*, 1983 S.C.C.R. 161.

5–38   Footnote 5. See also *Chan Wing-Siu* v. *The Queen* [1985] A.C. 168.

Footnote 6. In *Melvin* v. *H.M.A.*, 1984 S.C.C.R. 113 A and B were charged with robbery and murder, and A was convicted of murder and B of culpable homicide. In dismissing A's appeal on the ground that the verdicts were inconsistent, Lord Cameron said at page 117:

> "In determining the quality of the crime, *i.e.* as between culpable homicide and murder, a jury would be entitled, in a case where intent to kill was not suggested or established or indeed any antecedent concerted intention to carry out an assault and robbery on the deceased or any other person, to consider and assess the degree of recklessness displayed by each participant and return, if their judgment so required, a discriminating verdict in accordance with their assessment":

See also *Malone* v. *H.M.A.*, 1988 S.C.C.R. 498; *Johns* v. *The Queen* (1980) 54 A.L.J.R. 166.

5–39   In *Boyne* v. *H.M. Advocate*, 1980 S.L.T. 56 the victim of an assault and robbery committed by a number of people was killed by one of them with a knife. It was held that the others could be convicted of murder only if they knew that the assailant was carrying a knife at the time and was liable to use it, or if they carried on with the attack on the victim after the knife had been used. The Lord Justice-Clerk said, at page 59:

> "For instance, if an accused was one of a gang who attacked a victim, and says in a statement that he saw another member of the gang, he cannot say who, unexpectedly take out a knife and deliver a blow with it which proved fatal, but nonetheless he carried on with the attack on the victim, we do not see how that statement would not be competent evidence against him on a charge of murder art and part.
> Having considered the statements made by Boyne which were properly before the jury and which they manifestly accepted, we are satisfied that there is nothing in them which can be read or interpreted as an admission that he either knew or had reasonable cause to anticipate that Curley might use a knife on the victim or that he,

5–39 Boyne, carried on with the assault on the victim after Curley had used the knife. The advocate-depute suggested that the inference might be drawn from the statements that Boyne knew that Curley was likely to be carrying a knife on this occasion and was liable to use it. This stemmed from admissions by Boyne that he had seen Curley with a knife on previous occasions. These statements were qualified by assertions: (1) that Curley had told him that he only carried the knife in self-defence, having himself been attacked on a previous occasion; and (2) that while he had been involved with Curley in previous muggings he had never seen Curley use a knife. We reject the advocate-depute's suggestion and hold that there was nothing in Boyne's statements to constitute an acknowledgement that he was art and part in the murder (as distinct from an assault and robbery). The Crown accepted that if that were so there was not sufficient evidence to warrant the conviction of murder in his case. We shall accordingly quash that conviction."

See also *Robertson* v. *H.M. Advocate*, 1990 S.C.C.R. 345; *Jamieson* v. *Guild*, 1989 S.C.C.R. 583.

The fact that the accused knew that his co-accused had acted in a particular way towards the victim shortly before, *e.g.* by using a knife, does not make him guilty art and part even if he is present on the later occasion and involved in an attack with sticks in the course of which the co-accused uses a knife: *Carrick* v. *H.M.A.*, 1990 S.C.C.R. 286; *cf. Quinn* v. *H.M.A.*, 1990 S.C.C.R. 254. See also *Walker* v. *H.M. Advocate*, 1985 J.C. 53 where the appellant's conviction was quashed because of the absence of evidence that he persisted in the attack on the deceased after he realised his co-accused was using a knife.

In *O'Connell* v. *H.M. Advocate*, 1987 S.C.C.R. 459 a group of men assaulted the deceased with sticks, and during the attack one of the accused struck the deceased the fatal blow with a hammer which had belonged to the deceased. It was held that whether a hammer was to be regarded as sufficiently similar to a stick for its use to be within the reasonable contemplation of all the group was a jury question, and the jury were entitled to convict all the accused of culpable homicide.

5–44 See also *R.* v. *Calhaem* [1985] Q.B. 808.

5–46 In *R.* v. *Nathan* [1981] 2 N.Z.L.R. 473 the victim was attacked by a gang who kicked him and hit him with a weapon, but death was probably caused by a minor blow. It was held that since it was not possible to isolate the fatal blow or infer that it was delivered by someone with the requisite knowledge, the members of the gang were all guilty only of manslaughter: *cf. Ramnath Mohan* v. *The Queen* [1967] 2 A.C. 187; *Boyne* v. *H.M.A.*, 1980 S.L.T. 56; *supra*, para. 5.39.

5–50 Footnote 37. Contrast *Morton* v. *H.M.A.*, 1986 S.L.T. 622.

CHAPTER 6

INCHOATE CRIMES

6–15 English law is now governed by the Criminal Attempts Act 1981, section 1 of which provides: "If, with intent to commit an [indictable offence], a person does an act which is more than merely preparatory to the commission of the offence, he is guilty of [attempt]." Similar provision is made by s.3 of the Act for attempts under special statutory provision. See *R. v. Shivpuri* [1987] A.C. 1.

6–19 This theory appears now to be the law of England: Criminal Attempts Act 1981, ss.1 and 3; *supra*, para. 6–15.

6–21 Footnote 69. Add: *Cf. R. v. Matthews* [1981] Crim. L.R. 325.

6–42 It was held in *McKenzie v. H.M. Advocate*, 1988 S.L.T. 487 that to raise an action based on false averments constituted an attempt to defraud the person called as defender.

It was held in *Barrett v. Allan*, 1986 S.C.C.R. 479 that to stand in a queue at a stadium turnstile could constitute an attempt to enter the stadium.

6–47 Section 5 of the Road Traffic Act 1972 is now section 4 of the Road Traffic Act 1988, and section 175 of the 1972 Act is now section 178 of the 1988 Act.

6–48 Footnote 57. See now Road Traffic Offenders Act 1988, Sched. 2, Pt. II, which provides for disqualification for "stealing or attempting to steal a motor vehicle."

6–49 Footnote 59. See also Law Commission Report on Attempt and Impossibility in relation to Attempt, Conspiracy and Incitement (Law Com. No. 102, 1980); H.L.A. Hart, "The House of Lords on attempting the impossible," in *Crime, Proof and Punishment*, ed. Tapper (London, 1981), 1.

6–51 The Criminal Attempts Act 1981 provides that in England a person may be guilty of attempt even though the facts are such that the commission of the offence is impossible, and further that where a person's intention would constitute an intention to commit an offence only if the facts had been as he believed them, he shall be regarded as having such an intention: ss.1(2), (3) and 3(4), (5). Factual impossibility thus no longer prevents conviction for attempt in England, and the same is now true of legal impossibility: *R. v. Shivpuri* [1987] A.C. 1.

Footnote 69. It was held in *R. v. Taaffe* [1984] A.C. 539 that a person who imports what he mistakenly believes to be currency in the mistaken belief that its import is prohibited is not "knowingly concerned in any fraudulent evasion" of an import prohibition, although the goods imported were in fact the subject of a prohibition, being prohibited drugs. The question of attempt was not raised.

6–53 It is a crime to attempt to bribe a public official even if the purpose of the bribe is to persuade him to do something which he has no power to do: *Maxwell v. H.M.A.*, 1980 J.C. 40; the position in that case was, however, simplified by the fact that bribery is complete when the bribe is offered, whatever follows thereafter: *ibid.*; *cf. infra*, para. 44–08.

6–55   Conspiracy "is constituted by the agreement of two or more persons to further or achieve a criminal purpose. A criminal purpose is one which if attempted or achieved by action on the part of an individual would itself constitute a crime by the law of Scotland": *Maxwell* v. *H.M.A.*, 1980 J.C. 40, Lord Cameron at 43. See also *Sayers and Ors.* v. *H.M.A.*, 1981 S.C.C.R. 312.

6–63   Lord Cameron's definition of conspiracy in *Maxwell* v. *H.M. Advocate*, 1980 J.C. 40 clearly requires the conspiracy to involve conduct which would be criminal if committed by one person: see *supra*, para. 6–55.

6–67   Add new paragraph **6–67a**:

6–67a   IMPOSSIBILITY. In *Maxwell* v. *H.M. Advocate*, 1980 J.C. 40 the accused were convicted of conspiracy to bribe members of a licensing board to transfer a gaming licence. They appealed on the ground that the conspiracy was incapable of success since at the relevant time the transfer of gaming licences was a matter for the sheriff and not for the licensing board. The appeal failed. Lord Cameron said that a conspiracy was an agreement to achieve a criminal purpose, and that it was the criminality of the purpose and not the result which made the agreement criminal. A conspiracy whose purpose was to corrupt public officials was therefore criminal, whether or not it could have the desired result. This seems, with respect, an odd use of "purpose": the purpose was to get the licence transferred; bribery was the means of effecting that purpose. But, semantics aside, there was clearly a conspiracy to achieve the desired result by criminal means, and there is no question that the means proposed were criminal, and no question of error or impossibility in so far as the intention of giving bribes to public officials was concerned. The case is therefore distinguishable from, *e.g.* a conspiracy to abort a non-pregnant woman, or obtain a passport by arranging a bigamous marriage where the parties in question are in fact, unknown to the conspirators, free to marry. Lord Cameron distinguished the English case of *D.P.P.* v. *Nock* [1978] A.C. 979 where the House of Lords held that it was not a criminal conspiracy to conspire to produce cocaine from a powder from which such production was in fact impossible. There is no reason why that should not be a criminal conspiracy in Scotland by analogy with attempted theft from an empty pocket: para. 6–53 in the main work, and this seems to have been accepted in *Maxwell*: see Lord Cameron at 44–45. It is now a criminal conspiracy in England: Criminal Attempts Act 1981, s.5.

6–68   There is no case law on incitement to commit the impossible, but the law is doubtless the same as for conspiracy: *supra*, para. 6–67a. The position is different in England because the Criminal Attempts Act 1981 does not apply to incitement: *R.* v. *Fitzmaurice* [1983] Q.B. 1083; see also M. Cohen, "Inciting the Impossible" [1979] Crim.L.R. 239.

CHAPTER 7

THE CRIMINAL MIND

7–05   The High Court continues to use the concept of "evil intent," particularly in relation to assault: see *Roberts* v. *Hamilton*, 1989 S.L.T. 399; *Guest* v. *Annan*, 1988 S.C.C.R. 275; *Peebles* v. *MacPhail*, 1990 S.L.T. 245; *cf. Morton* v. *H.M.A.*, 1986 S.L.T. 622.

7–13   Footnote 35. See also Law Commission Report on the Mental Element in Crime (Law Com. No. 89, 1978), and articles thereon in [1978] Crim.L.R. 588; R.A. Duff, "Intention, Mens Rea and the Law Commission's Report" [1980] Crim.L.R. 147; "Intention, Recklessness and Probable Consequences," *ibid.* 404; "Recklessness," *ibid.* 282; see also Scottish Law Commission's Report on the Mental Element in Crime (Scot. Law Com. No. 80, 1983); John E. Stannard, "Subjectivism, Objectivism, and the Draft Criminal Code" (1985) 101 L.Q.R. 540; R.A. Duff, "The Obscure Intentions of the House of Lords" [1986] Crim.L.R. 771; Lord Goff of Chieveley, "The Mental Element in the Crime of Murder" (1988) 104 L.Q.R. 30; and Glanville Williams' rejoinder, "The *Mens Rea* for Murder: Ieave it Alone" (1989) 105 L.Q.R. 387; and the English Law Commission's Reports on Codification: L.C. Nos. 143 (1985) and 177 (1989).

7–14   Asquith L.J.'s definition was adopted by the trial judge in *Sayers and Ors.* v. *H.M. Advocate*, 1981 S.C.C.R. 312.

7–15   Footnote 4. The Law Commission's Draft Bill (1985, L.C. 143) offered "when he wants it to exist or occur, is aware that it exists or is almost certain that it exists or will exist or occur," but the later version, the 1989 Draft Code, s.18(*b*), provides that a person acts intentionally with respect to a circumstance when he hopes or knows that it exists or will exist, and to a result when he acts "in order to bring it about or being aware that it will occur in the ordinary course of events."

7–18   See also *R.* v. *Lemon* [1979] A.C. 617, especially Lord Diplock at 634E–F; *R.* v. *Maxwell* [1978] 1 W.L.R. 1350.

7–19   Footnote 60. *Cf.* J.C. Smith, *Justification and Excuse in the Criminal Law* (London, 1989), pp. 60–64.

7–27   *Cf. Gill* v. *Lockhart*, 1988 S.L.T. 189: A held to be in possession of articles about whose presence he had once known but had forgotten at the time they were found by the police.
On foresight as evidence of intention, see *R.* v. *Moloney* [1985] A.C. 905: *R.* v. *Hancock* [1986] A.C. 455; *R.* v. *Nedrick* [1986] 1 W.L.R. 1025.

7-34   It is now the law of England that "wilful" in the context of wilful neglect means intentional or reckless: *R.* v. *Sheppard* [1981] A.C. 394. Neglect to maintain one's dependants is something different again: see *Galt* v. *Turner*, 1981 S.C.C.R. 111.

7-35   Footnote 11. Add: D. Calligan, "Responsibility for Recklessness" (1978) 31 Curr. Leg. Problems 55; R.A. Duff, "Recklessness" [1980] Crim.L.R. 282.

7-49   Footnote 35. The 1989 Draft Code, s.18(*c*) provides that a person acts recklessly with respect to a circumstance when he is aware of a risk that it exists or will exist, and to a result when he is aware of a risk that it will occur, and it is, in the circumstances known to him, unreasonable to take the risk.

In his evidence to the House of Lords Select Committee on Murder and Life Imprisonment Lord Justice-General Emslie said:

> "The question for the jury is: 'Looking at the acts do you discover a mind as wicked and depraved as that of a deliberate killer?' It has got to be as near as no matter to the mind of the deliberate killer. I would certainly think in almost every case the classic definition of murder, which goes back to Hume, is given to a jury and judges may tend to add: 'What it comes to is this, if he did these terrible things you have heard about, are you satisfied on all the evidence that he did not care one way or t'other whether the victim lived or died? He did not even apply his mind to the question.' "

Report of the Select Committee, 1989, H.L. Paper 78, vol. III, para. 2024.

7-52   *Cf.* Lord Diplock in *R.* v. *Sheppard* [1981] A.C. 394, 404 A–B:

> "The concept of the reasonable man as providing the standard by which the liability of real persons for their actual conduct is to be determined is a concept of civil law, particularly in relation to the tort of negligence; the obtrusion into criminal law of conformity with the notional conduct of the reasonable man as relevant to criminal liability, though not unknown (e.g., in relation to provocation sufficient to reduce murder to manslaughter), is exceptional, and should not lightly be extended: *Andrews* v. *Director of Public Prosecutions* [1937] A.C. 576, 582–583. If failure to use the hypothetical powers of observation, ratiocination and foresight of consequences possessed by this admirable but purely notional exemplar is to constitute an ingredient of a criminal offence it must surely form part not of the actus reus but of the mens rea."

7-56   In *The Queen* v. *O'Connor* (1980) 54 A.L.J.R. 349, Barwick C.J. at 355, discussing the rule that self-induced intoxication is not a defence (see *infra*, para. 12–12) said: "A distrust of jurors and an anxiety that they may too readily be persuaded to an acquittal if evidence of the result of self-induced intoxication, particularly by drugs other than alcohol, were allowed, may have formed some part of the public policy on which the decision rests." He then quoted the trial judge, Starke J., as saying, "I, of course, have no knowledge of how English juries react . . . I do not share the fear held by many in England that if intoxication is accepted as a defence as far as general intent is concerned the floodgates will open and hordes of guilty men will descend on the community."

7–57 See *infra*, paras. 7–70 to 7–74.
to
7–61

7–57 Footnote 64. See now Road Traffic Act 1988, s.1.

7–63 The argument that "wicked recklessness" represents a moral judgment made by the jury as representatives of the public is considerably weakened by recent decisions of the High Court asserting the judge's right to withdraw culpable homicide from the jury where the court considers that no reasonable jury could have held that wicked recklessness was not present: see *infra*, para. 23–31.

7–67 See *People* v. *Murray* [1977] I.R. 360: advertent recklessness as to whether the victim was a police officer sufficient for capital murder requiring intention to kill or cause serious injury to a police officer.

7–70 It is now clear that recklessness in Scots law is basically objective,
to and that in both Scots and at least some areas of English law a person
7–74 who gives no thought to a risk may be reckless: *Allan* v. *Patterson*, 1980 J.C. 57; *R.* v. *Caldwell* [1982] A.C. 341; *R.* v. *Lawrence (Stephen)* [1982] A.C. 510; *Elliott* v. *C.* [1983] 1 W.L.R. 939. For criticisms of the English decisions see, *e.g.* Professors J.C. Smith and Glanville Williams in [1981] Crim.L.R. 392, 580, 658; E. Griew, "Reckless Damage and Reckless Driving," *ibid.* 743; Glanville Williams, "Recklessness Redefined," 1981 C.L.J. 252; R.A. Duff, "Professor Williams and Conditional Subjectivism," *ibid.*, 273; G. Syrota, "A Radical Change in the Law of Recklessness" [1982] Crim.L.R. 97. For later English cases, see *R.* v. *Moloney* [1985] A.C. 905; *R.* v. *Nedrick* [1986] 1 W.L.R. 1025; *R.* v. *Hancock* [1986] A.C. 455. *R.* v. *Spratt* [1990] 1 W.L.R. 1073, however, indicates that subjectivism is not yet dead. On the apparently special position of rape, see *R.* v. *Satnam S.* (1984) 78 Cr.App.R. 149.

In *Allan* v. *Patterson*, which was a charge of reckless driving contrary to section 2 of the Road Traffic Act 1972 which simply made it an offence to drive recklessly, Lord Justice-General Emslie said, at page 60:

> "There is nothing in the language of section 2 as amended to suggest an intention on the part of Parliament to penalise thereunder only a course of driving embarked upon wilfully or deliberately in the face of known risks of a material kind. Inquiry into the state of knowledge of a particular driver accused of the offence created by the section as amended, and into his intention at the time, is not required at all. The statute directs attention to the quality of the driving in fact but not to the state of mind or the intention of the driver. If it were otherwise, the section, and indeed section 1, would virtually become inoperable in all but the rarest of instances."

Cf. Peda v. *The Queen* [1969] S.C.R. 905.

That, of course, was said in the context of a statutory offence, and even in that context may overstate the irrelevance of the driver's knowledge of the situation with which he was faced. But the case

7–70 **to** **7–74**	was argued by the Crown on the basis of the ordinary meaning of the word "reckless" as an adverb qualifying "drives." "Recklessness," in other words, describes behaviour rather than a state of mind; and it can therefore be satisfied by a blank state of mind.

Allan v. *Patterson* has since been explicitly applied to the reckless discharge of firearms, a common law offence, in *Gizzi and Anr.* v. *Tudhope*, 1982 S.C.C.R. 442. In that case the firearms were discharged in ignorance of the presence of persons working behind some trees. The accused were convicted because they had done little or nothing to satisfy themselves that no one was within range: see also *W.* v. *H.M. Advocate*, 1982 S.C.C.R. 152.

It is also clear from the above cases that the degree of risk which is ignored, or to which the accused is "utterly indifferent," must be very high, and indeed the main question in the appeal in *Gizzi* was whether the risk had been shown to be sufficiently great, or sufficiently obvious to the reasonable man, to raise the accuseds' conduct from negligence to recklessness.

The statutory offence of wilfully or recklessly damaging property, contrary to section 78 of the Criminal Justice (Scotland) Act 1980, requires conduct creating an obvious and material risk of damage to the property which was in fact damaged: *Black* v. *Allan*, 1985 S.C.C.R. 11.

7–88   Footnote 39. See also 1989 Draft Code, s.49(2); R.A. Duff, "The Circumstances of an Attempt" [1991] C.L.J. 100 and Glanville Williams, "Intentions in the Alternative," *ibid.* 120.

7–90   It was held in *Brady* v. *H.M. Advocate*, 1986 S.L.T. 686 and *Salmond* v. *H.M. Advocate*, 1991 S.C.C.R. 43 that where the jury found that a person charged with attempted murder had acted under provocation the appropriate verdict was one of guilty of assault under provocation: *cf. H.M.A.* v. *Blake*, 1986 S.L.T. 661, where the defence was diminished responsibility.

CHAPTER 8

MENS REA IN STATUTORY OFFENCES

8–05   On the general question of *mens rea* or strict liability, see *Beaver* v. *The Queen* [1957] S.C.R. 531; *The Queen* v. *Sault Ste Marie* [1978] 2 S.C.R. 1299; *infra*, para. 8–33.

8–06   Section 301 of the Customs and Excise Act 1952 is now section 167 of the Customs and Excise Management Act 1979.

8–07   The offence of knowingly making a false statement to obtain a licence is now contained in section 174(1)(*a*) of the Road Traffic Act 1988, and that of making a false statement to obtain an insurance certificate is now in section 174(5) of that Act.

Footnote 29. See now Food Safety Act 1990, s.21; Weights and Measures Act 1985, ss.33, 34. Add: Hallmarking Act 1973, s.1; *Chilvers* v. *Rayner* [1984] 1 W.L.R. 328.

8–08   The Food and Drugs (Scotland) Act is replaced by the Food Safety Act 1990.

8–13   Footnote 50: See now Veterinary Surgeons Act 1966, s.19; Dentists Act 1984, s.39; Medical Act 1983, s.49.

8–14   *Alphacell* was followed in *Lockhart* v. *N.C.B.*, 1981 S.L.T. 161; *infra*, para. 8–29.

8–15   The current Regulations are the Road Vehicles (Construction and Use) Regulations 1986. See, *e.g. MacNeill* v. *Wilson*, 1981 J.C. 87; use of vehicle with dangerous load.

        Footnote 57. Lighting offences are now contained in the Road Vehicle Lighting Regulations 1989.

8–16   Most of these offences are now dealt with by Regulations made under the Health and Safety at Work etc. Act 1974: see *infra*, para. 8–64.

8–20   Footnote 85. See now Social Security Act 1986, s.55(1); Road Traffic Act 1988, s.174(1) as contrasted with s.174(5).

8–21   Footnote 94. *R.* v. *Manners-Astley* was overruled by the House of Lords in *R.* v. *Terry* [1984] A.C. 374, which held that "fraudulently" includes an intent to deceive a public official into doing or refraining from something he would not otherwise have done or refrained from doing.

8–23   In *Sutherland* v. *Aitchison*, 1975 J.C. 1, another case of failing to stop after an accident, the driver heard a bump as he squeezed past another car on a single track road. He thought the bump was caused by his exhaust hitting a stone and drove on. It was held that, having heard the bump, it was his duty to stop and see if there had been an accident. Where, therefore, something happens which should alert the accused to the possibility that the circumstances may be such as to require him to do something, he is not entitled to act on a belief that these circumstances do not exist, but is bound to make inquiry.

        Footnote 5. See now Road Traffic Act 1988, s.170.

8–24   Footnote 11. See now Mental Health (Scotland) Act 1984, s.106.

8–25   See also *Bellerby* v. *Carle* [1983] 2 A.C. 101, *infra*, para. 8–61.

8–27   Footnote 36. See now 1975 Act, ss.170, 369.

        Footnote 37. *Brennan* v. *H.M.A.* is now reported at 1977 J.C. 38.

8–28   See now *Ross* v. *H.M. Advocate,* 1991 S.L.T. 564, *supra,* paras. 3–18 to 3–22.

8–29   See M. Budd and A. Lynch, "Voluntariness, Causation and Strict Liability" [1978] Crim. L.R. 74.

8–29   *Alphacell Ltd.* v. *Woodward* was followed in *Lockhart* v. *N.C.B.*, 1981 S.L.T. 161 where the accused were convicted of causing polluting matter to enter a river from a mine which they had ceased to occupy, so that they were no longer able to carry out the pumping operations necessary to prevent the pollution: see *infra*, para. 8–69.

Add new paragraph **8–29a**:

8–29a   *Necessity and coercion.* Since these pleas are effective even when the accused acts freely and knowingly, and since they depend on the objective circumstances rather than on the accused's state of mind (see Chap. 13 in the main work), they are applicable to offences of strict responsibility. In *Tudhope* v. *Grubb*, 1983 S.C.C.R. 350 (Sh. Ct.) the defence of necessity was upheld where the accused who had an excess of alcohol in his blood tried to drive his car in order to escape from an assault.
   In *McLeod* v. *MacDougall*, 1989 S.L.T. 151 the High Court found it unnecessary to decide the general question of the application of the defence to such a charge, but held that it could not apply anyway where the accused, who claimed to be escaping from assailants, continued to drive after passing a police car from which he did not seek assistance.

8–30   See now Food Safety Act 1990, s.21(3)(*c*), and Weights and Measures Act 1985, s.34.
   Footnote 51. Section 96 of the Mental Health (Scotland) Act 1960 is now s.106 of the Mental Health (Scotland) Act 1984.
   Section 18 of the Children and Young Persons (Scotland) Act 1937 has been amended by s.27 of the Protection of Children (Tobacco) Act 1986 to enable the Crown to rely on a presumption that any substance sold in a container conforms to the description on the container.

8–33   In *The Queen* v. *Sault Ste Marie* [1978] 2 S.C.R. 1299 the Canadian Supreme Court divided offences into three categories:—those requiring *mens rea*; strict liability offences, in which *mens rea* need not be established but the defence of reasonable care or reasonable mistake is available; and absolute liability offences in which the accused cannot exculpate himself by showing he was free of fault; and held that public welfare offences were to be regarded as offences of strict liability unless the legislature clearly made them offences of absolute liability.

Footnote 73. *Lambie* v. *H.M.A.* is now reported at 1973 J.C. 53.

8–34   Footnotes 75 and 76. See now Food Safety Act 1990, s.21; Weights and Measures Act 1985, ss.33 and 34.

8–37   In *Valentine* v. *Mackie*, 1980 S.L.T. (Sh. Ct.) 122 A was convicted of aiding and abetting the driver of the car in which he was a passenger to drive with an excess of alcohol in his blood, on the basis that, given that they had been drinking together and the car was being driven erratically, a reasonable man in A's position would have realised that the driver was likely to be over the limit; following *Carter* v. *Richardson* [1974] R.T.R. 314. A was the owner of the car and was acting as supervisor of the driver who held a provisional licence.

8–41   Footnote 16. See now Representation of the People Act 1983, s.159. The Truck Amendment Act 1887 was repealed by the Wages Act 1986.

Footnote 18. Section 66 of the Offices, Shops and Railways Act 1963 was repealed by the Offices, Shops and Railway Premises Act 1963 (Repeals and Modifications) Regulations 1974 which followed on the Health and Safety at Work etc. Act 1974, and which also modified s.63 of the earlier Act.

8–46   See also *Skinner* v. *MacLean*, 1979 S.L.T. (Notes) 35.

8–47   It has been said in England that "use" by a passenger is limited to employers or to cases where the vehicle is being used directly for the accused's own purposes: *Bennett* v. *Richardson* [1980] R.T.R. 358. See also *Passmoor* v. *Gibbons* [1979] R.T.R. 53.

Where a group of people act together in stealing or unlawfully taking a vehicle, they are all treated as using the vehicle: *cf.* *Leathley* v. *Tatton* [1980] R.T.R. 21.

On the other hand, where a passenger becomes aware in the course of a journey that the car has been unlawfully taken and that the driver is therefore uninsured, he does not become a user by remaining in the car, and indeed he may not be a user even if he knows the position before he accepts a lift, albeit he will be guilty of allowing himself to be carried in an unlawfully taken vehicle: see *B (A Minor)* v. *Knight* [1981] R.T.R. 136.

In *Dickson* v. *Valentine*, 1989 S.L.T. 19 a car owner gave her car which was uninsured to another person to repair for her. That person left it parked on the road, and the owner was convicted of using the car without insurance at the place where it had been left. The court held that the concept of two persons having simultaneous use of a car was not confined to master and servant, but extended to principal and agent or even to friends between whom there was an arrangement that one should use the car on behalf of or in the interests of the other.

Footnote 46. *Swan* v. *MacNab* is now reported at 1977 J.C. 57.

8–56   But see *Bellerby* v. *Carle* [1983] 2 A.C. 101; *infra*, para. 8–61, which requires a degree of personal control.

8–59   See also *Byrne* v. *Tudhope*, 1983 S.C.C.R. 337.

8–61   The fact that a licensee is the only person who can lawfully use liquid measures for the sale of liquor does not in itself mean that he is in possession of them for the purpose of the offence of possessing unjust measures, contrary to the Weights and Measures Act 1985,

8-61 s.17; he must be shown to have a degree of control over them: *Bellerby* v. *Carle* [1983] 2 A.C. 101. The House of Lords seem to have been influenced by the fact that the section creates offences of using and possessing unjust weights, but provides a defence of lack of knowledge only in relation to use, making possession an offence of strict responsibility.

See also *MacDonald* v. *Smith*, 1979 J.C. 55; *Sopp* v. *Long* [1970] 1 Q.B. 518.

8-64 See now Weights and Measures Act 1985, section 34.

Footnote 22. See now Food Safety Act 1990, s.21; Road Traffic Act 1988, Sched. 1, para. 4(2). Section 161 of the Factories Act 1961 was superseded by the Health and Safety at Work etc. Act 1974, and was repealed by the Factories Act 1961 etc. (Repeals) Regulations 1976. The 1974 Act contains no general defences, but the principal duties under the Act require persons to do only what is reasonably practicable (ss.2–6) or to take reasonable care (s.7) and not to act intentionally or recklessly (s.8).

8-69 Where an offence of causing something to occur is strict, it is no defence that the forbidden result occurred because of a failure by someone else to take precautions, or that the accused was no longer in a position to prevent the result. In *Lockhart* v. *N.C.B.*, 1981 S.L.T. 161, the Coal Board were convicted of causing polluting matter to enter a river from disused workings which had some time before passed out of their control into that of someone else who had not kept up the precautions taken by the Board when they had been in occupation. It was held that as the Board had set up a system under which pollution was bound to occur in the absence of preventive measures they had caused the pollution. The only defences which might be open were acts of a third party or act of God; the mere fact that the accused could no longer legally enter the mine to take the necessary precautions was irrelevant. The High Court in this case accepted *Alphacell Ltd.* v. *Woodward* [1972] A.C. 824 as representing Scots law.

The Privy Council have held that causing requires control, and not just contributing to the principal actor's decision to act. The principal's conduct must be the result of "actual authority, express or implied, of the party said to have caused it or [be the] consequence of his exerting some capacity which he possesses in fact or law to control or influence the acts of the other": *Att.-Gen. of Hong Kong* v. *Tse Hung-Lit* [1986] A.C. 876, 883, approving *O'Sullivan* v. *Truth and Sportsman Ltd.* (1956) 96 C.L.R. 220.

8-70 "Use" in this context has been held to be limited to the actual driver and his employer: *Valentine* v. *MacBrayne Haulage Ltd.*, 1986 S.C.C.R. 692 (Sh. Ct.).

Footnote 39a. *Swan* v. *MacNab* is now reported at 1977 J.C. 57.

8-72 Footnote 44. *Smith of Maddiston Ltd.* v. *MacNab* is now reported at 1975 J.C. 48.

8–74   The "ought to have known" criterion was applied in *MacPhail* v. *Allan and Dey Ltd.*, 1980 S.L.T. (Sh. Ct.) 136 where the accused company's transport manager had no system for checking whether drivers had valid licences. See also *Carmichael* v. *Hannaway*, 1987 S.C.C.R. 236.

8–75   Footnote 57. Now s.143 of the Road Traffic Act 1988.

Add new paragraph **8–75a**:

8–75a   *Driving licences.* It was held in *Ferrymasters Ltd.* v. *Adams* [1980] R.T.R. 139 that the offence of causing or permitting someone to drive without a licence was in the same position as that of causing or permitting someone to drive uninsured. In *MacPhail* v. *Allan and Dey Ltd.*, 1980 S.L.T. (Sh. Ct.) 136 the sheriff refused to follow that decision, holding it to be inconsistent with *Smith of Maddiston Ltd.* v. *MacNab*, 1975 J.C. 48.

8–79   See *Dean* v. *John Menzies (Holdings) Ltd.*, 1981 J.C. 23, Lord Maxwell at 40–41.

8–80   See also *MacPhail* v. *Allan and Dey Ltd.*, 1980 S.L.T. (Sh. Ct.) 136: *Carmichael* v. *Hannaway*, 1987 S.C.C.R. 236, which may be an example of wilful blindness, *supra*, para. 8–64. *Smith of Maddiston Ltd.* v. *MacNab* is now reported at 1975 J.C. 48.

In *Brown* v. *W. Burns Tractors Ltd.*, 1986 S.C.C.R. 146 a clerical assistant was held to be a person to whom an important part of the administration of the accused's company had been delegated, he being responsible to the directors for supervising the company's drivers in relation to their work and rest hours and tachograph records, and the company were convicted of causing a large number of contraventions of the relevant Regulations by their drivers. The court also accepted that the contraventions had been so many and so flagrant that the accused must be regarded as having been wilfully blind to their assistant's behaviour.

8–84 to 8–90   There is now a decision of the Criminal Appeal Court on the responsibility of a company for a common law crime, *Dean* v. *John Menzies (Holdings) Ltd.*, 1981 J.C. 23 (see Steven L. Stuart, "The Case of the Shameless Company" (1981) 26 J.L.S. 176 and 222), but it does not make the law entirely clear. This is partly because the crime involved was the new form of shameless indecency which consisted in selling obscene articles. Lord Cameron, who was prominent in the development of this crime (see *supra*, para. 1–32; *infra*, para. 41–16), held that it could be committed by a company, but the majority of the court (Lord Stott and Lord Maxwell, who had not been in the earlier obscenity cases and some of whose comments suggest less than enthusiasm for them) held that a company could not be guilty of shameless indecency. The result is that while an individual who knowingly sells obscene books may be convicted of shameless indecency, a label carrying strongly stigmatic overtones, a limited company which is in business solely for the purpose of selling such materials can be convicted only of a contravention of the Civic Government (Scotland) Act 1982: its shop managers may be shamelessly indecent; it may not. If the company had been charged under the then applicable local statute it would have had no argument on the competency of the offence. But the Crown, having chosen instead to use their new toy, were hoist with their own petard. Shameless indecency connotes certain human characteristics and therefore cannot be committed by a company, and it does not matter that none of its original human characteristics is present when it takes the form of selling obscene magazines.

The result is that the incompetency of charging a company with an offence is limited to offences involving peculiarly human characteristics such as shame.

In *Dean* v. *John Menzies Holdings Ltd.*, the majority declined to answer the general question whether a company can commit a common law crime, but Lord Stott said, at p. 35:

> "It is I think self-evident that there are certain crimes and offences which cannot be committed by a corporate body. Murder is such a crime, not only, as the Advocate-Depute conceded, because a company cannot be imprisoned but because it is incapable of having that wicked intent or recklessness of mind necessary to constitute the crime of murder. Other examples which come to mind are reset and perjury. In my opinion the offence of conducting oneself in a shamelessly indecent manner falls into the same category."

That a company cannot commit perjury is due to the fact that it cannot be put on oath, but it is difficult to see why a company which has a policy of buying stolen goods should not be guilty of reset. Nor is it easy to see why a company should not be guilty of conspiracy to commit any crime. Lord Stott conceded that a company was capable of some degree of criminal intent, including an intent to deceive, and he accepted *D.P.P.* v. *Kent and Sussex Contractors* [1944] K.B. 146. It seems, therefore, that there are some kinds of intention which a company is capable of having, and others which it cannot have. It can be greedy, but it cannot harbour thoughts of violence; and it has no shame and no lustful thoughts.

Lord Maxwell was less inclined to admit the possibility of any form of common law *mens rea* in the case of a company than was Lord Stott. He regarded any attribution of *mens rea* to a company as necessarily a fiction, since a corporation is an abstraction. His Lordship said at p. 39:

> "Whatever may be the position as regards other common law crimes, it is perfectly apparent that the company as a legal abstraction could not, as matter of fact, have the knowledge, exercise the judgment and conduct itself in the manner alleged in the complaint. Accordingly the complaint can only become competent by the employment of a fiction (*Tesco* per Lord Reid). Fiction has frequently been employed both in England and Scotland to attribute to a corporation human characteristics which it cannot have, but the fiction which has been employed is not always the same fiction. It seems to me that the approach of the Courts has been this. Where the plain requirements of justice, the express provisions of statute, or the presumed intentions of Parliament require human characteristics to be attributed to corporations the courts provide the necessary fictions tailored to give effect to those requirements, provisions, or intentions."

As examples his Lordship referred to *Clydebank Co-operative Ltd.* v. *Binnie*, 1937 J.C. 17 and *Mackay Brothers* v. *Gibb*, 1969

J.C. 26 as involving different fictions from that of the controlling mind as discussed in *Tesco Supermarkets Ltd.* v. *Nattrass* [1972] A.C. 153: for a discussion of these cases see para. 8–90 in the main work. (His Lordship seems to have regarded all corporate responsibility as a form of vicarious responsibility, and so to have rejected any specific distinction between responsibility for offences which do and those which do not involve vicarious responsibility: his view seems to be that each offence has to be looked at separately to determine whether and if so in what manner responsibility can be attributed to a corporation.) His Lordship concluded, at p. 45:

> "In the light of the authorities cited to us I am not satisfied that the common law of Scotland recognises any clear single fiction which would, for purposes of criminal responsibility, in all matters attribute to a company the kind of human characteristics and conduct alleged in this complaint. It appears to me unrealistic to suggest that the accused company will be guilty if, but only if, some individuals or individual, whose status is not precisely defined, but who must be vaguely at or near director level, had knowledge of the contents of the magazines in question and acted in a shameless and indecent manner in deciding to sell them. That, however, seems to me to be the result of applying the controlling mind fiction. If some other fiction is to be applied I do not know what it is. I accordingly consider that the complaint here is incompetent. It may be that the criminal law of England would reach a different result (*R.* v. *I.C.R. Haulage Limited* [1944] K.B. 551). If so, it would not be the first time."

Lord Cameron, who would have upheld the competency of the charge, stressed that it concerned matters which were within the power of the company—sales in the course of its business, and this certainly seems a necessary limitation on corporate responsibility. His Lordship accepted *Tesco Supermarkets Ltd.* [1972] A.C. 153 and *Lennard's Carrying Co.* v. *Asiatic Petroleum Co. Ltd.* [1915] A.C. 705 as applicable in Scots law. On the specific question of shamelessness, Lord Cameron's view was that shamelessness in this particular offence was an objective matter which did not involve moral obloquy. His Lordship said, at p. 32:

> "The question is not whether a company is an entity which is endowed with a conscience to be appeased or a capacity for moral sensation or an absence of a sense of shame or even a capacity to overcome a sense of shame by the prospect of financial profit. It may well be that the offence libelled is one which falls within the category of offences against public morals, but in order to commit it the offender does not require to be possessed of capacity to feel a sense of personal shame or even to lack it."

Lord Cameron's view of the law in general can be found in his statement at pp. 28–29 that:

> "The criminal law has long recognised that a corporate body may be guilty of breaches of statute and incur a penalty, and therefore be susceptible to prosecution as a person recognised in the eyes of the law. Further, the law has also recognised that an incorporation may be guilty of statutory offences the commission of which is the result of intended or deliberate action or inaction. It was not Parliament which specifically provided that corporate bodies such as limited companies should be subject to prosecution: the various statutes assumed that no

distinction in capacity to offend should exist between natural and other persons recognised by law as legal entities with capacity to discharge certain functions and perform certain actions. The responsibility of both for breaches of statute is the same, and the individual and the company alike can be cited and charged in their own names . . . If Parliament had intended that a company in its individual capacity should not be liable to prosecution in respect of common law offences it could have said so, and at the same time prescribed where and on what natural persons within the structure or employment of the company responsibility and consequent criminal liability should fall. But Parliament has not so provided, and the authorities cited by the Advocate-Depute illustrate the extent to which companies in Scotland can be and are rendered liable to criminal prosecution, even where commission of the offence libelled involves a conscious exercise of will or demonstration of intent. It would seem therefore to follow that there should be no obstacle in principle to the same liability to prosecution where the offence is *malum in se* and not *malum prohibitum*. This distinction lay at the root of Mr Kerrigan's argument that the question of common law liability was a matter for Parliament and not for the Courts. The fallacy of this argument however would seem to lie in the fact this is not a case of creating or declaring a new crime or offence which never existed before, nor of extending the boundaries of criminal responsibility to a group of legal persons on whose shoulders criminal responsibility had not been rested before. If therefore a limited company has the capacity to form an intention, to decide on a course of action, to act in accordance with that deliberate intent within the scope and limits of its articles, it is difficult to see on what general principle it should not be susceptible to prosecution where that action offends against the common law."

It seems, therefore, that Lord Cameron might have regarded conduct which does involve a sense of shame as beyond the capacity of a corporation, and so as forming an exception, along with offences punishable only custodially or physically, to the general rule of corporate responsibility: see his Lordship's opinion at p. 31.

The court held in *Purcell Meats (Scotland) Ltd.* v. *McLeod*, 1987 S.L.T. 528 that it was competent to charge a limited company with an attempted common law fraud which consisted in an endeavour to obtain payments from a statutory board by applying false stamps to carcasses presented to inspectors of the Meat and Livestock Commission. The court did not really address the general question, contenting themselves with the Crown's concession that they would have to prove *mens rea*. It seems, therefore, to be accepted that a company is capable of *mens rea*, at least in relation to fraud.

The offence in *Purcell* was alleged to have been committed "by the hands of persons unknown," but the Crown conceded that they would have to show that the hands in question were those of "an employee of such status and at such a level that the sheriff could reasonably conclude that the acts had been done by the company," and the Crown also accepted the applicability of Lord Reid's statement that for the company to be guilty the actual offenders must act as "the directing mind of the company." (*Tesco Supermarkets Ltd.* v. *Nattrass* [1972] A.C. 153 at p. 170.) It was on the authority of that statement that the High Court held that it would only be after the facts had emerged that it would be possible to decide whether the actual offenders were of the necessary status to make their acts those of the company.

It remains to be seen what, if any, will be the effect of *Docherty* v. *Stakis Hotels Ltd.*, 1991 S.C.C.R. 6 in which the High Court held that a company could not be a person having the management of food premises.

For an example of the attribution to a company of the wilful blindness of an employee, see *Brown* v. *W. Burns Tractors Ltd.*, 1986 S.C.C.R. 146; *supra*, para. 8–80.

The cases are reviewed in Jenifer M. Ross, "Corporate Liability for Crime," 1990 S.L.T. (News) 265.

8–93   Neglect is attributable where the accused has failed to take steps to prevent the commission of an offence by a corporation, if taking these steps falls or should be held to fall within the scope of the functions of his office: *Wotherspoon* v. *H.M.A.*, 1978 J.C. 74, L.J.–G. at 78.

A local authority director of roads is a "manager, secretary or other similar officer" of the authority: *Armour* v. *Skeen*, 1977 J.C. 15.

CHAPTER 9

ERROR

9–06   On rape, see *infra*, paras. 9–25 to 9–33.

9–08   *C.* v. *H.M. Advocate*, 1987 S.C.C.R. 104 is an example of an irrelevant error: belief that a girl under the age of twelve was a consenting party is irrelevant in a charge of indecent assault, on the view, which was accepted by the defence, that she is incapable of consenting to such behaviour. It must be said, however, that where there is actual consent the charge is, at least usually, not one of assault but of lewd practices.

9–12   The general position adopted in the main work has been rejected
to   by the High Court. It was held in *Roberts* v. *Hamilton*, 1989 S.L.T.
9–14   399 and *Connor* v. *Jessop*, 1988 S.C.C.R. 624 that if A aims a blow at B and hits C instead, he is guilty of assaulting C, at least if C is sufficiently close to B for it to be likely that he will be injured. In *Connor* v. *Jessop* the ground of decision was that the circumstances were such that injury to the victim was likely. A threw a tumbler at someone with whom he had been fighting in a disco and the tumbler struck another person who was standing nearby. That decision was said in *Roberts* to be consistent with the decision in the latter case where A tried to intervene in a fight between two combatants by hitting one of them with a stick and in fact struck a third party who was trying to separate the combatants. *Roberts*, however, specifically applied the doctrine of transferred intent as stated by Hume, and held that provided there is an intention to assault someone it does not matter that the act directed against that person takes effect on someone else. Statements to the contrary in the main work in

**9–12
to
9–14** paragraph 9–12 and at page 825 were disapproved. It will be seen that on the facts of these two cases A behaved recklessly with regard to the victims, but it remains to be seen whether *Roberts* is confined to such cases, or extends, for example, to the case where the actual victim unexpectedly intervenes between the assailant and his intended victim. *Quaere* also, whether provocation by the intended victim is relevant in a charge of assaulting the actual victim. Presumably self-defence against the intended victim would be relevant since it would exclude what the court in *Roberts* called "the necessary evil intention," and all that would remain would be a possible charge of recklessly injuring the actual victim.

9–12 For a criticism of this section, see J.H. Pain, "Aberratio Ictus. A Comedy of Errors—and Deflection" (1978) 95 S.A.L.J. 480, 482–484.

9–16 It has been held in South Africa that an error of law is no different from an error of fact, so that even an unreasonable error of law will excuse, provided that where the crime is one of negligence there was nothing to put the accused on his guard as to the possibility that his behaviour was illegal: *S.* v. *De Bloom*, 1977 (3) S.A. 513 (A.D.), where the offence was illegally exporting jewellery; see R.C. Whiting "Changing the Face of Mens Rea" (1978) 95 S.A.L.J. 1. The court's view was that "At this stage of our legal development it must be accepted that the cliché that 'every person is presumed to know the law' has no ground for its existence and that the view that 'ignorance of the law is no excuse' is not legally applicable in the light of present day concept of mens rea in our law."

In *Secretary of State for Trade and Industry* v. *Hart* [1982] 1 W.L.R. 481 A was charged with acting as a company auditor when he knew he was disqualified by reason of being a director of the company, contrary to section 13(5) of the Companies Act 1976, which provides that "No person shall act as auditor of a company at a time when he knows that he is disqualified . . . " The court held that it was necessary for conviction not merely that the accused knew he was a director, but that he knew that directors were disqualified from acting as auditors. Woolf, J. said, at 485F, "The words in their ordinary interpretation are wholly consistent with a view of the subsections which means that a person in the position of the defendant must be aware of the statutory restrictions which exist against his holding the appointment."

It is not yet clear how far this decision will extend. Woolf, J. referred to the possibility of amending the Act. Ormrod, L.J. said, "If that means that he is entitled to rely on ignorance of the law as a defence, in contrast to the usual practice and the usual rule, the answer is that the section gives him that right. Whether it does so intentionally or not is another matter": at 487–488. His Lordship also referred to the difficulty of proving ignorance, but if the offence requires knowledge it will be for the prosecution to prove knowledge.

It may, therefore, be the law that where a statute requires knowledge of some particular circumstances which involves a rule of law, ignorance of that rule of law is a defence where it leads to lack of the knowledge required by the statute.

9–17   A belief by a property owner that a person who is actually a protected tenant is a squatter may be relevant in a charge of harassment: *R.* v. *Phekoo* [1981] 1 W.L.R. 1117; but *cf. R.* v. *Kimber* [1983] 1 W.L.R. 1118.

Footnote 44. It was held in the Canadian case of *The Queen* v. *Prue* [1979] 2 S.C.R. 547 that as the offence of driving while disqualified was one requiring *mens rea*, it required knowledge of the disqualification, even where the disqualification was an automatic consequence of the accused's earlier convictions. Where, therefore, the accused knew that he had been convicted but had not been told that he was disqualified, he was not guilty of driving while disqualified, his error being treated as one of fact. The case is, however, complicated by reason of the disqualification being the result of provincial legislation while the offence of driving while disqualified is a federal one.

9–21   Add new paragraph **9–21a**:

9–21a   *Entrapment*
It appears that Scots law may recognise a limited form of a defence of entrapment, or at least accept that certain evidence of the commission of a crime is inadmissible as where it has been obtained by entrapment, *i.e.* by a police officer or other person in authority disguising himself and inciting the accused to commit a crime, *e.g.* by supplying him with controlled drugs, or with liquor in breach of the licensing laws. Such a defence will succeed only where it can be said that the accused would not have committed the offence but for the inducement, and was not already predisposed or willing to commit crimes of the kind involved. A distinction is also drawn between proper police activities designed to detect and stop a course of criminal activity already embarked on, and activity designed to pressurise, encourage or induce the commission of an offence of a kind the accused would not otherwise be involved in: See *Weir* v. *Jessop (No. 2)*, 1991 S.C.C.R. 636.

See also *Tudhope* v. *Lee*, 1982 S.C.C.R. 409 (Sh. Ct.); *Cook* v. *Skinner*, 1977 J.C. 9. For a general discussion of entrapment, see *Amato* v. *The Queen* [1982] 2 S.C.R. 418.

**9–25
to
9–33**   These paragraphs must now be read subject to the dictum in *Meek and Ors.* v. *H.M. Advocate*, 1982 S.C.C.R. 613 that the Scots courts would answer the question in *Morgan* in the same way as did the House of Lords: see the commentary at 1982 S.C.C.R. 620; Peter Ferguson, "Rape and Reasonable Belief," 1983 S.L.T. (News) 89; the Scottish Law Commission do not regard *Meek* as an authority on recklessness—see their Report on the Mental Element in Crime 1983 (Scot. Law Com. No. 80), para. 4.30, n.1.
There have been suggestions in England that *Morgan* is limited to rape, or at least does not apply to certain statutory offences where

error to be relevant must be based on reasonable grounds: *R. v. Phekoo* [1981] 1 W.L.R. 1117; *Albert* v. *Lavin* [1982] A.C. 546; but these cases were doubted in *R. v. Kimber* [1983] 1 W.L.R. 1118, where *Morgan* was applied to indecent assault, and it is difficult to see any halfway house between the application of *Morgan* and strict responsibility.

There is specific statutory provision in England that in determining whether or not the man believed the woman was a consenting party the jury may take into account the presence or absence of reasonable grounds for the belief: Sexual Offences (Amendment) Act 1976, s.1(2). It seems that recklessness in relation to error in rape depends on *Morgan* and on that statutory provision, and is unaffected by later development in the general law of recklessness such as *R. v. Caldwell* [1982] A.C. 341; *supra*, paras. 7–70 to 7–74: see *R. v. Satnam, S.* (1984) 78 Cr.App.R. 149; *cf. R. v. Pigg* [1983] 1 W.L.R. 6. Drunken error is irrelevant: *R. v. Woods* (1981) 74 Cr.App.R. 312.

On the question of when it is necessary to direct a jury on the defence of belief in consent, see *Meek, supra*, which follows *Morgan* in this too, as does *Pappajohn* v. *The Queen* [1980] 2 S.C.R. 121; see also *R. v. Bashir* (1982) 77 Cr.App.R. 59.

It has been held in Australia that a plea of self-defence requires that the accused's belief that he was being attacked in such a way as to justify his retaliation must be reasonable, and is to be judged on the basis of what the accused himself might reasonably believe in the circumstances: *Viro* v. *The Queen* (1976–1978) 141 C.L.R. 88, 146; *R. v. Wills* [1983] 2 V.R. 201. However, *Morgan* was applied to self-defence in *R. v. Williams (Gladstone)* [1987] 3 All E.R. 411 and *Beckford* v. *The Queen* [1988] A.C. 130. *Jones* v. *H.M. Advocate*, 1990 J.C. 160 suggests that Scots law still requires an error as to self-defence or provocation to be reasonable. For an approach to this problem based on general moral principles, see Jeremy Hordern, "Cognition, Emotion and Criminal Culpability" (1990) 106 L.Q.R. 469.

CHAPTER 10

INSANITY

10–01   Footnote 2. *Brennan* v. *H.M.A.* is now reported at 1977 J.C. 38.

10–03   Footnote 7. See Mental Health (Scotland) Act 1984, ss.1, 17–18.

10–04   *Cunningham* has been overruled by *Ross* v. *H.M. Advocate*, 1991 S.L.T. 564, *supra*, paras. 3–18 to 3–22.

10–05   Section 1(3) of the Mental Health (Scotland) Act 1984 provides that no one shall be treated under the Act "as suffering from mental disorder by reason only of promiscuity or other immoral conduct, sexual deviancy or dependence on alcohol or drugs." Section 17(1) of the 1984 Act provides that no one may be compulsorily admitted to hospital under section 18 of that Act for mental illness unless it is appropriate for him to receive medical treatment in a hospital and it is necessary for his health or safety or the protection of others that he should receive such treatment and it cannot be provided unless he is detained.

Cf. Nicola Lacy, *State Punishment* (London and New York, 1988), p. 74: "Insane offenders must thus be removed from the ambit of normal criminal regulation not because they lack normal capacities of understanding and control, but because they do not and cannot participate in the normal discourse which underpins the enterprise of criminal justice," an approach which also offers an explanation of the rule that the insane cannot be tried: see R.A. Duff, *Trials and Punishments* (C.U.P., 1986).

10–07   Footnote 19. This should read "1975 Act, ss.174, 375, 376(3)."

Footnote 23a. *Brennan* v. *H.M.A.* is now reported at 1977 J.C. 38.

10–15   The 1989 Draft Code seems to have abandoned causal criteria and requires proof only that at the time of the offence the accused was suffering from severe mental illness or severe mental handicap: see s.35.

10–22   Footnote 73. *Brennan* v. *H.M.A.* is now reported at 1977 J.C. 38.

10–40   The 1989 Draft Code's definition of severe mental illness such as to justify a "mental disorder verdict" is very wide, but includes "thinking so disordered as to prevent reasonable appraisal of the defendant's situation or reasonable communication with others": s.34(*e*). For an interesting discussion of the difference between appreciation and knowledge, see *The Queen* v. *Barnier* [1980] 1 S.C.R. 1124.

10–45   The current English provisions are in the Criminal Procedure (Insanity and Unfitness to Plead) Act 1991.

CHAPTER 11

DIMINISHED RESPONSIBILITY

11–03   See also M. Wasik, "Partial Excuses in Criminal Law" (1982) 45 M.L.R. 516.

It seems, however, that diminished responsibility may apply to a charge of attempted murder, resulting in a verdict of guilty of assault under deletion of attempted murder on the ground of diminished responsibility: *H.M.A.* v. *Blake*, 1986 S.L.T. 661.

11–05   Footnote 20. ⎫   *Brennan* v. *H.M.A.* is now reported at 1977
        Footnote 30a. ⎭   J.C. 38.

11–06   See also *Duff* v. *H.M. Advocate*, 1983 S.C.C.R. 461; *L.T.* v. *H.M. Advocate*, 1990 S.C.C.R. 540.

11–19   *Savage* was approved by the High Court in *Connelly* v. *H.M. Advocate*, 1990 J.C. 349 where the need for some element of mental disorder was stressed.

11–21   *Carraher* and *Savage* were approved, and the need for mental disorder was stressed, in *Connelly* v. *H.M. Advocate*, 1990 J.C. 349.

11–22   Section 1(3) of the Mental Health (Scotland) Act 1984 provides that no one shall be treated under the Act "as suffering from mental disorder by reason only of promiscuity or other immoral conduct, sexual deviancy or dependence on alcohol or drugs."

    The distinction between persons under and persons over 21 is removed by section 17(1) of the 1984 Act so that a hospital order under section 18 of that Act can be made on any person whose mental disorder is a persistent one manifested only by abnormally aggressive or seriously irresponsible conduct only where it is appropriate for him to receive medical treatment in a hospital which is likely to alleviate or prevent a deterioration of his condition, and such treatment is necessary for his own health or safety or for the protection of others and cannot be provided unless he is detained under the Act. In view of current psychiatric attitudes psychopaths are unlikely to be dealt with under the Act.

11–23   Footnote 15a. *Brennan* v. *H.M.A.* is now reported at 1977 J.C. 38.

11–24   Section 1(2) of the Mental Health (Scotland) Act 1984 replaces the term "mental deficiency" with the term "mental handicap." A mentally handicapped person of any age may be compulsorily detained in the same circumstances as any other mentally disordered person, provided the handicap is severe mental impairment, or, where the impairment is not severe, the appropriate treatment "is likely to alleviate or prevent a deterioration of his condition": Mental Health (Scotland) Act 1984, s.17(1)(*a*)(ii). "Impairment" and "severe impairment" are defined in s.1(2) of the Act.

CHAPTER 12

INTOXICATION

12–01   *Brennan* v. *H.M. Advocate* is now reported at 1977 J.C. 38. See
et seq. on that case J.W.R. Gray, "The Expulsion of Beard from Scotland: Murder North of the Border" [1979] Crim.L.R. 369.

12–12   The Australian High Court by a majority refused to follow *Majewski* in *The Queen* v. *O'Connor* (1980) 54 A.L.J.R. 349, a case of unlawful wounding by a person under the influence of drugs and alcohol. He had stabbed a police officer who was about to arrest him for stealing *inter alia* the knife involved from the officer's car. The jury had been directed that while intoxication was a relevant defence to the charges of theft and of wounding with intent to resist arrest with which he was indicted, they were not relevant to the offence of unlawful wounding of which they were entitled to convict. Barwick, C.J. said, " . . . proof of a state of intoxication, whether self-induced or not, so far from constituting itself a matter of defence or excuse, is at most merely part of the totality of the evidence which may raise a reasonable doubt as to the existence of essential elements of criminal responsibility": at 351–352; *cf. Kennedy* v. *H.M.A.*, 1944 J.C. 171, L.J.-G. at 177; *Leary* v. *The Queen* [1978] 1 S.C.R. 29, Dickson, J. diss. at 43–44. Barwick, C.J. went on to point out that while there are doubtless cases where a person sets out to become intoxicated, there are also cases where "the state of intoxication may be reached by inadvertence, even though the drug . . . may be taken voluntarily," as where a diner "does not observe the frequency with which the waiter tops up his glass," 54 A.L.J.R. at 353, and that *Majewski* (and *a fortiori Brennan*, we might add) would apply to such a case. He therefore suggested that if voluntary intoxication is to be a basis of criminal responsibility, a distinction ought to be made between wantonly taking drink or drugs with a view to becoming intoxicated, and cases where such wantonness or indifference is absent. Recklessness was used in *Majewski*, he said, outside its usual use in relation to criminal responsibility: at 355; see also the comments at p. 357. It should, however, be pointed out that Australia (as did England at the time of *Majewski*) adopts a subjective approach to recklessness.

Barwick, C.J. also pointed out that the evidence in *Majewski* did not support a conclusion of involuntariness, and that the House of Lords was not concerned with the voluntariness of Majewski's actings as distinct from their intentional nature: *ibid.* 353–354. It is, however, accepted in Britain that intoxication is irrelevant to automatism, *i.e.* that it cannot exclude voluntariness: *supra*, para. 3–23.

The *O'Connor* approach has now been followed in South Africa in *S.* v. *Chretien*, 1981 (1) S.A. 1097 (A.D.), rejecting the earlier case of *S.* v. *Johnson*, 1969 (1) S.A. 201 (A.D.); see J.M. Burchell, "Intoxication and the Criminal Law" (1981) 98 S.A.L.J. 177. The majority of the Canadian Supreme Court preferred *Majewski* in *Leary* v. *The Queen, supra.*

12–14   Add new paragraph **12–14a**:

12–14a   *Error.* There is no Scots law on the effect of intoxication on the law of error. The English view is that where a statute provides a defence of honest belief, a belief induced by drink is relevant: *Jaggard* v. *Dickinson* [1981] Q.B. 527, but that drunken error does not exclude recklessness: *R.* v. *Woods* (1981) 74 Cr.App.R. 312. On the other hand an error of fact induced by voluntary intoxication has been held not to be capable of supporting a plea of self-defence: *R.* v. *O'Grady* [1987] Q.B. 995. Drunken error is irrelevant in the context of a statutory defence requiring the absence of reasonable grounds for suspicion: *R.* v. *Young (Robert)* [1984] 1 W.L.R. 654.

12–14a   The 1989 Draft Code treats drunken error as generally irrelevant: s.22.

It is possible that Scots law will disregard any error caused by self-induced intoxication, even perhaps one which negatives an essential part of the definition of the crime, such as a drunken belief that one is taking one's own umbrella.

12–16   In *H.M. Advocate* v. *Raiker*, 1989 S.C.C.R. 149 one of a number of persons charged with offences committed during a prison riot gave evidence that he had taken part in the riot because he had been given a drug forcibly and perhaps also by stealth. Lord McCluskey directed the jury, at page 154, that where a person acts under the influence of a drug given to him without his consent which, like hypnosis, puts his will under the control of another, he is entitled to be acquitted. It was held in *Ross* v. *H.M. Advocate,* 1991 S.L.T. 564 that automatism caused by involuntary intoxication where the accused's beer had been laced with drugs without his knowledge was a good defence entitling him to an acquittal.

12–18   It has been held in England that the effects of taking valium by someone who believed it to be harmless can negative recklessness: *R.* v. *Hardie* [1985] 1 W.L.R. 64.

12–20   Barwick, C.J. suggested in *The Queen* v. *O'Connor* (1980) 54 A.L.J.R. 349, 358, that juries should be entitled to acquit on the ground of intoxication, and to bring in a verdict that the accused had brought on his own irresponsibility, and that such a verdict should make the accused liable to a substantial penalty.

CHAPTER 13

NECESSITY, COERCION AND SUPERIOR ORDERS

13–06   In *Tudhope* v. *Grubb*, 1983 S.C.C.R. 350 (Sh. Ct.) the need to escape assault was accepted as a defence to a charge of attempting to drive with an excess of alcohol in one's blood. The situation was essentially one of self-defence, but the prima facie crime was not directed at the assailants: see *infra*, para. 13–18.

13–09   Footnote 16. See also *Downie* v. *H.M.A.* 1984 S.C.C.R. 365: removal of a child from its lawful custodian without recourse to the courts justifiable only in the most dire circumstances.

13–10   The High Court has so far declined to state whether necessity is
to   available as a defence to a charge of reckless driving: *Morrison* v.
13–12   *Valentine*, 1990 S.C.C.R. 692; *McNab* v. *Guild*, 1989 S.C.C.R. 138, but has held that if it is available it will be limited to cases of immediate danger to life or of serious injury. It has been held in England that necessity of this limited kind, known as duress of circumstances, is available in charges of reckless driving: *R.* v.

Conway [1989] Q.B. 290, and of driving while disqualified: *R. v. Martin* [1989] R.T.R. 63. The 1989 Draft Code makes it available generally: s.43.

13–13   See Glanville Williams, "The Theory of Excuses" [1982] Crim.L.R. 732.

On the distinction between justification and excuse see J.C. Smith, *Justification and Excuse in the Criminal Law* (London, 1989), Chap. 1; Miriam Gur-Arye, "Should the Criminal Law distinguish between Necessity as a Justification and Necessity as an Excuse" (1986) 102 L.Q.R. 71.

13–15   Footnote 33. For a full account of this and similar cases, see A.W.B. Simpson, *Cannibalism in the Common Law* (University of Chicago Press, 1984).

13–16   Footnote 43. See A.W.B. Simpson, *op. cit.*, Chap. 7.

13–18   Necessity was accepted as a defence to a charge of attempting to drive with an excess of alcohol in one's blood where the accused was trying to escape from three men who had already inflicted substantial injuries on him and were trying to smash the windows of his car which he had entered in an attempt to protect himself from further injury: *Tudhope* v. *Grubb*, 1983 S.C.C.R. 350 (Sh. Ct.), but the position is still unclear: see *MacLeod* v. *MacDougall*, 1989 S.L.T. 151.

13–20   For an example of the treatment of coercion as involving an overpowering of the will, see *Paquette* v. *The Queen* [1977] 2 S.C.R. 189, 197: "A person whose actions have been dictated by fears of death or of grievous bodily injury cannot be said to have formed a genuine intention to carry out an unlawful purpose with the person who has threatened him with those consequences if he fails to co-operate."

13–25   In *R.* v. *Fitzpatrick* [1977] N.I. 20 it was held that a member of an illegal organisation cannot plead duress in respect of crimes committed against his will or in respect of his continued but unwilling association with the organisation. "If a person behaves immorally by, for example, committing himself to an unlawful conspiracy, he ought not to be able to take advantage of the pressure exercised on him by his fellow criminals in order to put on when it suits him the breastplate of righteousness" at 31 D–E. The court also referred to the American rule that coercion is not available to someone who is culpably negligent or reckless in exposing himself to the risk of coercion.

13–26   It was held in *Thomson* v. *H.M. Advocate*, 1983 J.C. 69 that the defence of coercion can succeed only where the harm threatened is so imminent that it is not possible for the accused to seek the protection of the authorities. The extent of his participation in the crime and/or his restoration of the spoils or disclosure of the crime are not conditions for the application of the plea, but go only to

13–26 credibility. The degree of coercion applied must be such that it would affect a reasonable person of normal resolution: *cf.* the law on provocation, *infra*, paras. 25–32 *et seq.*; *R.* v. *Graham (Paul)* [1982] 1 W.L.R. 294. The plea is not normally available to someone who joins what he knows to be a criminal gang: *cf. R.* v. *Fitzpatrick, supra*, para. 13–25; *R.* v. *Sharp* [1987] Q.B. 853. The law laid down in *Thomson* seems in line with that in other Commonwealth countries; *e.g. R.* v. *Teichelman* [1981] 2 N.Z.L.R. 64; *R.* v. *Dawson* [1978] V.R. 536; for a criticism of *Thomson*, see Alan Norrie, "The Defence of Coercion in Scots Criminal Law," 1984 S.L.T. (News) 13.

For another example of coercion, see *H.M. Advocate* v. *Raiker*, 1989 S.C.C.R. 149.

13–27 The availability of coercion as a defence to murder was conceded in the particular circumstances of *R.* v. *Graham (Paul)* [1982] 1 W.L.R. 294. The position of murder was reserved in *Thomson* v. *H.M. Advocate*, 1983 J.C. 69.

D.P.P. v. *Lynch* was overruled in *R.* v. *Howe* [1987] A.C. 417 which applied *R.* v. *Dudley and Stephens* (*supra*, para. 13–15 in the main work) to coercion, and held that it is not a defence to murder. It has also been held that it is not a defence to attempted murder: *R.* v. *Gotts* [1991] 2 W.L.R. 878.

13–36 For a modern case on superior orders, see *Attorney-General's Reference (No. 1 of 1975)* [1977] A.C. 105.

CHAPTER 14

THEFT

14–08 Footnote 75. See now Road Traffic Act 1988, s.192.

14–15 It has been held in England that to take an article from a shelf in a supermarket, remove its price label and substitute one from a cheaper article, constitutes appropriation and is a completed theft, even though there is an intention to pay the lesser price: *R.* v. *Morris* [1984] A.C. 320; *Oxford* v. *Peers* (1980) 72 Cr.App.R. 19. Such a case should, it is submitted, be treated in Scotland as an attempt to defraud the store of the goods or at least of the difference in price: compare *Kaur* v. *Chief Constable for Hampshire* [1981] 1 W.L.R. 578, which was disapproved in *R.* v. *Morris*.

It has also been held in England that where a person puts goods into the store's trolley intending not to pay for them, but changes his mind and abandons the trolley in the store there is no theft: *Eddy* v. *Niman* (1981) 73 Cr.App.R. 237.

In Scotland, however, where any movement of the goods may constitute *amotio*, the question is one of evidence of intention to steal. In *Barr* v. *O'Brien*, 1991 S.C.C.R. 67 it was held that intention to steal could be inferred where the accused took articles from the shelf and put them in his pocket, and then, on noticing that he was being watched as he approached the door, turned back before reaching the last check-out.

14-21   The unusual case of *Mackenzie* v. *MacLean*, 1981 S.L.T. (Sh.Ct.) 40 perhaps owes more to a sense of proportion than to strict law.

14-22   For a modern example of theft by finding, see *MacMillan* v. *Lowe*, 1991 S.C.C.R. 113.

14-24   The Burgh Police (Scotland) Act provisions are now replaced by ss.67 to 75 of the Civic Government (Scotland) Act 1982.

Section 67(1) of that Act obliges any person taking possession of any property without the owner's authority in circumstances making it reasonable to infer that it has been lost or abandoned to take reasonable care of it and to deliver it, or report his finding of it, to a constable (or to its owner or possessor, or to the owner or occupier of any premises or land on which it was found, or to anyone apparently authorised to act on behalf of any of these persons) without unreasonable delay. Any person other than a constable, or the owner or possessor of the property to whom a finder makes a report under these provisions, is himself obliged to report the matter to a constable or to the owner or possessor: s.67(4). Failure to do so without reasonable excuse is a summary offence: maximum penalty a fine of level 2: s.67(6).

Any person who reports to a constable that he has taken possession of lost or abandoned property may be directed by the chief constable to deliver it to such person as the latter may direct, and failure to do so without reasonable excuse is an offence under the section punishable as above: s.67(4); *quaere* whether "chief constable" here requires the personal intervention of that officer or of a specifically appointed deputy.

The chief constable is empowered to make arrangements for the custody of lost property, and is obliged to try to find the owner. After two months he may dispose of it if he thinks this appropriate in the circumstances, but he may do so earlier if it cannot be safely or conveniently kept, and he may return it to the owner at any time. If it is not claimed he can offer it to the finder or sell it. The chief constable may also order the owner to pay him such sum as he determines as a reward to the finder: ss.68, 70.

It has been held that the chief constable has no power to adjudicate in cases where the ownership of property is in dispute, and that the provisions of the Act have no application to stolen property: *Fleming* v. *Chief Constable of Strathclyde*, 1987 S.C.L.R. 303 (Sh.Ct.).

A disposal of property under these provisions to a person taking it in good faith vests ownership in that person subject to a right in the previous owner to recover possession within a year thereof: s.71. This is the only way in which ownership of lost or abandoned property can be transferred: s.73.

These provisions do not apply to property found on public transport premises or vehicles, or to dogs: s.67(2).

14-31
to
14-33   Whatever the nature of the crime discussed in these paragraphs it does not extend to the mere copying of information where no unlawful taking of any object is involved, even if the information is

14–31
to   commercially valuable and is offered for sale: *Grant* v. *Allan*, 1988
14–33 S.L.T. 11.

14–33 For water see now Water (Scotland) Act 1980, Sched. 4, para. 31: max. pen. a fine of level 1.

14–34 Delete the first paragraph of footnote 87.
Delete footnote 88 and substitute:
Paragraph 3(2) of Sched. 6 to the Electricity Act 1989 makes it an offence to restore a supply of electricity by a public supplier which has been cut off, and para. 11(1) of Sched. 7 to that Act makes it an offence to alter the register of any electricity meter or to prevent it duly registering the quantity of electricity supplied by any supplier: max. pen. in each case a fine of level 3.

14–35 It is an offence under section 42 of the Telecommunications Act 1984 dishonestly to obtain a service provided by means of a licensed telecommunication system with intent to avoid payment of any applicable charge: max. pen. two years and a fine on indictment, six months on summary conviction. That section does not apply to the dishonest receipt of a television or sound broadcasting service provided from a place in the United Kingdom, such receipt being an offence under section 297 of the Copyright, Designs and Patents Act 1988: max. pen. a fine of level 5: see *infra*, para. 15–58a.

14–40 See *Valentine* v. *Kennedy*, 1985 S.C.C.R. 89 (Sh.Ct.).

14–42 Footnote 21. The reference should be to s.536(2)(*c*); max. fine now level 3: Merchant Shipping Act 1979, Sched. 6.
Footnote 22. Max. fine now level 4: Merchant Shipping Act 1979, Sched. 6.

14–43 In the latest reported High Court case of plagium it was held that the father of an illegitimate child who did not hold a custody decree in respect of the child could be guilty of stealing her: *Downie* v. *H.M.A.*, 1984 S.C.C.R. 365; see also *Hamilton* v. *Mooney*, 1990 S.L.T. (Sh.Ct.) 105.

14–44 Footnote 34. The Anatomy Act 1832 was repealed and replaced by the Anatomy Act 1984.

14–47 Footnote 65. See now Sale of Goods Act 1979, s.18, r. 4.

14–50 A charge of embezzlement by a partner of funds received by him for the partnership was upheld by the High Court in *Peter Anthony Sumner*, Nov. 1983, unreported.

14–62 For a discussion of the position where a person who has complete control of a company is charged with theft from the company, see *Att.-Gen.'s Reference (No 2 of 1982)* [1984] Q.B. 624.

Footnote 48. See now Sale of Goods Act 1979, ss.24, 25.

14–65 See Glanville Williams, "Temporary Appropriation should be Theft" [1981] Crim.L.R. 129.

14–65 It seems now to be accepted that temporary appropriation for a
to nefarious purpose is theft. In *Milne* v. *Tudhope*, 1981 J.C. 53 a
14–76 builder who was doing work on a house on a fixed price contract
refused to carry out remedial work without further payment, and
removed parts of the house without the consent of the owner whom
he told he would not return them unless he received more money.
He was convicted of theft, on the view that "a clandestine taking,
aimed at achieving a nefarious purpose, constitutes theft, even if the
taker intends all along to return the thing when his purpose has
been achieved." The conviction was upheld, the court saying that in
certain exceptional cases an intention to deprive temporarily will
suffice, and disapproving *Herron* v. *Best*. The exceptional circumstances in this case were that the accused was seeking to achieve an
unlawful, even if not a criminal, purpose. The element of clan-
destinity is unimportant, since it means nothing more than that the
owner was not aware of and had not authorised the removal, and
indeed only the latter matters.

Milne v. *Tudhope* leaves us without any general principle for
determining when temporary appropriation is enough. It might be
argued that where the intention to return is conditional on the
owner doing something which the accused is not entitled to require
him to do, there is a theft; or alternatively, and this may indeed be
the same thing, it might be argued that there is theft where the
circumstances also involve some other crime, such as extortion. But
the court approved a general reference to taking for a nefarious
purpose, which would mean, for example, that to borrow a key in
order to commit housebreaking was clearly theft, and indeed that to
borrow it to gain entry to premises in order there to engage in
shamelessly indecent conduct was enough. *Milne* v. *Tudhope* may
be another example of the tendency of Scots law to make broad
"moral" pronouncements. It was followed by the trial judge in
Sandlan v. *H.M. Advocate*, 1983 S.C.C.R. 71 where it was suggested that stock and books had been temporarily removed from a
company's premises by its director in order to prevent auditors
discovering shortages. Lord Stewart told the jury that where goods
are removed clandestinely, that is to say, secretly, "such a taking
. . . , aimed at achieving a nefarious purpose, constitutes theft even
if the taker intends all along to return the things taken when his
purpose has been achieved.": at 83.

See now also *Kidston* v. *Annan*, 1984 S.C.C.R. 20 in which *Milne*
v. *Tudhope* was followed in the case of a person who was given
property in order to make an estimate of the cost of repairing it and
who refused to return the property unless he was paid for an
uninstructed repair. In that case a reference to "holding goods to
ransom" which had been made in *Milne* v. *Tudhope* was approved
as describing a situation which constituted theft.

The law of England still requires an intention to deprive permanently: Theft Act 1968, s.1(1); *R.* v. *Lloyd* [1985] Q.B. 829.

14–71 See also D. W. Ellott, "Dishonesty in Theft. A Dispensable
Concept" [1982] Crim.L.R. 395. For the current state of English
law, see Archbold (43rd ed.) para. 18–32.

**14–77
to
14–79**
It was held in *Kivlin* v. *Milne*, 1979 S.L.T. (Notes) 2 that where a car was unlawfully taken and left in a place where the owner was not liable to discover it by his own investigations the sheriff was entitled to infer an intention permanently to deprive. It was accepted, however, that it would always be a question of circumstances in each case whether that intention had been established. On the other hand, *McLeod* v. *Mason and Ors.*, 1981 S.C.C.R. 75 indicates that in the absence of evidence that the accused intended only to contravene section 178 of the Road Traffic Act an intention to steal is to be presumed: see the commentary at 1981 S.C.C.R. 78.

14–78
Footnote 22. The current provision is s.178 of the Road Traffic Act 1988.
Footnote 24. Sched. 4 to the Road Traffic Act 1972 is replaced by Part II of Sched. 2 to the Road Traffic Offenders Act 1988. Section 175 is re-enacted without substantial alteration in s.178 of the Road Traffic Act 1988.

14–79
Footnote 31. *Lambie* v. *H.M.A.* is now reported at 1973 J.C. 53.

14–85
Footnote 45. See also *supra*, paras. 14–65 to 14–76.

14–86
Footnote 86. See *Harrison* v. *Jessop*, 1991 S.C.C.R. 329.

CHAPTER 15

AGGRAVATED THEFTS AND ALLIED OFFENCES

15–06
A burglar alarm is an integral part of the security of a building, and to disconnect it constitutes attempted housebreaking: *Burns* v. *Allan*, 1987 S.C.C.R. 449. Presumably if the disconnection enables the thief to enter the premises without actual violence to the building, that entry will constitute housebreaking, the security of the alarm having been overcome.

15–22
The relevant value is now level 4: Criminal Justice Act 1982, Sched. 7.

15–29
Footnote 9. See now the 2nd edition of Walker on *Delict* (Edinburgh, 1981).

15–30
Footnote 16. The current provision is s.178 of the Road Traffic Act 1988.

15–33
The statutory offence is now contained in section 178(1) of the Road Traffic Act 1988 whose terms are identical to those of section 175(1) of the 1972 Act save that "shall" is replaced by "is," and "be" is deleted.

Footnote 24. See now Road Traffic Offenders Act 1988, Sched. 4.

15–34   The *McKnight* v. *Davies* approach was preferred in *Barclay* v. *Douglas*, 1983 S.C.C.R. 224 where A was given the keys of B's car so that he might drive a short distance to B's house. On his way to the car A met his girl friend and took her for a run in the car in the course of which he was stopped by the police. He was convicted of a contravention of section 175.

Where consent is obtained by fraud and the use of the vehicle is within the terms of that consent, there is no contravention of section 175: *Whittaker* v. *Campbell* [1984] Q.B. 318.

Footnote 33a. See now Road Traffic Act 1988, s.143.

15–35   Footnote 35. Section 23(3) of the Road Traffic Offenders Act 1988 applies the same rule to charges of contravening s.178 of the Road Traffic Act 1988 which re-enacts s.175 of the Road Traffic Act 1972.

15–37   See now section 178(2) of the Road Traffic Act 1988 whose terms are substantially the same as those of section 175(2) of the Road Traffic Act 1972.

15–41   Footnote 39. Section 34 of the Mental Health (Scotland) Act 1960 was repealed by the Mental Health (Amendment) (Scotland) Act 1983.

15–42   The word "destroys" was removed by the Schedule to the Criminal Damage Act 1971.

15–45   See now section 100 of the Customs and Excise Management Act 1979 and section 17 of the Alcoholic Liquor Duties Act 1979 respectively.

15–47   Footnote 51. See now Road Traffic Act 1988, s.25.

15–49   Max. fine now level 1: Criminal Justice Act 1982, Sched. 15.

15–51   Section 4 of the Vagrancy Act 1824 was repealed by the Civic Government (Scotland) Act 1982.

15–52   Footnote 63. Max. fine now level 3: Merchant Shipping Act 1979, Sched. 6.

Footnote 64. Max. fine now level 2: Merchant Shipping Act 1979, Sched. 6.

15–54   Section 21 of the Copyright Act 1956 is replaced by section 107 of the Copyright, Designs and Patents Act 1988, which provides:

> "(1) A person commits an offence who, without the licence of the copyright owner—
> (*a*) makes for sale or hire, or
> (*b*) imports into the United Kingdom otherwise than for his private and domestic use, or
> (*c*) possesses in the course of a business with a view to committing any act infringing the copyright, or

(*d*) in the course of a business—
    (i) sells or lets for hire, or
    (ii) offers or exposes for sale or hire, or
    (iii) exhibits in public, or
    (iv) distributes, or

(*e*) distributes otherwise than in the course of a business to such an extent as to affect prejudicially the owner of the copyright,

an article which is, and which he knows or has reason to believe is, an infringing copy of a copyright work.

(2) A person commits an offence who—

(*a*) makes an article specifically designed or adapted for making copies of a particular copyright work, or

(*b*) has such an article in his possession,

knowing or having reason to believe that it is to be used to make infringing copies for sale or hire or for use in the course of a business.

(3) Where copyright is infringed (otherwise than by reception of a broadcast or cable programme)—

(*a*) by the public performance of a literary, dramatic or musical work, or

(*b*) by the playing or showing in public of a sound recording or film,

any person who caused the work to be so performed, played or shown is guilty of an offence if he knew or had reason to believe that copyright would be infringed.

(4) A person guilty of an offence under subsection (1)(*a*), (*b*), (*d*)(iv) or (*e*) is liable—

(*a*) on summary conviction to imprisonment for a term not exceeding six months or a fine not exceeding the statutory maximum, or both;

(*b*) on conviction on indictment to a fine or imprisonment for a term not exceeding two years, or both.

(5) A person guilty of any other offence under this section is liable on summary conviction to imprisonment for a term not exceeding six months or a fine not exceeding level 5 on the standard scale, or both.

(6) Sections 104 to 106 (presumptions as to various matters connected with copyright) do not apply to proceedings for an offence under this section; but without prejudice to their application in proceedings for an order under section 108 below.''

In terms of section 1 of the Copyright, Designs and Patents Act 1988 copyright subsists in original literary, dramatic, musical or artistic works, in sound recordings, films, broadcasts or cable programmes, and in the typographical arrangement of published editions. Further definitions are to be found in sections 3 to 8 of the Act.

Section 18 of the Copyright Act 1956 is replaced by section 27 of the Copyright, Designs and Patents Act 1988 subss. (2) to (6) of which provide the following definition of "infringing copy."

"(2) An article is an infringing copy if its making constituted an infringement of the copyright in the work in question.

(3) An article is also an infringing copy if—

(*a*) it has been or is proposed to be imported into the United Kingdom, and

(*b*) its making in the United Kingdom would have constituted an infringement of the copyright in the work in question, or a breach of an exclusive licence agreement relating to that work.

(4) Where in any proceedings the question arises whether an article is an infringing copy and it is shown—

(*a*) that the article is a copy of the work, and

(*b*) that copyright subsists in the work or has subsisted at any time,
it shall be presumed until the contrary is proved that the article was
made at a time when copyright subsisted in the work.

(5) Nothing in subsection (3) shall be construed as applying to an
article which may lawfully be imported into the United Kingdom by
virtue of any enforceable Community right within the meaning of
section 2(1) of the European Communities Act 1972.

(6) In [Part I of this Act] 'infringing copy' includes a copy falling to
be treated as an infringing copy by virtue of any of the following
provisions—

section 32(5) (copies made for purposes of instruction or examination),

section 35(3) (recordings made by educational establishments for educational purposes),

section 36(5) (reprographic copying by educational establishments for
purposes of instruction),

section 37(3)(*b*) (copies made by librarian or archivist in reliance on
false declaration),

section 56(2) (further copies, adaptations, &c. of work in electronic
form retained on transfer of principal copy),

section 63(2) (copies made for purpose of advertising artistic work for
sale),

section 68(4) (copies made for purpose of broadcast or cable programme), or

any provision of an order under section 141 (statutory licence for
certain reprographic copying by educational establishments)."

15–55 These provisions are replaced by section 198 of the Copyright,
15–56 Designs and Patents Act 1988 which provides:

"(1) A person commits an offence who without sufficient consent—
(*a*) makes for sale or hire, or
(*b*) imports into the United Kingdom otherwise than for his private
and domestic use, or
(*c*) possesses in the course of a business with a view to committing any
act infringing the rights conferred by this Part [Part II], or
(*d*) in the course of a business—
    (i) sells or lets for hire, or
    (ii) offers or exposes for sale or hire, or
    (iii) distributes,
a recording which is, and which he knows or has reason to believe is,
an illicit recording.

(2) A person commits an offence who causes a recording of a
performance made without sufficient consent to be—
(*a*) shown or played in public, or
(*b*) broadcast or included in a cable programme service,
thereby infringing any of the rights conferred by this Part, if he knows
or has reason to believe that those rights are thereby infringed.

(3) In subsections (1) and (2) 'sufficient consent' means—
(*a*) in the case of a qualifying performance, the consent of the
performer, and
(*b*) in the case of a non-qualifying performance subject to an exclusive
recording contract—
    (i) for the purposes of subsecton (1)(*a*) (making of recording),
the consent of the performer or the person having recording
rights, and
    (ii) for the purposes of subsection (1)(*b*), (*c*) and (*d*) and
subsection (2) (dealing with or using recording), the consent
of the person having recording rights.

The references in this subsection to the person having recording
rights are to the person having those rights at the time the consent is
given or, if there is more than one such person, to all of them.

15–55
15–56 (4) No offence is committed under subsection (1) or (2) by the commission of an act which by virtue of any provision of Schedule 2 may be done without infringing the right conferred by this Part.

(5) A person guilty of an offence under subsection (1)(*a*), (*b*) or (*d*)(iii) is liable—

  (*a*) on summary conviction to imprisonment for a term not exceeding six months or a fine not exceeding the statutory maximum, or both;

  (*b*) on conviction on indictment to a fine or imprisonment for a term not exceeding two years, or both.

(6) A person guilty of any other offence under this section is liable on summary conviction to a fine not exceeding level 5 on the standard scale or imprisonment for a term not exceeding six months, or both."

15–57 The 1958 Act was repealed by the Copyright, Designs and Patents Act 1988.

15–58 Section 4 of the Performers Protection Act 1963 is replaced by section 201 of the Copyright, Designs and Patents Act 1988 which makes it an offence to represent falsely that one is authorised to give consent in relation to a performance, unless one believes on reasonable grounds that one is so authorised: max. pen. six months and a fine of level 5.

Add new paragraph **15–58a**:

15–58a *Fraudulent receipt of transmissions*

Section 297 of the Copyright, Designs and Patents Act 1988 makes it an offence dishonestly to receive a programme included in a programme service (as defined in the Broadcasting Act 1990) provided from a place in the U.K. with intent to avoid payment of any applicable charge: max. pen. a fine of level 5.

15–61 In a charge of opening a lockfast car with intent to steal it is not necessary to specify or prove whether the intention was to steal the car or its contents: *McLeod* v. *Mason & Ors.*, 1981 S.C.C.R. 75, a case which appears to achieve much the same result as section 9 of the English Criminal Attempts Act 1981.

15–62
to
15–71 Sections 7 and 20 of the Prevention of Crimes Act 1871, section 4 of the Vagrancy Act 1824 and section 409 of the Burgh Police (Scotland) Act 1892 were repealed by the Civic Government (Scotland) Act 1982.

Section 57(1) of the Civic Government (Scotland) Act 1982 provides:

"Any person who, without lawful authority to be there, is found in or on a building or other premises, whether enclosed or not, or in its curtilage or in a vehicle or vessel so that, in all the circumstances, it may reasonably be inferred that he intended to commit theft there shall be guilty of an offence and liable, on summary conviction, to a fine not exceeding [level 4] or to imprisonment for a period not exceeding 3 months or to both."

"Theft" includes any aggravation of theft including robbery: *ibid.*, s.57(2).

Section 58(1) of the Civic Government (Scotland) Act 1982 provides:

"Any person who, being a person to whom this section applies—

(a) has or has recently had in his possession any tool or other object from the possession of which it may reasonably be inferred that he intended to commit theft or has committed theft; and

(b) is unable to demonstrate satisfactorily that his possession of such tool or other object is or was not for the purposes of committing theft

shall be guilty of an offence and liable, on summary conviction, to a fine not exceeding [level 4] or to imprisonment for a period not exceeding 3 months or to both."

The section applies to persons with two or more convictions for theft which are not spent in terms of the Rehabilitation of Offenders Act 1974: s.58(4). "Theft" includes any aggravation of theft, including robbery: s.58(5).

"Recent possession" in this context means possession within 14 days of the accused's arrest for contravention of s.58(1) or of the issue of a warrant for his arrest therefor, or of any earlier date at which he is first served with a complaint therefor: s.58(2). The circumstances of the possession, as well as the nature of the articles themselves, may be taken into account in making the inference of theftuous intention: *Newlands* v. *MacPhail*, 1991 S.C.C.R. 88.

It will be noted that these provisions are much narrower than the older ones. In particular, they are limited to theft and robbery, and do not extend even to other crimes of dishonesty.

15–72   It is a defence to a charge under section 4 that the object of making the explosive was to protect the accused or his family or property against imminent apprehended attack by means he believed to be reasonably necessary for the purpose, but such a defence will rarely succeed where the explosives are petrol bombs: *Attorney-General's Reference (No. 2 of 1983)* [1984] Q.B. 456.

For the meaning of "explosive," see *infra*, paras. 22–18 to 22–19.

Where the Crown lead evidence giving rise to a suspicion of an unlawful object, it does not matter whether that object is intended to be achieved in the United Kingdom or abroad: *R.* v. *Berry* [1985] A.C. 246.

CHAPTER 16

ROBBERY

16–02   Theft no longer requires an intention permanently to deprive (*supra*, paras. 14–65 to 14–76) and therefore neither does robbery: *Harrison* v. *Jessop*, 1991 S.C.C.R. 329.

It is robbery to take money by force or threat, even if the money is taken in part satisfaction of a debt: *Harrison* v. *Jessop*, *supra*.

16–11   In *Cromar* v. *H.M. Advocate*, 1987 S.C.C.R. 635 the accused was convicted of robbery on a charge that he placed his hands on a bag being carried by the victim, pulled at the bag, tried to force the

16–11 victim to release the bag and seized hold of the bag. The handle of the bag snapped and the accused made off with it.

16–19 The Hijacking Act 1971 was repealed by the Aviation Security Act 1982. Section 1 is replaced by section 1 of the latter Act, which provides:

> "(1) A person on board an aircraft in flight who unlawfully, by the use of force or by threats of any kind, seizes the aircraft or exercises control of it commits the offence of hijacking, whatever his nationality, whatever the State in which the aircraft is registered and whether the aircraft is in the United Kingdom or elsewhere, but subject to subsection (2) below.
>
> (2) If—
>
> (*a*) the aircraft is used in military, customs or police service, or
>
> (*b*) both the place of take-off and the place of landing are in the territory of the State in which the aircraft is registered,
>
> subsection (1) above shall not apply unless—
>
> > (i) the person seizing or exercising control of the aircraft is a United Kingdom national; or
> >
> > (ii) his act is committed in the United Kingdom; or
> >
> > (iii) the aircraft is registered in the United Kingdom or is used in the military or customs service of the United Kingdom or in the service of any police force in the United Kingdom.
>
> (3) A person who commits the offence of hijacking shall be liable, on conviction on indictment, to imprisonment for life.
>
> (4) If the Secretary of State by order made by statutory instrument declares—
>
> (*a*) that any two or more States named in the order have established an organisation or agency which operates aircraft; and
>
> (*b*) that one of those States has been designated as exercising, for aircraft so operated, the powers of the State of registration,
>
> the State declared under paragraph (*b*) of this subsection shall be deemed for the purposes of this section to be the State in which any aircraft so operated is registered; but in relation to such an aircraft subsection (2)(*b*) above shall have effect as if it referred to the territory of any one of the States named in the order.
>
> (5) For the purposes of this section the territorial waters of any State shall be treated as part of its territory."

A United Kingdom national is someone who is
(a) a British citizen, a British Dependent Territories citizen or a British overseas citizen; or
(b) a person who under the British Nationality Act 1981 is a British subject; or
(c) a British protected person (within the meaning of that Act): Aviation Security Act 1982, s.38(1).

CHAPTER 17

EMBEZZLEMENT

17–08 Footnote 52. The relevant sum is now £25: Consumer Credit (Increase of Monetary Amounts) Order 1983.

17–28   A partner may be convicted of embezzlement from his firm: *Peter Anthony Sumner*, High Court on appeal, November 1983, unreported.

17–33   Footnote 53. The provisions of s.4 of the Solicitors (Scotland) Act 1965 are now contained in s.36 of the Solicitors (Scotland) Act 1980, as amended by s.25 of the Law Reform (Miscellaneous Provisions) (Scotland) Act 1980.

CHAPTER 18

COMMON LAW FRAUD

18–06   The applicability of *R.* v. *Charles* [1977] A.C. 177 to credit cards was affirmed by the House of Lords in *R.* v. *Lambie* [1982] A.C. 449. Presentation of a cheque card or credit card constitutes a representation of actual authority from the bank or the card company to use the card for the transaction in question. It is for the jury to decide whether it was that representation which induced the dupe to hand over the goods, and it is to be expected that in practice they will decide that it was.

18–19   It has been held to be a fraud to induce a solicitor to raise an action against a third party by giving him false instructions: *McKenzie* v. *H.M.A.*, 1988 S.L.T. 487. It may also be the case that to induce the police to make unnecessary investigations, or to bring out a doctor or the fire brigade by raising a false alarm, would now be regarded as frauds: *cf. Waddell* v. *MacPhail*, 1986 S.C.C.R. 593, *infra*, para. 48–45.

Footnote 13. The provisions of s.78 of the Post Office Act 1969 are now contained in s.42 of the Telecommunications Act 1984, and apply to programme services within the meaning of the Broadcasting Act 1990, other than any to which s.297(1) of the Copyright, Designs and Patents Act 1988 applies: see *supra*, para. 15–58a.

18–33   A policeman who induces someone to commit a crime, such as selling him drugs, or liquor out of hours, by concealing his identity or assuming a false identity, will have a defence of public duty, provided he acted within the bounds set by the law of entrapment: *Weir* v. *Jessop*, 1991 S.C.C.R. 242.

18–54   See also *Macdonald* v. *Tudhope*, 1983 S.C.C.R. 341.

CHAPTER 19

STATUTORY FRAUDS

19–01   All the earlier legislation was repealed by the Bankruptcy (Scotland) Act 1985.

19–03   Bankruptcy frauds are now dealt with under section 67 of the Bankruptcy (Scotland) Act 1985 which provides, *inter alia*:

"(1) A debtor who during the relevant period makes a false statement in relation to his assets or his business or financial affairs to any creditor or to any person concerned in the administration of his estate shall be guilty of an offence, unless he shows that he neither knew nor had reason to believe that his statement was false.

(2) A debtor, or other person acting in his interest whether with or without his authority, who during the relevant period destroys, damages, conceals or removes from Scotland any part of the debtor's estate or any document relating to his assets or his business or financial affairs shall be guilty of an offence, unless the debtor or other person shows that he did not do so with intent to prejudice the creditors.

(3) A debtor who is absent from Scotland and who after the date of sequestration of his estate fails, when required by the court, to come to Scotland for any purpose connected with the administration of his estate, shall be guilty of an offence.

(4) A debtor, or other person acting in his interest whether with or without his authority, who during the relevant period falsifies any document relating to the debtor's assets or his business or financial affairs, shall be guilty of an offence, unless the debtor or other person shows that he had no intention to mislead the permanent trustee, a commissioner or any creditor.

(5) If a debtor whose estate is sequestrated—

(*a*) knows that a person has falsified any document relating to the debtor's assets or his business or financial affairs; and

(*b*) fails, within one month of the date of acquiring such knowledge, to report his knowledge to the interim or permanent trustee,

he shall be guilty of an offence.

(6) A person who is absolutely insolvent and who during the relevant period transfers anything to another person for an inadequate consideration or grants any unfair preference to any of his creditors shall be guilty of an offence, unless the transferor or grantor shows that he did not do so with intent to prejudice the creditors.

(7) A debtor who is engaged in trade or business shall be guilty of an offence if at any time in the period of one year ending with the date of sequestration of his estate, he pledges or disposes of, otherwise than in the ordinary course of his trade or business, any property which he has obtained on credit and has not paid for unless he shows that he did not intend to prejudice his creditors.

(8) A debtor who is engaged in trade or business shall be guilty of an offence if at any time in the period of 2 years ending with the date of sequestration, he has failed to keep or preserve such records as are necessary to give a fair view of the state of his assets or his business and financial affairs and to explain his transactions, unless he shows that such failure was neither reckless nor dishonest:

Provided that a debtor shall not be guilty of an offence under this subsection if, at the date of sequestration, his unsecured liabilities did not exceed the prescribed amount; but, for the purposes of this proviso, if at any time the amount of a debt (or part of a debt) over which a security is held exceeds the value of the security, that debt (or part) shall be deemed at that time to be unsecured to the extent of the excess. . . .

(10) For the purposes of subsection (9) above—

(*a*) 'debtor' means—

    (i) a debtor whose estate has been sequestrated, or

    (ii) a person who has been adjudged bankrupt in England and Wales or Northern Ireland,

and who, in either case, has not been discharged;

(b) the reference to the debtor obtaining credit includes a reference to a case where goods are hired to him under a hire-purchase agreement or agreed to be sold to him under a conditional sale agreement; and

(c) the relevant information about the status of the debtor is the information that his estate has been sequestrated and that he has not received his discharge or, as the case may be, that he is an undischarged bankrupt in England and Wales or Northern Ireland.

(11) In this section—

(a) 'the relevant period' means the period commencing one year immediately before the date of sequestration of the debtor's estate and ending with his discharge;

(b) references to intent to prejudice creditors shall include references to intent to prejudice an individual creditor.

(12) A person convicted of any offence under this section shall be liable—

(a) on summary conviction, to a fine not exceeding the statutory maximum or—

    (i) to imprisonment for a term not exceeding 3 months; or

    (ii) if he has previously been convicted of an offence inferring dishonest appropriation of property or an attempt at such appropriation, to imprisonment for a term not exceeding 6 months,

or (in the case of either sub-paragraph) to both such fine and such imprisonment; or

(b) on conviction on indictment to a fine or—

    (i) in the case of an offence under subsection (1), (2), (4) or (7) above to imprisonment for a term not exceeding 5 years,

    (ii) in any other case to imprisonment for a term not exceeding 2 years.

or (in the case of either sub-paragraph) to both such fine and such imprisonment."

19–04   Section 67(9) of the Bankruptcy (Scotland) Act 1985 provides:

"(9) If a debtor, either alone or jointly with another person, obtains credit to the extent of £100 (or such other sum as may be prescribed) or more without giving the person from whom he obtained it the relevant information about his status he shall be guilty of an offence."

For penalties see *supra*, para. 19–03.

19–05   Section 187 is replaced by section 17 of the Company Directors Disqualification Act 1986 which makes it an offence for an undischarged bankrupt to act as director of, or directly or indirectly to take part in or be concerned in the promotion, formation or management of, a company except with leave of the court which awarded sequestration.

19–06   Section 22 of the Bankruptcy (Scotland) Act 1985 provides, *inter alia*:

"Submission of claims for voting purposes at statutory meeting

22.—(1) For the purposes of voting at the statutory meeting, a creditor shall submit a claim in accordance with this section to the interim trustee at or before the meeting.

(2) A creditor shall submit a claim under this section by producing to the interim trustee—

19–06
    (*a*) a statement of claim in the prescribed form; and
    (*b*) an account or voucher (according to the nature of the debt) which
        constitutes *prima facie* evidence of the debt:
    Provided that the interim trustee may dispense with any requirement
under this subsection in respect of any debt or any class of debt . . .
    (5) If a creditor produces under this section a statement of claim,
account, voucher or other evidence which is false—
    (*a*) the creditor shall be guilty of an offence unless he shows that he
        neither knew nor had reason to believe that the statement of
        claim, account, voucher or other evidence was false;
    (*b*) the debtor shall be guilty of an offence if he—
        (i) knew or became aware that the statement of claim, account,
            voucher or other evidence was false; and
        (ii) failed as soon as practicable after acquiring such knowledge
            to report it to the interim trustee or permanent trustee. . . .
    (10) A person convicted of an offence under subsection (5) above
shall be liable—
    (*a*) on summary conviction to a fine not exceeding the statutory
        maximum or—
        (i) to imprisonment for a term not exceeding 3 months; or
        (ii) if he has previously been convicted of an offence inferring
            dishonest appropriation of property or an attempt at such
            appropriation, to imprisonment for a term not exceeding 6
            months,
    or (in the case of either sub-paragraph) to both such fine and such
    imprisonment; or
    (*b*) on conviction on indictment to a fine or to imprisonment for a
        term not exceeding 2 years or to both."

19–07   There are no comparable provisions in the Bankruptcy (Scotland) Act 1985.

19–08   The current law is contained in the Insolvency Act 1986.

19–09   Section 328 is now contained in sections 206, 208, 210 and 211 of the Insolvency Act 1986 which provide as follows:

    "**206.**—(1) When a company is ordered to be wound up by the court, or passes a resolution for voluntary winding up, any person, being a past or present officer of the company, is deemed to have committed an offence if, within the 12 months immediately preceding the commencement of the winding up, he has—
    (*a*) concealed any part of the company's property to the value of £120
        or more, or concealed any debt due to or from the company, or
    (*b*) fraudulently removed any part of the company's property to the
        value of £120 or more, or
    (*c*) concealed, destroyed, mutilated or falsified any book or paper
        affecting or relating to the company's property or affairs, or
    (*d*) made any false entry in any book or paper affecting or relating to
        the company's property or affairs, or
    (*e*) fraudulently parted with, altered or made any omission in any
        document affecting or relating to the company's property or
        affairs, or
    (*f*) pawned, pledged or disposed of any property of the company
        which has been obtained on credit and has not been paid for
        (unless the pawning, pledging or disposal was in the ordinary way
        of the company's business).
    (2) Such a person is deemed to have committed an offence if within the period above mentioned he has been privy to the doing by others of

any of the things mentioned in paragraphs (*c*), (*d*) and (*e*) of subsection (1); and he commits an offence if, at any time after the commencement of the winding up, he does any of the things mentioned in paragraphs (*a*) to (*f*) of that subsection, or is privy to the doing by others of any of the things mentioned in paragraphs (*c*) to (*e*) of it.

(3) For purposes of this section, 'officer' includes a shadow director.

(4) It is a defence—

(*a*) for a person charged under paragraph (*a*) or (*f*) of subsection (1) (or under subsection (2) in respect of the things mentioned in either of those two paragraphs) to prove that he had no intent to defraud, and

(*b*) for a person charged under paragraph (*c*) or (*d*) of subsection (1) (or under subsection (2) in respect of the things mentioned in either of those two paragraphs) to prove that he had no intent to conceal the state of affairs of the company or to defeat the law.

(5) Where a person pawns, pledges or disposes of any property in circumstances which amount to an offence under subsection (1)(*f*), every person who takes in pawn or pledge, or otherwise receives, the property knowing it to be pawned, pledged or disposed of in such circumstances, is guilty of an offence.

(6) A person guilty of an offence under this section is liable to imprisonment or a fine, or both.

(7) The money sums specified in paragraphs (*a*) and (*b*) of subsection (1) are subject to increase or reduction by order under section 416 in Part XV.

. . . .

208.—(1) When a company is being wound up, whether by the court or voluntarily, any person, being a past or present officer of the company, commits an offence if he—

(*a*) does not to the best of his knowledge and belief fully and truly discover to the liquidator all the company's property, and how and to whom and for what consideration and when the company disposed of any part of that property (except such part as has been disposed of in the ordinary way of the company's business), or

(*b*) does not deliver up to the liquidator (or as he directs) all such part of the company's property as is in his custody or under his control, and which he is required by law to deliver up, or

(*c*) does not deliver up to the liquidator (or as he directs) all books and papers in his custody or under his control belonging to the company and which he is required by law to deliver up, or

(*d*) knowing or believing that a false debt has been proved by any person in the winding up, fails to inform the liquidator as soon as practicable, or

(*e*) after the commencement of the winding up, prevents the production of any book or paper affecting or relating to the company's property or affairs.

(2) Such a person commits an offence if after the commencement of the winding up he attempts to account for any part of the company's property by fictitious losses or expenses; and he is deemed to have committed that offence if he has so attempted at any meeting of the company's creditors within the 12 months immediately preceding the commencement of the winding up.

(3) For purposes of this section, 'officer' includes a shadow director.

(4) It is a defence—

(*a*) for a person charged under paragraph (*a*), (*b*) or (*c*) of subsection (1) to prove that he had no intent to defraud, and

(*b*) for a person charged under paragraph (*e*) of that subsection to prove that he had no intent to conceal the state of affairs of the company or to defeat the law.

59

(5) A person guilty of an offence under this section is liable to imprisonment or a fine, or both.

.   .   .   .   .   .

210.—(1) When a company is being wound up, whether by the court or voluntarily, any person, being a past or present officer of the company, commits an offence if he makes any material omission in any statement relating to the company's affairs.

(2) When a company has been ordered to be wound up by the court, or has passed a resolution for voluntary winding up, any such person is deemed to have committed that offence if, prior to the winding up, he has made any material omission in any such statement.

(3) For purposes of this section, 'officer' includes a shadow director.

(4) It is a defence for a person charged under this section to prove that he had no intent to defraud.

(5) A person guilty of an offence under this section is liable to imprisonment or a fine, or both.

211.—(1) When a company is being wound up, whether by the court or voluntarily, any person, being a past or present officer of the company—

(a) commits an offence if he makes any false representation or commits any other fraud for the purpose of obtaining the consent of the company's creditors or any of them to an agreement with reference to the company's affairs or to the winding up, and

(b) is deemed to have committed that offence if, prior to the winding up, he has made any false representation, or committed any other fraud, for that purpose.

(2) For purposes of this section, 'officer' includes a shadow director.

(3) A person guilty of an offence under this section is liable to imprisonment or a fine, or both.''

19–10   Section 329 is now section 209 of the Insolvency Act 1986 which provides as follows:

"(1) When a company is being wound up, an officer or contributory of the company commits an offence if he destroys, mutilates, alters or falsifies any books, papers or securities, or makes or is privy to the making of any false or fraudulent entry in any register, book of account or document belonging to the company with intent to defraud or deceive any person.

(2) A person guilty of an offence under this section is liable to imprisonment or a fine, or both.''

19–11   The current provision is section 207 of the Insolvency Act 1986 which provides:

"(1) When a company is ordered to be wound up by the court or passes a resolution for voluntary winding up, a person is deemed to have committed an offence if he, being at the time an officer of the company—

(a) has made or caused to be made any gift or transfer of, or charge on, or has caused or connived at the levying of an execution against, the company's property, or

(b) has concealed or removed any part of the company's property since, or within 2 months before, the date of any unsatisfied judgment or order for the payment of money obtained against the company.

(2) A person is not guilty of an offence under this section—

(*a*) by reason of conduct constituting an offence under subsection (1)(*a*) which occurred more than 5 years before the commencement of the winding up, or

(*b*) if he proves that, at the time of the conduct constituting the offence, he had no intent to defraud the company's creditors.

(3) A person guilty of an offence under this section is liable to imprisonment or a fine, or both."

Max. pen. two years and a fine on indictment, six months on summary conviction.

Add new paragraph **19–11a**:

19–11a   *Fraudulent trading.* Section 458 of the Companies Act 1985 provides:

> "If any business of a company is carried on [with intent to defraud creditors of the company or creditors of any other person or for any fraudulent purpose], every person who was knowingly a party to the carrying on of the business in that manner is liable to imprisonment or a fine or both.
>
> This applies whether or not the company has been, or is in the course of being, wound up."

Max. pen. seven years and a fine on indictment, six months on summary conviction: Companies Act 1985, Sched. 24.

It has been held that the collection and distribution of assets constitutes "carrying on business," which is not the same as carrying on trade: *Re Sarflax Ltd.* [1979] Ch. 592. The same case held that merely to prefer one creditor to another was not fraudulent.

The section applies to an intent to defraud any customers of the company who are not creditors at the relevant time: *R.* v. *Kemp* [1988] Q.B. 645.

"Intent to defraud" includes an intention to prejudice creditors in receiving payment by getting further credit when there is no good reason for expecting money to become available for payment, even without proof of knowledge at the time the debt was incurred that it was not likely to be paid: *R.* v. *Grantham* [1984] 1 Q.B. 675.

19–12   Section 438 of and Sched. 15 to the Companies Act 1948 were repealed by the Companies Act 1980.

19–13   Section 44 is now superseded by section 47 of the Financial Services Act 1986, *infra*, para. 19–19. The other provisions mentioned are repealed.

19–14   Section 71 is now section 141 of the Companies Act 1985: max. pen. a fine on indictment: Companies Act 1985, Sched. 24.

19–15   Section 439 is now section 34 of the Companies Act 1985. The corresponding offence in relation to the term "public limited company" is created by section 33(1) of the 1985 Act. Section 33(2) of that Act makes it an offence for a public limited company to use a name which may reasonably be expected to give the impression that it is a private company, in circumstances where the fact that it is

19–15   a public company is likely to be material: max. pen. £400 on summary conviction, and £40 a day for any continuing contravention after conviction: Companies Act 1985, Sched. 24.

19–16   Section 85 is now section 189 of the Companies Act 1985: max. pen. seven years' imprisonment and a fine on indictment, six months' on summary conviction: Companies Act 1985, Sched. 24.

19–17   The duty to keep accounts is now contained in section 221 of the Companies Act 1985, as substituted by section 2 of the Companies Act 1989. Every officer of a company in default is guilty of an offence unless he shows that he acted honestly and that in the circumstances in which the company's business was carried on the default was excusable: max. pen. two years and a fine on indictment, six months on summary conviction. The duty to lay the accounts before a general meeting is now contained in section 241 of the 1935 Act, as substituted by section 11 of the 1989 Act, with a defence that the accused took all reasonable steps to comply with the statutory requirements: max. pen. on indictment, a fine of the statutory maximum, and a fine of one-tenth thereof on summary conviction.

Footnote 40. Section 4(3) is now s.242A(3) of the Companies Act 1985.

19–18   The Prevention of Fraud (Investments) Act 1958 is repealed by
to   the Financial Services Act 1986, section 4 of which makes it an
19–24   offence for anyone not authorised or exempted under the Act to carry on an investment business: max. pen. two years and a fine on indictment, six months on summary conviction.
Section 200 of the Act provides:

"(1) A person commits an offence if—
(a) for the purposes of or in connection with any application under this Act; or
(b) in purported compliance with any requirement imposed on him by or under this Act,
he furnishes information which he knows to be false or misleading in a material particular or recklessly furnishes information which is false or misleading in a material particular.
(2) A person commits an offence if, not being an authorised person or exempted person, he—
(a) describes himself as such a person; or
(b) so holds himself out as to indicate or be reasonably understood to indicate that he is such a person.
(3) A person commits an offence if, not having a status to which this subsection applies, he—
(a) describes himself as having that status, or
(b) so holds himself out as to indicate or be reasonably understood to indicate that he has that status.
(4) Subsection (3) above applies to the status of recognised self-regulating organisation, recognised professional body, recognised investment exchange or recognised clearing house.
(5) A person guilty of an offence under subsection (1) above shall be liable—
(a) on conviction on indictment, to imprisonment for a term not exceeding two years or to a fine or to both;

(*b*) on summary conviction, to imprisonment for a term not exceeding six months or to a fine not exceeding the statutory maximum or to both.

(6) A person guilty of an offence under subsection (2) or (3) above shall be liable on summary conviction to imprisonment for a term not exceeding six months or to a fine not exceeding the fifth level on the standard scale or to both.

(7) Where a contravention of subsection (2) or (3) above involves a public display of the offending description or other matter the maximum fine that may be imposed under subsection (6) above shall be an amount equal to the fifth level on the standard scale multiplied by the number of days for which the display has continued.

(8) In proceedings brought against any person for an offence under subsection (2) or (3) above it shall be a defence for him to prove that he took all reasonable precautions and exercised all due diligence to avoid the commission of the offence."

19–19 *Misleading statements.* Section 47 of the Financial Services Act 1986 provides:

"(1) Any person who—
(*a*) makes a statement, promise or forecast which he knows to be misleading, false or deceptive or dishonestly conceals any material facts; or
(*b*) recklessly makes (dishonestly or otherwise) a statement, promise or forecast which is misleading, false or deceptive,
is guilty of an offence if he makes the statement, promise or forecast or conceals the facts for the purpose of inducing, or is reckless as to whether it may induce, another person (whether or not the person to whom the statement, promise or forecast is made or from whom the facts are concealed) to enter or offer to enter into, or to refrain from entering or offering to enter into, an investment agreement or to exercise, or refrain from exercising, any rights conferred by an investment.

(2) Any person who does any act or engages in any course of conduct which creates a false or misleading impression as to the market in or the price or value of any investments is guilty of an offence if he does so for the purpose of creating that impression and of thereby inducing another person to acquire, dispose of, subscribe for or underwrite those investments or to refrain from doing so or to exercise, or refrain from exercising, any rights conferred by those investments.

(3) In proceedings brought against any person for an offence under subsection (2) above it shall be a defence for him to prove that he reasonably believed that his act or conduct would not create an impression that was false or misleading as to the matters mentioned in that subsection.

(4) Subsection (1) above does not apply unless—
(*a*) the statement, promise or forecast is made in or from, or the facts are concealed in or from, the United Kingdom;
(*b*) the person on whom the inducement is intended to or may have effect is in the United Kingdom; or
(*c*) the agreement is or would be entered into or the rights are or would be exercised in the United Kingdom.

(5) Subsection (2) above does not apply unless—
(*a*) the act is done or the course of conduct is engaged in in the United Kingdom; or
(*b*) the false or misleading impression is created there.

(6) A person guilty of an offence under this section shall be liable—
(*a*) on conviction on indictment, to imprisonment for a term not exceeding seven years or to a fine or to both;

19–19 (*b*) on summary conviction, to imprisonment for a term not exceeding six months or to a fine not exceeding the statutory maximum or to both."

19–20 The current provision is section 133 of the Financial Services Act 1986 which provides:

"(1) Any person who—
(*a*) makes a statement, promise or forecast which he knows to be misleading, false or deceptive or dishonestly conceals any material facts; or
(*b*) recklessly makes (dishonestly or otherwise) a statement, promise or forecast which is misleading, false or deceptive,
is guilty of an offence if he makes the statement, promise or forecast or conceals the facts for the purpose of inducing, or is reckless as to whether it may induce, another person (whether or not the person to whom the statement, promise or forecast is made or from whom the facts are concealed) to enter into or offer to enter into, or to refrain from entering or offering to enter into, a contract of insurance with an insurance company (not being an investment agreement) or to exercise or refrain from exercising, any rights conferred by such a contract.
(2) Subsection (1) above does not apply unless—
(*a*) the statement, promise or forecast is made in or from, or the facts are concealed in or from, the United Kingdom;
(*b*) the person on whom the inducement is intended to or may have effect is in the United Kingdom; or
(*c*) the contract is or would be entered into or the rights are or would be exercisable in the United Kingdom.
(3) A person guilty of an offence under this section shall be liable—
(*a*) on conviction on indictment, to imprisonment for a term not exceeding seven years or to a fine or to both;
(*b*) on summary conviction, to imprisonment for a term not exceeding six months or to a fine not exceeding the statutory maximum or to both."

19–23 The Banking Act 1979, which repealed the Protection of Depositors Act 1963, is itself repealed and replaced by the Banking Act 1987, section 3 of which makes it an offence, subject to certain exceptions set out in section 4, for any person to accept a deposit in the United Kingdom in the course of carrying on a business (there or elsewhere) which is a deposit-taking business, unless that person is an institution authorised by the Bank of England: max. pen. two years and a fine on indictment, six months on summary conviction.

19–24 The current provision is section 35 of the Banking Act 1987 which is restricted to acts done in or from the United Kingdom in order to influence persons in the United Kingdom or in relation to a deposit or agreement to be made or entered into there. The offence is defined as follows:

"(1) Any person who—
(*a*) makes a statement, promise or forecast which he knows to be misleading, false or deceptive, or dishonestly conceals any material facts; or
(*b*) recklessly makes (dishonestly or otherwise) a statement, promise or forecast which is misleading, false or deceptive,
is guilty of an offence if he makes the statement, promise or forecast or conceals the facts for the purpose of inducing, or is reckless as to

whether it may induce, another person (whether or not the person to whom the statement, promise or forecast is made or from whom the facts are concealed)—

      (i) to make, or refrain from making, a deposit with him or any other person; or

      (ii) to enter, or refrain from entering, into an agreement for the purpose of making such a deposit.

(2) This section does not apply unless—

(a) the statement, promise or forecast is made in or from, or the facts are concealed in or from, the United Kingdom or arrangements are made in or from the United Kingdom for the statement, promise or forecast to be made or the facts to be concealed;

(b) the person on whom the inducement is intended to or may have effect is in the United Kingdom; or

(c) the deposit is or would be made, or the agreement is or would be entered into, in the United Kingdom.

(3) A person guilty of an offence under this section shall be liable—

(a) on conviction on indictment, to imprisonment for a term not exceeding seven years or to a fine or to both;

(b) on summary conviction, to imprisonment for a term not exceeding six months or to a fine not exceeding the statutory maximum or to both.

(4) For the purposes of this section the definition of deposit in section 5 above shall be treated as including any sum that would be otherwise excluded by subsection (3) of that section."

"Deposit" is defined in section 5 of the Banking Act 1987, which provides:

"(1) Subject to the provisions of this section, in this Act 'deposit' means a sum of money paid on terms—

(a) under which it will be repaid, with or without interest or a premium, and either on demand or at a time or in circumstances agreed by or on behalf of the person making the payment and the person receiving it; and

(b) which are not referable to the provision of property or services or the giving of security;

and references in this Act to money deposited and to the making of a deposit shall be construed accordingly.

(2) For the purposes of subsection (1)(b) above, money is paid on terms which are referable to the provision of property or services or to the giving of security if, and only if—

(a) it is paid by way of advance or part payment under a contract for the sale, hire or other provision of property or services, and is repayable only in the event that the property or services is not or are not in fact sold, hired or otherwise provided;

(b) it is paid by way of security for the performance of a contract or by way of security in respect of loss which may result from the non-performance of a contract; or

(c) without prejudice to paragraph (b) above, it is paid by way of security for the delivery up or return of any property, whether in a particular state of repair or otherwise.

(3) Except so far as any provision of this Act otherwise provides, in this Act 'deposit' does not include—

(a) a sum paid by the Bank or an authorised institution;

(b) a sum paid by a person for the time being specified in Schedule 2 to this Act;

(c) a sum paid by a person, other than a person within paragraph (a) or (b) above, in the course of carrying on a business consisting wholly or mainly of lending money;

19–24   (*d*) a sum which is paid by one company to another at a time when one is a subsidiary of the other or both are subsidiaries of another company or the same individual is a majority or principal share-holder controller of both of them; or

(*e*) a sum which is paid by a person who, at the time when it is paid, is a close relative of the person receiving it or who is, or is a close relative of, a director, controller or manager of that person.

(4) In the application of paragraph (*e*) of subsection (3) above to a sum paid by a partnership that paragraph shall have effect as if for the reference to the person paying the sum there were substituted a reference to each of the partners.

(5) In subsection (3)(*e*) 'close relative,' in relation to any person, means—

(*a*) his spouse;

(*b*) his children and step-children, his parents and step-parents, his brothers and sisters and step-brothers and step-sisters; and

(*c*) the spouse of any person within paragraph (*b*) above."

19–27   The concept of "trade or business" involves a degree of regularity, such as to make the activity involved part of the normal practice of a business, although a one-off transaction with a view to profit can constitute a trade in itself: *Davies* v. *Sumner* [1984] 1 W.L.R. 1301. While the sale of his stock-in-trade by a car hirer may form part of his trade or business, as in *Havering B.C.* v. *Stevenson* [1970] 1 W.L.R. 1375, the sale of business equipment such as a courier's car will normally lack the necessary element of regularity: *Davies* v. *Sumner, supra*; see also *Devlin* v. *Hall* [1990] R.T.R. 320. It has also been held that a person who buys, works on and sells cars as a hobby does not sell them in the course of a trade or business: *Blakemore* v. *Bellamy* [1983] R.T.R. 303. See Ian Lloyd, "Consumer Protection: Sales 'in the course of a business' " (1984) 29 J.L.S. 147; *Buchanan-Jardine* v. *Hamilink and Anr.*, 1981 S.L.T. (Notes) 60.

19–32   The Food and Drugs (Scotland) Act is now replaced by the Food Safety Act 1990.

19–34   The Trade Descriptions Act 1972 was repealed by the Consumer Protection Act 1987.

19–36   Section 11 was repealed by the Consumer Protection Act 1987, sections 20 to 24 of which provide:

"**20.**—(1) Subject to the following provisions of this Part, a person shall be guilty of an offence if, in the course of any business of his, he gives (by any means whatever) to any consumers an indication which is misleading as to the price at which any goods, services, accommodation or facilities are available (whether generally or from particular persons).

(2) Subject as aforesaid, a person shall be guilty of an offence if—

(*a*) in the course of any business of his, he has given an indication to any consumers which, after it was given, has become misleading as mentioned in subsection (1) above; and

(*b*) some or all of those consumers might reasonably be expected to rely on the indication at a time after it has become misleading; and

(*c*) he fails to take all such steps as are reasonable to prevent those consumers from relying on the indication.

(3) For the purposes of this section it shall be immaterial—

(*a*) whether the person who gives or gave the indication is or was acting on his own behalf or on behalf of another;

(*b*) whether or not that person is the person, or included among the persons, from whom the goods, services, accommodation or facilities are available; and

(*c*) whether the indication is or has become misleading in relation to all the consumers to whom it is or was given or only in relation to some of them.

(4) A person guilty of an offence under subsection (1) or (2) above shall be liable—

(*a*) on conviction on indictment, to a fine;

(*b*) on summary conviction, to a fine not exceeding the statutory maximum.

(5) No prosecution for an offence under subsection (1) or (2) above shall be brought after whichever is the earlier of the following, that is to say—

(*a*) the end of the period of three years beginning with the day on which the offence was committed; and

(*b*) the end of the period of one year beginning with the day on which the person bringing the prosecution discovered that the offence had been committed.

(6) In this Part—

'consumer'—

(*a*) in relation to any goods, means any person who might wish to be supplied with the goods for his own private use or consumption;

(*b*) in relation to any services or facilities, means any person who might wish to be provided with the services or facilities otherwise than for the purposes of any business of his; and

(*c*) in relation to any accommodation, means any person who might wish to occupy the accommodation otherwise than for the purpose of any business of his;

'price,' in relation to any goods, services, accommodation or facilities, means—

(*a*) the aggregate of the sums required to be paid by a consumer for or otherwise in respect of the supply of the goods or the provision of the services, accommodation or facilities; or

(*b*) except in section 21 below, any method which will be or has been applied for the purpose of determining that aggregate.

21.—(1) For the purposes of section 20 above an indication given to any consumers is misleading as to a price if what is conveyed by the indication, or what those consumers might reasonably be expected to infer from the indication or any omission from it, includes any of the following, that is to say—

(*a*) that the price is less than in fact it is;

(*b*) that the applicability of the price does not depend on facts or circumstances on which its applicability does in fact depend;

(*c*) that the price covers matters in respect of which an additional charge is in fact made;

(*d*) that a person who in fact has no such expectation—

    (i) expects the price to be increased or reduced (whether or not at a particular time or by a particular amount); or

    (ii) expects the price, or the price as increased or reduced, to be maintained (whether or not for a particular period); or

(*e*) that the facts or circumstances by reference to which the consumers might reasonably be expected to judge the validity of any relevant comparison made or implied by the indication are not what in fact they are.

(2) For the purposes of section 20 above, an indication given to any consumers is misleading as to a method of determining a price if what is conveyed by the indication, or what those consumers might reasonably be expected to infer from the indication or any omission from it, includes any of the following, that is to say—

(*a*) that the method is not what in fact it is;

(*b*) that the applicability of the method does not depend on facts or circumstances on which its applicability does in fact depend;

(*c*) that the method takes into account matters in respect of which an additional charge will in fact be made;

(*d*) that a person who in fact has no such expectation—

    (i) expects the method to be altered (whether or not at a particular time or in a particular respect); or

    (ii) expects the method, or that method as altered, to remain unaltered (whether or not for a particular period); or

(*e*) that the facts or circumstances by reference to which the consumers might reasonably be expected to judge the validity of any relevant comparison made or implied by the indication are not what in fact they are.

(3) For the purposes of subsections (1)(*e*) and (2)(*e*) above a comparison is a relevant comparison in relation to a price or method of determining a price if it is made between that price or that method, or any price which has been or may be determined by that method, and—

(*a*) any price or value which is stated or implied to be, to have been or to be likely to be attributed or attributable to the goods, services, accommodation or facilities in question or to any other goods, services, accommodation or facilities; or

(*b*) any method, or other method, which is stated or implied to be, to have been or to be likely to be applied or applicable for the determination of the price or value of the goods, services, accommodation or facilities in question or of the price or value of any other goods, services, accommodation or facilities.

22.—(1) Subject to the following provisions of this section, references in this Part to services or facilities are references to any services or facilities whatever including, in particular—

(*a*) the provision of credit or of banking or insurance services and the provision of facilities incidental to the provision of such services;

(*b*) the purchase or sale of foreign currency;

(*c*) the supply of electricity;

(*d*) the provision of a place, other than on a highway, for the parking of a motor vehicle;

(*e*) the making of arrangements for a person to put or keep a caravan on any land other than arrangements by virtue of which that person may occupy the caravan as his only or main residence.

(2) References in this Part to services shall not include references to services provided to an employer under a contract of employment.

(3) References in this Part to services or facilities shall not include references to services or facilities which are provided by an authorised person or appointed representative in the course of the carrying on of an investment business.

(4) In relation to a service consisting in the purchase or sale of foreign currency, references in this Part to the method by which the price of the service is determined shall include references to the rate of exchange.

(5) In this section—

'appointed representative,' 'authorised person' and 'investment business' have the same meanings as in the Financial Services Act 1986;

'caravan' has the same meaning as in the Caravan Sites and Control of Development Act 1960;

'contract of employment' and 'employer' have the same meanings as in the Employment Protection (Consolidation) Act 1978;
'credit' has the same meaning as in the Consumer Credit Act 1974.

23.—(1) Subject to subsection (2) below, references in this Part to accommodation or facilities being available shall not include references to accommodation or facilities being available to be provided by means of the creation or disposal of an interest in land except where—

(*a*) the person who is to create or dispose of the interest will do so in the course of any business of his; and

(*b*) the interest to be created or disposed of is a relevant interest in a new dwelling and is to be created or disposed of for the purpose of enabling that dwelling to be occupied as a residence, or one of the residences, of the person acquiring the interest.

(2) Subsection (1) above shall not prevent the application of any provision of this Part in relation to—

(*a*) the supply of any goods as part of the same transaction as any creation or disposal of an interest in land; or

(*b*) the provision of any services or facilities for the purposes of, or in connection with, any transaction for the creation or disposal of such an interest.

(3) In this section—

'new dwelling' means any building or part of a building in Great Britain which—

(*a*) has been constructed or adapted to be occupied as a residence; and

(*b*) has not previously been so occupied or has been so occupied only with other premises or as more than one residence,

and includes any yard, garden, out-houses or appurtenances which belong to that building or part or are to be enjoyed with it;

'relevant interest'—

(*a*) in relation to a new dwelling in England and Wales, means the freehold estate in the dwelling or a leasehold interest in the dwelling for a term of years absolute of more than twenty-one years, not being a term of which twenty-one years or less remains unexpired;

(*b*) in relation to a new dwelling in Scotland, means the *dominium utile* of the land comprising the dwelling, or a leasehold interest in the dwelling where twenty-one years or more remains unexpired.

24.—(1) In any proceedings against a person for an offence under subsection (1) or (2) of section 20 above in respect of any indication it shall be a defence for that person to show that his acts or omissions were authorised for the purposes of this subsection by regulations made under section 26 below.

(2) In proceedings against a person for an offence under subsection (1) or (2) of section 20 above in respect of an indication published in a book, newspaper, magazine or film or in a programme included in a programme service (within the meaning of the Broadcasting Act 1990), it shall be a defence for that person to show that the indication was not contained in an advertisement.

(3) In proceedings against a person for an offence under subsection (1) or (2) of section 20 above in respect of an indication published in an advertisement it shall be a defence for that person to show that—

(*a*) he is a person who carries on a business of publishing or arranging for the publication of advertisements;

(*b*) he received the advertisement for publication in the ordinary course of that business; and

(*c*) at the time of publication he did not know and had no grounds for suspecting that the publication would involve the commission of the offence.

19-36   (4) In any proceedings against a person for an offence under subsection (1) of section 20 above in respect of any indication, it shall be a defence for that person to show that—

(*a*) the indication did not relate to the availability from him of any goods, services, accommodation or facilities;

(*b*) a price had been recommended to every person from whom the goods, services, accommodation or facilities were indicated as being available;

(*c*) the indication related to that price and was misleading as to that price only by reason of a failure by any person to follow the recommendation; and

(*d*) it was reasonable for the person who gave the indication to assume that the recommendation was for the most part being followed.

(5) The provisions of this section are without prejudice to the provisions of section 39 below.

(6) In this section—

'advertisement' includes a catalogue, a circular and a price list;''

19-37   "Facilities" has been held to include a guarantee of goods sold, as being the provision of the customer with the wherewithal to arrange for the repair of the goods: *Smith* v. *Dixons Ltd.*, 1986 S.C.C.R. 1 (Sh.Ct.). "Facilities" does not normally include the supply of goods, nor does section 14 apply to statements regarding price. Where, therefore, a video recorder is offered "free" to anyone who buys a car, but in fact any customer taking advantage of the offer will receive a reduced trade-in allowance or discount, the offer is not a statement as to the provision of a facility, although it might be a false indication of price, contrary to section 20 of the Consumer Protection Act 1987: *Newell* v. *Hicks* [1984] R.T.R. 135.

A person may be guilty of knowingly making a false statement if he knows of the falsity of the statement at the time it was read by the customer, even if he did not know of its falsity at the time it was made, as when a travel agent learns after the publication of a brochure that it contains a false statement: *Wings Ltd.* v. *Ellis* [1985] A.C. 272.

19-41   Footnote 16. See now also *Amag Ltd.* v. *Jessop*, 1989 S.C.C.R. 186.

19-42   It has been said that a defence of due diligence cannot succeed unless the precaution of making a disclaimer has been taken: *Simmons* v. *Potter* [1975] R.T.R. 347; *Crook* v. *Howells Garages (Newport) Ltd.* [1980] R.T.R. 434. On the other hand, it has been pointed out that a disclaimer is not a defence in terms of s.24, but evidence that no representation was made: *Wandsworth LBC* v. *Bentley* [1980] R.T.R. 429. It has also been suggested that to wind down an odometer to nought might be a way of avoiding making any representation as to mileage, since no one would be misled by it into believing it to be a true record: *Lill Holdings* v. *White* [1979] R.T.R. 120.

Amag Ltd. v. *Jessop*, 1989 S.C.C.R. 186; *Costello* v. *Lowe*, 1990 J.C. 231; and *Ford* v. *Guild*, 1990 J.C. 55 are examples of how difficult it is for a section 24 defence to succeed.

Footnote 20. Add: *Wandsworth LBC* v. *Bentley* [1980] R.T.R. 429.

19–44   It has been said that the act or default must be an unlawful one: *Lill Holdings* v. *White* [1979] R.T.R. 120, Wien J. at 125. It has been held that section 23 is not limited to persons acting in the course of a trade or business, and that a private individual who sells a car to a garage with what he knows is a false odometer reading may be guilty of an offence in terms of section 23 when the garage subsequently sells the car to a customer: *Olgeirsson* v. *Kitching* [1986] 1 W.L.R. 304.

19–46   Sections 162 and 164 of the Customs and Excise Act 1952 were repealed by the Alcoholic Liquor Duties Act 1979 and re-enacted by ss.71 and 73 respectively of the latter Act: maximum penalty a fine of level 3, and forfeiture. Section 45 of the Act of 1952 is now section 50 of the Customs and Excise Management Act 1979.

19–47   Section 33 of the Road Traffic Act 1972 is now section 17 of the Road Traffic Act 1988: max. pen. a fine of level 3.

19–48   Section 91 of the Patents Act 1949 was repealed by the Patents Act 1977. Section 91(1) was replaced by s.110 of that Act which provides, *inter alia*:

> "(1) If a person falsely represents that anything disposed of by him for value is a patented product he shall, subject to the following provisions of this section, be liable on summary conviction to a fine [of level 4]."

Subsection (2) provides that where the article has on it "patent" or any other expression implying that it is patented, anyone who disposes of it for value is taken to represent that it is a patented product. Subsection (3) provides that s.110(1) shall not apply where the patent is revoked and a sufficient period has not elapsed to enable the accused to take steps to ensure that the representation is not made. Subsection (4) provides a general defence of due diligence.

Section 91(2) was replaced by s.112 of the 1977 Act: max. fine now level 5.

It is also an offence falsely to represent that a patent has been applied for in respect of an article disposed of for value where no application has been made, or where any application made has been withdrawn or refused. There is a defence of due diligence: Patents Act 1977, s.111; max. pen. a fine of level 4.

For the current form of section 35 of the Registered Designs Act 1949, see the Copyright, Designs and Patents Act 1988, Sched. 3: max. pen. now a fine of level 3.

19–49   The fraudulent application or use of trade marks is penalised by section 58A of the Trade Marks Act 1938, as inserted by section 300 of the Copyright, Designs and Patents Act 1988, which provides:

> "(1) It is an offence, subject to subsection (3) below for a person—
> (*a*) to apply a mark identical to or nearly resembling a registered trade mark to goods, or to material used or intended to be used for labelling, packaging or advertising goods, or
> (*b*) to sell, let for hire, or offer or expose for sale or hire, or distribute—

(i) goods bearing such a mark, or

(ii) material bearing such a mark which is used or intended to be used for labelling, packaging or advertising goods, or

(*c*) to use material bearing such a mark in the course of a business for labelling, packaging or advertising goods, or

(*d*) to possess in the course of a business goods or material bearing such a mark with a view to doing any of the things mentioned in paragraphs (*a*) to (*c*).

when he is not entitled to use the mark in relation to the goods in question and the goods are not connected in the course of trade with a person who is so entitled.

(2) It is also an offence, subject to subsection (3) below, for a person to possess in the course of a business goods or material bearing a mark identical to or nearly resembling a registered trademark with a view to enabling or assisting another person to do any of the things mentioned in subsection (1)(*a*) to (*c*), knowing or having reason to believe that the other person is not entitled to use the mark in relation to the goods in question and that the goods are not connected in the course of trade with a person who is so entitled.

(3) A person commits an offence under subsection (1) or (2) only if—

(*a*) he acts with a view to gain for himself or another, or with intent to cause loss to another, and

(*b*) he intends that the goods in question should be accepted as connected in the course of trade with a person entitled to use the mark in question;

and it is a defence for a person charged with an offence under subsection (1) to show that he believed on reasonable grounds that he was entitled to use the mark in relation to the goods in question.

(4) A person guilty of an offence under this section is liable—

(*a*) on summary conviction to imprisonment for a term not exceeding six months or a fine not exceeding the statutory maximum, or both;

(*b*) on conviction on indictment to a fine or imprisonment for a term not exceeding ten years, or both.

(5) Where an offence under this section committed by a body corporate is proved to have been committed with the consent or connivance of a director, manager, secretary or other similar officer of the body, or a person purporting to act in any such capacity, he as well as the body corporate is guilty of the offence and liable to be proceeded against and punished accordingly.

In relation to a body corporate whose affairs are managed by its members 'director' means a member of the body corporate.

(6) In this section 'business' includes a trade or profession."

19–51 to 19–59 The Food and Drugs (Scotland) Act 1956 is repealed and replaced by the Food Safety Act 1990, "the 1990 Act."

"Food" in the 1990 Act includes drink, and articles and substances of no nutritional value which are used for human consumption, chewing gum and like products and ingredients used to prepare food as so defined: 1990 Act, s.1(1).

It does not include live animals, birds or fish which are not eaten while live, feeding stuffs for animals, birds or fish, controlled drugs, or medicines not specified by order: *ibid.*, s.1(2).

19–51 Section 2 of the 1956 Act is now section 14 of the 1990 Act which provides:

"(1) Any person who sells to the purchaser's prejudice any food which is not of the nature or substance or quality demanded by the purchaser shall be guilty of an offence.

(2) In subsection (1) above the reference to sale shall be construed as a reference to sale for human consumption; and in proceedings under that subsection it shall not be a defence that the purchaser was not prejudiced because he bought for analysis or examination."

Max. pen. two years and a fine on indictment, six months on summary conviction: s.35(2).

19–52 See now Sale of Goods Act 1979. "Sale" includes a supply, otherwise than by sale, in the course of a business: Food Safety Act 1990, s.2(1)(*a*).

19–53 Footnote 44. See *Skinner* v. *MacLean*, 1979 S.L.T. (Notes) 35 which treats *Frew* v. *Gunning* as very special, and makes it clear that the facts that a sale is made in error and the error later brought to the notice of the buyer do not affect the seller's responsibility.

19–54 See now *infra*, paras. 19–58 and 19–59.

19–55 *Morton* v. *Green* was followed in the recent case of *Goldup* v. *Manson Ltd.* [1982] Q.B. 161 where it was held that the court is not obliged to accept uncontradicted expert evidence as to what the standard should be in relation to the fat content of beef. It is for the prosecution to show that the customer was demanding mince containing significantly less fat than was supplied.

19–56 Labelling is now dealt with by section 15 of the 1990 Act which provides:

"(1) Any person who gives with any food sold by him, or displays with any food offered or exposed by him for sale or in his possession for the purpose of sale, a label, whether or not attached to or printed on the wrapper or container, which—
(*a*) falsely describes the food; or
(*b*) is likely to mislead as to the nature or substance or quality of the food,
shall be guilty of an offence.

(2) Any person who publishes, or is a party to the publication of, an advertisement (not being such a label given or displayed by him as mentioned in subsection (1) above) which—
(*a*) falsely describes any food; or
(*b*) is likely to mislead as to the nature or substance or quality of any food,
shall be guilty of an offence.

(3) Any person who sells, or offers or exposes for sale, or has in his possession for the purpose of sale, any food the presentation of which is likely to mislead as to the nature or substance or quality of the food shall be guilty of an offence.

(4) In proceedings for an offence under subsection (1) or (2) above, the fact that a label or advertisement in respect of which the offence is alleged to have been committed contained an accurate statement of the composition of the food shall not preclude the court from finding that the offence was committed.

(5) In this section references to sale shall be construed as references to sale for human consumption.

19–56   Max. pen. two years and a fine on indictment, six months on summary conviction: s.35(2). Exposure for sale includes the offering of food as a prize in connection with any entertainment: 1990 Act, s.2(2).

Footnote 57. Section 25 of the Agriculture Act 1970 was repealed by the Agriculture Act 1986.

19–58   Sections 3 and 45 of the 1956 Act are replaced by section 21 of the
and   1990 Act which provides:
19–59
> "(1) In any proceedings for an offence under any of the preceding provisions of this Part (in this section referred to as "the relevant provision"), it shall, subject to subsection (5) below, be a defence for the person charged to prove that he took all reasonable precautions and exercised all due diligence to avoid the commission of the offence by himself or by a person under his control.
>
> (2) Without prejudice to the generality of subsection (1) above, a person charged with an offence under section 8, 14 or 15 above who neither—
>
> (a) prepared the food in respect of which the offence is alleged to have been committed; nor
>
> (b) imported it into Great Britain,
>
> shall be taken to have established the defence provided by that subsection if he satisfies the requirements of subsection (3) or (4) below.
>
> (3) A person satisfies the requirements of this subsection if he proves—
>
> (a) that the commission of the offence was due to an act or default of another person who was not under his control, or to reliance on information supplied by such a person;
>
> (b) that he carried out all such checks of the food in question as were reasonable in all the circumstances, or that it was reasonable in all the circumstances for him to rely on checks carried out by the person who supplied the food to him; and
>
> (c) that he did not know and had no reason to suspect at the time of the commission of the alleged offence that his act or omission would amount to an offence under the relevant provision.
>
> (4) A person satisfies the requirements of this subsection if he proves—
>
> (a) that the commission of the offence was due to an act or default of another person who was not under his control, or to reliance on information supplied by such a person;
>
> (b) that the sale or intended sale of which the alleged offence consisted was not a sale or intended sale under his name or mark; and
>
> (c) that he did not know, and could not reasonably have been expected to know, at the time of the commission of the alleged offence that his act or omission would amount to an offence under the relevant provision. . . . . "

Where the defence provided by section 21(1) involves the act or default of or information supplied by another person, the accused cannot rely on that defence without leave of the court unless he has given prior written notice thereof to the prosecutor giving such information as he has of the identity of the other person: 1990 Act, s.21(5).

For an example of an unsuccessful defence of due diligence, see *Alex Munro (Butchers) Ltd.* v. *Carmichael*, 1990 S.C.C.R. 275.

Section 46 of the 1956 Act is not re-enacted.

19–60   The Weights and Measures Act 1963 was repealed and replaced by the Weights and Measures Act 1985 ("the 1985 Act").

19–61   The lawful units of measurement are set out in section 1 of and Schedules 1–3 to the 1985 Act. The use for trade of other measurements is made an offence by section 8(4) of the Act: max. pen. level 3 on the standard scale and forfeiture: s.84(1).

19–62   Section 9 is replaced by section 7 of the 1985 Act which provides:

"**7.**—(1) In this Act "use for trade" means, subject to subsection (3) below, use in Great Britain in connection with, or with a view to, a transaction falling within subsection (2) below where—

(*a*) the transaction is by reference to quantity or is a transaction for the purposes of which there is made or implied a statement of the quantity of goods to which the transaction relates, and

(*b*) the use is for the purpose of the determination or statement of that quantity.

(2) A transaction falls within this subsection if it is a transaction for—

(*a*) the transferring or rendering of money or money's worth in consideration of money or money's worth, or

(*b*) the making of a payment in respect of any toll or duty.

(3) Use for trade does not include use in a case where—

(*a*) the determination or statement is a determination or statement of the quantity of goods required for despatch to a destination outside Great Britain and any designated country, and

(*b*) the transaction is not a sale by retail, and

(*c*) no transfer or rendering of money or money's worth is involved other than the passing of the title to the goods and the consideration for them.

(4) The following equipment, that is to say—

(*a*) any weighing or measuring equipment which is made available in Great Britain for use by the public, whether on payment or otherwise, and

(*b*) any equipment which is used in Great Britain for the grading by reference to their weight, for the purposes of trading transactions by reference to that grading, of hens' eggs in shell which are intended for human consumption.

shall be treated for the purposes of this Part of this Act as weighing or measuring equipment in use for trade, whether or not it would apart from this subsection be so treated.

(5) Where any weighing or measuring equipment is found in the possession of any person carrying on trade or on any premises which are used for trade, that person or, as the case may be, the occupier of those premises shall be deemed for the purposes of this Act, unless the contrary is proved, to have that equipment in his possession for use for trade."

Footnote 65. Section 17 is now s.7(5) of the 1985 Act, *supra*.

Footnote 66. Section 58 is now s.94(2) of the 1985 Act.

19–63   Footnote 68. See now 1985 Act, s.11(2); Units of Measurement Regulations 1986: max. pen. as for s.8(4).

19–64   Section 15 is now section 16 of the 1985 Act: max. pen. a fine of
level 5 on the standard scale: s.84(6).

Footnote 70. See now 1985, s.16(3).

19–65   Section 16 is now section 17 of the 1985 Act: max. pen. under
subs. (1) as for s.16 of the 1985 Act; max. pen. under subs. (3), six
months and a fine of level 5: s.84(4), (6).
The offence of possession under this section is one of strict
responsibility, but can be committed only by a person who has
actual control of the weights; the mere fact that a licensee is the
only person who can lawfully use liquor measures in a sale does not
make him their possessor: *Bellerby* v. *Carle* [1983] 2 A.C. 101,
although if short measure is actually sold he is liable as the seller:
MacDonald v. *Smith*, 1979 J.C. 55.

19–66   On the vexed question of the "head" of a glass of beer, see *Dean*
v. *Scottish and Newcastle Breweries*, 1977 J.C. 90.

Footnote 72. See now s.25(1) of the 1985 Act: max. pen. now a
fine of level 5: 1985 Act, s.84(6).

Footnote 73. Sched. 4 was repealed by the 1985 Act.

19–67   Sections 22 and 23 are now sections 25 and 26 respectively of the
to   1985 Act.
19–70
Footnote 75. Section 58 is now s.94(1) of the 1985 Act.

19–70   Section 24(1) is now section 28 of the 1985 Act.
A licensee is responsible for a sale by a barman even if they are
fellow employees: *MacDonald* v. *Smith*, 1979 J.C. 55.

19–71   Footnotes 84 to 89. Section 24(3) to (6) is now part of s.30 of the
1985 Act, and s.26(2) is now s.35(2) of the 1985 Act.

19–72   Section 24(2) is now section 29 of the 1985 Act and section 24(7)
is now section 31 of that Act.

Footnote 93. Section 24(8) is now s.28(2) of the 1985 Act, and
applies also to ss.29, 30 and 31 of the Act.

19–73   For "section 24," read "sections 28 and 29 of the 1985 Act." The
exemptions are set out in section 24 of that Act.

19–74   The defences are now in sections 33 to 36 of the 1985 Act.

19–75   Section 25 is now section 33 of the 1985 Act.
to   Section 26(1) is replaced by section 34(1) and (2) of the 1985 Act
19–78   which provides:

"(1) In any proceedings for an offence under this Part of this Act or
any instrument made under this Part, it shall be a defence for the

person charged to prove that he took all reasonable precautions and exercised all due diligence to avoid the commission of the offence.

(2) If in any case the defence provided by subsection (1) above involves an allegation that the commission of the offence in question was due to the act or default of another person or due to reliance on information supplied by another person, the person charged shall not, without the leave of the court, be entitled to rely on the defence unless, before the beginning of the period of seven days ending with the date when the hearing of the charge began, he served on the prosecutor a notice giving such information identifying or assisting in the identification of the other person as was then in his possession."

Section 26(4) was repealed by the Weights and Measures Act 1979. Section 35(2) of the 1985 Act provides that in relation to the goods formerly dealt with in section 26(4) it shall be a defence for the accused to prove that the deficiency arose after the making up, etc., of the goods and was attributable wholly to factors for which reasonable allowance was made when the goods were made up, etc.

19–79   Footnote 2. See now 1985 Act, s.35(3).

19–80   Footnote 5. See now 1985 Act, s.35(4).

19–81   Footnote 6. See now 1985 Act, s.36.

19–82   Section 26(7) is now section 37 of the 1985 Act.

19–83   Section 27(3) was repealed by the Weights and Measures Act 1979, as was section 28. Section 32 of the 1985 Act provides that where the commission of any offence under the Act is due to the act or default of another person that other person may be dealt with whether or not proceedings are taken against the first person.

19–84   It is an offence under section 80 of the 1985 Act wilfully to obstruct an inspector acting in pursuance of the Act, and an offence under section 81 to fail to comply with a requirement properly made by such an inspector, to fail to give him information, or to give him false information, but there is no obligation to give any self-incriminating information: max. pen. in each case level 5 on the standard scale: s.84(6).

19–85   The Coinage Offences Act 1936, the Bank Notes Forgery Act
to   1801 and the Bank Notes (Forgery) Act 1805 are repealed by the
19–101   Forgery and Counterfeiting Act 1981 which creates the following offences. (The Act followed on the Law Commission's Report on Forgery and Counterfeit Currency, 1973 (Law Com. No. 55)).

COUNTERFEITING. Section 14:

"(1) It is an offence for a person to make a counterfeit of a currency note or of a protected coin, intending that he or another shall pass or tender it as genuine.

(2) It is an offence for a person to make a counterfeit of a currency note or of a protected coin without lawful authority or excuse."

Maximum penalty under subs. (1) is ten years' imprisonment and a fine on indictment, and under subs. (2) two years' imprisonment and a fine on indictment. The maximum imprisonment on summary conviction is six months in each case: s.22.

PASSING COUNTERFEIT NOTES OR COINS. Section 15:

"(1) It is an offence for a person—
(*a*) to pass or tender as genuine any thing which is, and which he knows or believes to be, a counterfeit of a currency note or of a protected coin; or
(*b*) to deliver to another any thing which is, and which he knows or believes to be, such a counterfeit, intending that the person to whom it is delivered or another shall pass or tender it as genuine.
(2) It is an offence for a person to deliver to another, without lawful authority or excuse, any thing which is, and which he knows or believes to be, a counterfeit of a currency note or of a protected coin."

Maximum penalty as for s.14(1) and (2) respectively.

POSSESSION OF COUNTERFEIT NOTES AND COINS. Section 16:

"(1) It is an offence for a person to have in his custody or under his control any thing which is, and which he knows or believes to be, a counterfeit of a currency note or of a protected coin, intending either to pass or tender it as genuine or to deliver it to another with the intention that he or another shall pass or tender it as genuine.
(2) It is an offence for a person to have in his custody or under his control, without lawful authority or excuse, any thing which is, and which he knows or believes to be, a counterfeit of a currency note or of a protected coin.
(3) It is immaterial for the purposes of subsections (1) and (2) above that a coin or note is not in a fit state to be passed or tendered or that the making or counterfeiting of a coin or note has not been finished or perfected."

Maximum penalties as for s.14(1) and (2) respectively.

POSSESSION OF IMPLEMENTS. It is an offence to make or have in one's custody or control anything intended for use by oneself or others to make a counterfeit note or coin intended to be passed as genuine: s.17(1); maximum penalty as for s.14(1).

It is also an offence to make or have in one's custody or control, without lawful authority or excuse, anything one knows to be designed or adapted for making a counterfeit currency note: s.17(2); maximum penalty as for s.14(2). It is also an offence to make or have in one's custody or control anything one knows to be capable of imparting to anything a resemblance to all or part of either side of a protected coin or of the reverse of the image on either side of a protected coin: s.17(3); maximum penalty as for s.14(2). It is a defence to this last offence to prove that one acted with Treasury permission or with other lawful authority or excuse: s.17(4).

REPRODUCTION OF IMITATIONS. It is an offence to reproduce any British currency note or any part of such a note on any substance or scale without written permission from the relevant authority: s.18. It is also an offence to make, sell or distribute, or have custody or control of, an imitation British coin in connection with a scheme intended to promote the sale of any product or the making of contracts for the supply of any service, without prior Treasury consent in writing to such sale or distribution: s.19; maximum penalty under these sections is a fine on indictment.

DEFINITIONS. "Currency note" is defined by s.27(1) as follows:

"(a) any note which—
   (i) has been lawfully issued in England and Wales, Scotland, Northern Ireland, any of the Channel Islands, the Isle of Man or the Republic of Ireland; and
   (ii) is or has been customarily used as money in the country where it was issued; and
   (iii) is payable on demand; or
(b) any note which—
   (i) has been lawfully issued in some country other than those mentioned in paragraph (a)(i) above; and
   (ii) is customarily used as money in that country."

A British currency note, in terms of section 18 is a currency note issued in England and Wales, Scotland or Northern Ireland.

"Protected coin" is any coin customarily used as money in any country, or specified in the Forgery and Counterfeiting (Protected Coins) Order 1981, section 27(1).

"British coin" in section 19 is any coin which is legal tender in the United Kingdom (see Coinage Act 1971, s.2), and imitation British coin is anything resembling a British coin in shape, size and substance.

"Counterfeiting" is defined by section 28 as follows:

"(1) For the purposes of this Part of this Act a thing is a counterfeit of a currency note or of a protected coin—
(a) if it is not a currency note or a protected coin but resembles a currency note or protected coin (whether on one side only or on both) to such an extent that it is reasonably capable of passing for a currency note or protected coin of that description; or
(b) if it is a currency note or protected coin which has been so altered that it is reasonably capable of passing for a currency note or protected coin of some other description.
(2) For the purposes of this Part of this Act—
(a) a thing consisting of one side only of a currency note, with or without the addition of other material, is a counterfeit of such a note;
(b) a thing consisting—
   (i) of parts of two or more currency notes; or
   (ii) of parts of a currency note, or of parts of two or more currency notes, with the addition of other material,
   is capable of being a counterfeit of a currency note.
(3) References in this Part of this Act to passing or tendering a counterfeit of a currency note or a protected coin are not to be construed as confined to passing or tendering it as legal tender."

19–99 Footnote 36. The Bank Notes (Forgery) (Scotland) Act 1820 and s.380(15) of the Burgh Police (Scotland) Act 1892 were repealed by the Forgery and Counterfeiting Act 1981.

19–101 The Counterfeit Currency (Convention) Act 1935 was repealed by the Forgery and Counterfeiting Act 1981.

19–102 National Insurance and Industrial Injuries Insurance are now abolished.

19–105 Section 169 is now section 173 of the Road Traffic Act 1988. Delete "section 233" and substitute "section 173."

19–107 Section 170(1) is now section 174(1) of the Road Traffic Act 1988, and section 170(6) is now section 174(5) of the 1988 Act.

19–108 Section 171 is now section 175 of the Road Traffic Act 1988; section 170(6) of the 1972 Act is now section 174(5) of the 1988 Act. "Fraudulently" means with intent to deceive, and does not require an intent to defraud: *R.* v. *Clayton* (1980) 72 Cr.App.R. 135.

19–109 Section 174 is now section 177 of the Road Traffic Act 1988; section 43 of the 1972 Act is now section 45 of the 1988 Act.

19–110 On the meaning of "fraudulently," see *R.* v. *Terry* [1984] A.C. 374, *supra*, para. 8–21.

Add new paragraph **19–110a**:

COMPUTER MISUSE

19–110a Section 1 of the Computer Misuse Act 1990 provides:
> "(1) A person is guilty of an offence if—
> (*a*) he causes a computer to perform any function with intent to secure access to any program or data held in any computer;
> (*b*) the access he intends to secure is unauthorised; and
> (*c*) he knows at the time when he causes the computer to perform the function that that is the case.
> (2) The intent a person has to have to commit an offence under this section need not be directed at—
> (*a*) any particular program or data;
> (*b*) a program or data of any particular kind; or
> (*c*) a program or data held in any particular computer.
> (3) A person guilty of an offence under this section shall be liable on summary conviction to imprisonment for a term not exceeding six months or to a fine not exceeding level 5 on the standard scale or to both."

Where the offence is committed with intent to commit or to facilitate the commission on the same or any future occasion of an offence punishable by five years' imprisonment, the maximum penalty is five years and a fine on indictment, six months on summary conviction: *ibid.*, s.2.

Unauthorised modification of computer material is dealt with in section 3 of the Act: *infra*, para. 22–21a.

19–114 The Post Office (Protection) Act was repealed by the Telecommunications Act 1984.

19–117   These provisions were repealed by the Civic Government (Scotland) Act 1982.

19–119   This provision disappeared with the repeal of s.4 of the Vagrancy Act 1824 by the Civic Government (Scotland) Act 1982.

19–123   Max. pen. a fine of level 4 or three months' imprisonment: Criminal Justice Act 1982, Sched. 6.

19–125   Footnote 86. Section 31 is now s.49 of the Medical Act 1983: max. pen. a fine of level 5 payable to the General Medical Council and recoverable by any person in the sheriff or district court together with expenses.

19–126   The Dentists Act 1957 was repealed by the Dentists Act 1984.

    Footnote 87. See now s.39 of the Dentists Act 1984.

19–129   See now Opticians Act 1989, s.28.

19–130   Section 12 of the Nurses (Scotland) Act 1951 and section 9 of the Midwives (Scotland) Act 1951 were repealed by the Nurses, Midwives and Health Visitors Act 1979, section 14 of which penalises the making and the causing or permitting others to make false representations as to one's qualifications or registered status, as well as making such representations about other people, all with intent to deceive: max. pen. a fine of level 4.

19–131   The Solicitors (Scotland) Act 1933 was repealed by the Solicitors (Scotland) Act 1980, and section 36 was re-enacted in section 31(*a*) of the latter Act: max. pen. a fine of level 3 and one month's imprisonment: s.63(1); 1975 Act, s.289F(3), (8).
    It is also an offence for any person or body corporate wilfully and falsely to pretend to be an incorporated practice or to use any name or description implying that he is an incorporated practice: Solicitors (Scotland) Act 1980, s.31(2), as inserted by Sched. 1 to the Law Reform (Miscellaneous Provisions) (Scotland) Act 1985.

19–132   Section 94 is now section 104 of the Mental Health (Scotland) Act 1984.

19–133   For an example of an offence against section 165, see *Aitchison* v. *Rizza*, 1985 S.C.C.R. 297.

19–135 to 19–137   The current Act is the Social Security Act 1986, section 55(1) of which provides:

    "(1) If a person for the purpose of obtaining any benefit or other payment under any of the benefit Acts, whether for himself or some other person, or for any other purpose connected with any of those Acts—
    (*a*) makes a statement or representation which he knows to be false; or

(*b*) produces or furnishes, or knowingly causes or knowingly allows to be produced or furnished, any document or information which he knows to be false in a material particular,
he shall be guilty of an offence."

Max. pen. three months and a fine of level 5.

The "benefit Acts" are the Social Security Act 1973, the Social Security Acts 1975 to 1986, the Industrial Injuries and Diseases (Old Cases) Act 1975, and the Child Benefit Act 1975, the last having replaced the Family Allowances Act 1965. Section 21 of the Supplementary Benefits Act 1976 is repealed by the Social Security Act 1986 along with the provisions of the 1976 Act conferring a right to supplementary benefit.

It was held in *Barrass* v. *Reeve* [1981] 1 W.L.R. 408 that it is an offence under this section to make any statement known to be untrue, even if the statement is not made with intent to obtain benefit to which one is not entitled, but only in order to deceive an employer. The false statement in that case was made on a sickness benefit claim form and related to the date on which the accused became unfit for work, he having in fact worked for someone else for two days after that date, and being unwilling to admit this lest he lose his job. The accused was not aware that he was entitled to benefit for these two days. Waller L.J. said, " . . . the plain words of this subsection are covered if a person, for the purpose of obtaining any benefit or other payments under this Act, knowingly makes any false statement. . . . There are no words to say 'with intent to obtain money' or anything of that sort": at 413C–D.

In *Clear* v. *Smith* [1981] 1 W.L.R. 399 the accused was charged with falsely declaring that he had not worked when in fact he had delivered scrap metal to dealers on behalf of others without payment, although he sometimes received petrol for the journeys he made. It was held that "work" was not limited to paid work, and that provided a statement was made dishonestly it was not necessary to show an intention to defraud. The justices had held that the accused knew that he was doing work dealing in scrap so that no defence of error was available, even assuming that an error as to the meaning of "work" was one of fact. Lord Widgery, C.J. said that the question was one of fact and degree, and went on, "One cannot possibly lay down as a general proposition that an unpaid activity is not work. As was suggested in argument, no housewife would be ready to accept that proposition with equanimity. On the other hand, it does not follow that every activity which is backed up by remuneration is work": at 406A–B.

19–138   Footnote 1. The reference to the Gas Act 1972 should be to Sched. 4, para. 20. For water see now Water (Scotland) Act 1980, Sched. 4, para. 32. For electricity see Electricity Act 1989, Sched. 7, para. 11(1); max. pen. a fine of level 3.

Add new paragraph **19–138a**:

19–138a   *Telephones.* Dishonest use of a service provided by a licensed telecommunication system other than a service broadcast from the U.K. (as to which see Copyright, Designs and Patents Act 1988, s.297(1), *supra*, para. 14–35) with intent to avoid payment is an offence under section 42 of the Telecommunications Act 1984: max. pen. two years and a fine on indictment, six months on summary conviction.

19–139   The Protection of Aircraft Act 1973 was repealed by the Aviation Security Act 1982. Section 2(3) and (4) are re-enacted by section 3(3) and (4) of the latter Act. The offence of making false statements in response to a requirement made by the Secretary of State of aircraft operators or aerodrome managers is now contained in section 11(5)(*b*) of the Act of 1982.

19–142   Footnote 7. Section 16(7) of the Dentists Act 1957 was repealed by s.13(2) of the Dentists Act 1983. The Nurses (Scotland) Act 1951 and the Midwives (Scotland) Act 1951 were repealed by the Nurses, Midwives and Health Visitors Act 1979; for the offence of falsely claiming to possess a relevant professional qualification, see s.14: max. pen. a fine of level 4.

19–143   Section 159 of the Factories Act 1961 was repealed by the Factories Act 1961 etc. (Repeals and Modifications) Order 1974.

CHAPTER 20

RESET

20–02   Footnote 6. See also *McRae* v. *H.M.A.*, 1975 J.C. 34.

20–05   A husband is not entitled to the benefit of this rule which is limited to a wife, and even in her case to the concealment of property in order to protect her husband from detection or punishment: *Smith* v. *Watson*, 1982 J.C. 34. It does not apply to a wife who uses the property, or to her continued concealment of it after her husband has been sentenced, so that *Clark* v. *Mone* is of little value as an authority.

20–10   Footnote 42. Section 439 of the Burgh Police (Scotland) Act 1892 and s.13 of the Prevention of Crimes Act 1871 were repealed by the Civic Government (Scotland) Act 1982.

20–15   In *People* v. *Egan* [1989] I.R. 681 A was asked by some people to let them use his premises to hide the proceeds of what he said he thought was going to be a minor theft, "a small stroke." They then brought the proceeds of an armed robbery to his premises. He was convicted of the robbery, and acquitted of a charge of reset.

    Footnote 54. Insert at the beginning of the note: *Backhurst* v. *MacNaughton*, 1981 S.C.C.R. 6.

20–17   Where, however, the passenger remains silent and does not attempt to run away when the vehicle is stopped by the police, there

20–17 may be insufficient evidence to convict him of reset: *Hipson* v. *Tudhope*, 1983 S.C.C.R. 247.

20–21 Section 7 of the Public Stores Act 1875 was repealed by the Criminal Law Act 1977, Sched. 12.

Add new paragraph **20–21a**:

20–21a *Value Added Tax.* Section 39(4) of the Value Added Tax Act 1983 (*infra*, para. 38–21) makes it an offence to acquire possession of or deal with any goods having reason to believe that tax on the supply or importation of the goods has been or will be evaded: max. pen. a fine of level 5 or three times the amount of tax whichever is greater.

20–22 Section 13 of the Prevention of Crimes Act 1871 was repealed by the Civic Government (Scotland) Act 1982 and metal dealing is controlled by sections 28 to 37 of the latter Act.

20–23 These provisions were repealed by the Forgery and Counterfeit-
20–24 ing Act 1981.

20–25 Section 409 of the Burgh Police (Scotland) Act 1892 was repealed by the Civic Government (Scotland) Act 1982, and replaced by section 58 of the latter Act which is in the following terms:

> "(1) Any person who, being a person to whom this section applies—
> (*a*) has or has recently had in his possession any tool or other object from the possession of which it may reasonably be inferred that he intended to commit theft or has committed theft; and
> (*b*) is unable to demonstrate satisfactorily that his possession of such tool or other object is or was not for the purposes of committing theft
> shall be guilty of an offence and liable, on summary conviction, to a fine not exceeding [level 4] or to imprisonment for a period not exceeding 3 months or to both.
> (2) For the purposes of subsection (1) above, a person shall have recently had possession of a tool or other object if he had possession of it within 14 days before the date of—
> (*a*) his arrest without warrant for the offence of having so possessed it in contravention of subsection (1) above; or
> (*b*) the issue of a warrant for his arrest for that offence; or
> (*c*) if earlier, the service upon him of the first complaint alleging that he has committed that offence.
> (3) Where a court convicts a person of an offence under this section or discharges him absolutely or makes a probation order in relation to him in respect of such an offence it may order the forfeiture of any tool or other object in respect of the possession of which he was convicted or discharged absolutely, or, as the case may be, the probation order was made.
> (4) This section applies to a person who has two or more convictions for theft which are not, for the purposes of the Rehabilitation of Offenders Act 1974, spent convictions.
> (5) In this section 'theft' includes any aggravation of theft including robbery."

Section 438 was also repealed by the Civic Government (Scotland) Act 1982.

Section 26 of the latter Act makes it an offence for anyone to give a false name or address when selling anything to a second-hand dealer: max. pen. a fine of level 3.

20–27   See now section 206(5) and 206(1)(*f*) of the Insolvency Act 1986: max. pen. seven years and a fine on indictment, six months on summary conviction.

CHAPTER 21

EXTORTION AND CORRUPTION

21–10   See also *Rae* v. *Donnelly*, 1982 S.C.C.R. 148: threat to expose sexual relationship if victim did not drop action for wrongful dismissal.

21–16   The current provisions are contained in the Rent (Scotland) Act 1984, the "1984 Act."

21–17   See now 1984 Act, sections 82 and 83: max. pen. a fine of level 3.

Footnote 43. See now 1984 Act, s.90(1).

21–18   See now 1984 Act, section 16: max. pen. as above.

21–19   See now 1984 Act, section 87(1)(*a*): max pen. as above.

Add new paragraph **21–19a**:

21–19a   The above provisions (other than section 16 of the 1984 Act) are applied to assured tenancies by section 27 of the Housing (Scotland) Act 1988.

21–20   See now 1984 Act, section 22(2).
Section 22(2A) of the 1984 Act, as inserted by section 38 of the Housing (Scotland) Act 1988, extends the provisions in section 22(2) to acts done (or services withheld) by a landlord or his agents in the knowledge or with reasonable cause to believe that they are likely to cause the occupier to give up the occupation of all or part of the premises or to refrain from exercising any right or pursuing any remedy in respect of all or part of the premises. It is a defence to a charge under section 22(2A) that services were withdrawn or withheld on reasonable grounds: s.22(2B).
Conduct may constitute harassment even if it does not constitute a breach of contract or other civil wrong: *R.* v. *Burke* [1991] 1 A.C. 135.
It has been held in England that it is necessary for the Crown to prove a specific intent to harass a person believed to be a residential occupier, and that no offence is committed where the accused

21–20   believes on reasonable grounds that the person harassed is a squatter: *R.* v. *Phekoo* [1981] 1 W.L.R. 1117; but *cf. R.* v. *Kimber* [1983] 1 W.L.R. 1118.

21–22   The maximum period of imprisonment is now seven years in all cases: Criminal Justice Act 1988, s.47.

21–26   No offence is committed under this paragraph where the document is an internal one passing only between an employee and his employers: *R.* v. *Tweedie* [1984] 2 Q.B. 729.

21–27   Max. pen. a fine of level 2 in each case: Merchant Shipping Act 1979, Sched. 6.

CHAPTER 22

DAMAGE TO PROPERTY

22–01   Malicious mischief may be committed by causing economic loss even where there is no damage to any corporeal property, at least where the loss is caused by doing something to such property as, for example, by turning a switch on or off and so activating or preventing the activation of machinery or power: *H.M.A.* v. *Wilson*, 1984 S.L.T. 117. It may also be caused by deflating a tyre: *Peter Penman*, High Court on appeal, March 1984, unreported.

22–13   Add new paragraph **22–13a**:

22–13a   *Vandalism.* Section 78(1) and (2) of the Criminal Justice (Scotland) Act 1980 provides:

> "(1) Subject to subsection (2) below, any person who, without reasonable excuse, wilfully or recklessly destroys or damages any property belonging to another shall be guilty of the offence of vandalism.
> (2) It shall not be competent to charge acts which constitute the offence of wilful fire-raising as vandalism under this section."

Max. pen. in the district court 60 days and a fine of level 3, in the sheriff court three (or in the case of a subsequent offence six) months and a fine of level 5: see 1975 Act, s.289E(4)(*b*), as inserted by Criminal Justice Act 1982, s.54.

This provision appears to have been designed to single out those kinds of malicious mischief commonly referred to as vandalism, but it is frequently used for any kind of malicious mischief, even on indictment (as an additional charge where section 457A(4) of the 1975 Act, as inserted by section 55(1) of the Criminal Justice Act 1982, applies) where the only effect of libelling the statutory charge is to limit the court's powers of punishment.

For conduct to constitute vandalism it must create an obvious and material risk of damage: *Black* v. *Allan*, 1985 S.C.C.R. 11.

On reasonable excuse see *MacDougall* v. *Ho*, 1985 S.C.C.R. 199.

22–15   The Telegraph Act 1878 was repealed by the Telecommunications Act 1984.

References to telephone kiosks or cabinets were removed from the Post Office Act 1953 by the British Telecommunications Act 1981.

Footnote 37. Penalty now payable to British Telecommunications.

Footnote 42. For aircraft see now the Air Navigation Order 1989 (S.I. 1989 No. 2004), arts. 46 and 47.

22–16   The Protection of Aircraft Act 1973 was repealed and re-enacted by the Aviation Security Act 1982.

22–17   The principal provision dealing with interference with water supplies is now the Water (Scotland) Act 1980, Schedule 4, para. 33. Section 380(14) of the Burgh Police (Scotland) Act 1892 was repealed by the Civic Government (Scotland) Act 1982.

The current provision relating to electricity is paragraph 4 of Schedule 6 to the Electricity Act 1989 which makes it an offence to damage or allow to be damaged, intentionally or by "culpable negligence," any electric plant, line or meter belonging to a public electricity supplier: max. pen. a fine of level 3.

Injury to water meters etc. is now dealt with under the Water (Scotland) Act 1980, Schedule 4, paragraph 32.

22–18   "Explosive" is defined in section 3 of the Explosives Act 1875 as including substances "used or manufactured with a view to produce a practical effect by explosion or a pyrotechnic effect," and includes petrol bombs: *R.* v. *Bouch* [1983] Q.B. 246.

22–19   "Explosive" has the same meaning in the Explosive Substances Act 1883 as in the Explosives Act 1875: *R.* v. *Wheatley* [1979] 1 W.L.R. 144, and includes a petrol bomb made in a milk bottle whose main effect is to produce a fireball: *R.* v. *Bouch* [1983] Q.B. 246. Although the ingredients of a mixture of air and petrol in a milk bottle may not in themselves be in such proportions as to be an explosive substance the fact that the bottle will become a fireball when it is broken makes the petrol, bottle and accompanying wick, materials for making an explosive substance as defined in section 9.

22–20   "Lawful object" may in some exceptional cases include the defence of person or property from imminent attack: *Att.-Gen.'s Reference (No. 2 of 1983)* [1984] Q.B. 456.

The "lawful object" is not confined to objects intended to be achieved in the United Kingdom, or to ones which would be lawful there. Where, therefore, there was evidence that the accused had manufactured timing devices in England for use abroad, he had to show that they were meant for a lawful object abroad: *R.* v. *Berry* [1985] A.C. 246.

Footnote 49. *Black* v. *H.M.A.* is now reported at 1974 J.C. 43.

22–21   Footnote 50. The Burgh Police (Scotland) Act 1892 was repealed by the Civic Government (Scotland) Act 1982.

Add new paragraph **22–21a**:

22–21a   *Computer misuse.* Section 3 of the Computer Misuse Act 1990 provides:

> "(1) A person is guilty of an offence if—
> (*a*) he does any act which causes an unauthorised modification of the contents of any computer; and
> (*b*) at the time when he does the act he has the requisite intent and the requisite knowledge.
> (2) For the purposes of subsection (1)(*b*) above the requisite intent is an intent to cause a modification of the contents of any computer and by so doing—
> (*a*) to impair the operation of any computer;
> (*b*) to prevent or hinder access to any program or data held in any computer; or
> (*c*) to impair the operation of any such program or the reliability of any such data.
> (3) The intent need not be directed at—
> (*a*) any particular computer;
> (*b*) any particular program or data or a program or data of any particular kind; or
> (*c*) any particular modification or a modification of any particular kind.
> (4) For the purposes of subsection (1)(*b*) above the requisite knowledge is knowledge that any modification he intends to cause is unauthorised.
> (5) It is immaterial for the purposes of this section whether an unauthorised modification or any intended effect of it of a kind mentioned in subsection (2) above is, or is intended to be, permanent or merely temporary. . . .
> (7) A person guilty of an offence under this section shall be liable—
> (*a*) on summary conviction, to imprisonment for a term not exceeding six months or to a fine not exceeding the statutory maximum or to both; and
> (*b*) on conviction on indictment, to imprisonment for a term not exceeding five years or to a fine or to both."

22–23   In one strange case, where A had allegedly set fire to the shoe laces of a sleeping person "recklessly," he was charged with recklessly setting fire to the laces to the wearer's danger "while he was dozing and the fire took effect thereon and on his trousers to the injury of his leg": *Wither* v. *Adie*, 1986 S.L.T. (Sh.Ct.) 32. The charge was held to be relevant as a charge of burning objects aggravated by injury to the person, and it was also held that the absence in the charge of the word "culpably" did not affect the relevancy of the complaint. The charge sounds more like something in an examination paper than something in real life, and it is difficult to understand why it was not libelled as culpable and reckless injury.

22–24   *Angus* was applied in *Blane* v. *H.M. Advocate*, 1991 S.C.C.R. 576, where a conviction of wilful fire-raising by setting fire to bedding which fire took effect on the premises was quashed, and a conviction of the crime of setting fire to bedding wilfully was substituted.

22–26   The *mens rea* of wilful fire-raising was considered by the appeal court in *Blane* v. *H.M. Advocate*, 1991 S.C.C.R. 576. In that case the accused had set fire to his bedding, and the fire had spread to the premises. The sheriff had applied the doctrine of transferred intent, and directed the jury that the only *mens rea* which had to be proved was an intention to set fire to the bedding. The High Court held that that was wrong, that transferred intent did not apply to wilful fire-raising, and that the Crown had to establish the necessary *mens rea* in relation to the actual result. It is not altogether clear, however, whether the court held that that *mens rea* extended to recklessness, or whether it was limited to intention and recklessness was relevant only as proof of intention.

22–31   Footnote 1. Max. fine now £200: Wildlife and Countryside Act 1981, s.72(3).

CHAPTER 23

MURDER

23–01   See also D.J. Lanham, "Murder by Instigating Suicide" [1980] Crim. L.R. 215.

23–02   It is homicide in Scotland as well as in England to injure a child in the womb so as to cause its death after it has been born alive: *McCluskey* v. *H.M. Advocate*, 1989 S.L.T. 175, a case of causing death by reckless driving. It has, however, also been held in England that to threaten a woman that one will injure her foetus is not to threaten her with injury to "another person": *R.* v. *Tait* (1990) 90 Cr.App.R. 44.

23–05   See also *Lourie* v. *H.M. Advocate*, 1988 S.C.C.R. 634, in which the Crown failed because they did not prove that the deceased householder had seen the accused stealing her handbag.

23–08   Footnote 29. Add: Walking into the path of a car so as to cause the driver to take action to avoid a collision, and then hitting the car, shouting, swearing, opening the driver's door, struggling with him, trying to let one of the tyres down, and placing the driver who had a weak heart in such a state of fear, alarm and exhaustion that he died there and then: *John Mason Taylor*, Criminal Appeal Court, June 1975, unreported; pushing someone who falls against another person who falls and sustains an injury from which he dies: *R.* v. *Mitchell* [1983] Q.B. 741; injecting a dangerous drug: *Finlayson* v. *H.M.A.*, 1979 J.C. 33. There is a form of manslaughter in English law known as "manslaughter by flight" which occurs when the victim dies as a result of, *e.g.* tripping while running away

23–08   from an attack from which he fears imminent injury, the fear being caused by the conduct of the accused: *D.P.P.* v. *Daley* [1980] A.C. 237.

23–18   Footnote 78. *Brennan* v. *H.M.A.* is now reported at 1977 J.C. 38.

23–20   In *H.M. Advocate* v. *Hartley*, 1989 S.L.T. 135 Lord Sutherland directed the jury that murder might be constituted by an intentional act causing the destruction of life with intent to kill or cause grievous bodily harm. That direction was criticised by Lord Justice-General Emslie in his evidence to the House of Lords Select Committee on Murder and Life Imprisonment on the ground that an intent to do serious bodily harm was not in itself enough to constitute the *mens rea* of murder, which required that the intention be carried out in circumstances displaying a degree of wicked recklessness. His Lordship's view was that there were only two "parts" to the definition of the *mens rea* of murder: intention to kill and wicked recklessness: Report of the Select Committee, 1989, H.L. Paper 78, Vol. III, para. 2017. See also Timothy H. Jones and S. Griffin, "Serious Bodily Harm and Murder," 1990 S.L.T. (News) 305.

23–21   The withdrawal of culpable homicide in a lethal weapon case (where the accused struck the deceased several times with a weapon) was approved on appeal in *Parr* v. *H.M. Advocate*, 1991 S.L.T. 208 and *Broadley* v. *H.M. Advocate*, 1991 S.L.T. 218.

23–26   Footnote 16. See also *Robt. Paul Dunn*, Criminal Appeal Court, Jan. 1980, unreported. *D.P.P.* v. *Stonehouse* is now reported at [1978] A.C. 55.

23–29   Footnote 33a. *Brennan* v. *H.M.A.* is now reported at 1977 J.C. 38.

23–31   The High Court have affirmed in recent cases that a judge is entitled to withdraw culpable homicide from the jury in any case in which the evidence is such that no reasonable jury could hold that wicked recklessness was not present, and have made it clear that *Miller and Denovan* is not limited to robbery cases: *Parr* v. *H.M.A.* 1991 S.L.T. 208, *Broadley* v. *H.M.A.*, 1991 S.L.T. 218; both cases of multiple blows with a lethal weapon.

Quaere whether homicidal force would nowadays but justifiable in defence of property, even against a mob: *cf.* P.W. Ferguson, *Crimes against the Person* (Edinburgh, 1990), para. 2.05.

CHAPTER 24

SELF-DEFENCE

24–10   Where there is a single incident during which blows are exchanged and which concludes with the accused inflicting a fatal wound on the deceased the incident should be treated as a whole for the purpose of determining whether the accused acted in self-defence: *Surman* v. *H.M.A.*, 1988 S.L.T. 371.

In practice, an accused's defence is often a mixture of self-defence and accident: he hit me and I was defending myself, but I never meant to strike the blow which killed him. The two defences, self-defence and accident, although theoretically contradictory, are not necessarily mutually exclusive in practice. *Surman, supra*; *cf. McKenzie* v. *H.M.A.* 1983 S.L.T. 220; *H.M.A.* v. *Woods*, 1972 S.L.T. (Notes) 77.

24–13   The essential feature of this aspect of self-defence is that there should not be "cruel excess," references to the heat of the moment are merely illustrative, and it is not necessary to include them in a charge to the jury: *Fenning* v. *H.M.A.*, 1985 J.C. 76.

24–17   *McCluskey* was followed in *Elliott* v. *H.M.Advocate*, 1987 S.C.C.R. 278.

CHAPTER 25

VOLUNTARY CULPABLE HOMICIDE

25–01   In one unusual case a verdict of "culpable homicide without evil intent" was described by the jury as meaning that "although he struck the blow he did not actually mean to kill him," and was held to be a verdict of guilty of culpable homicide: *Morton* v. *H.M.A.*, 1986 S.L.T. 622.

25–08   Footnote 3.   ⎫   *Brennan* v. *H.M.A.* is now reported at 1977
            Footnote 17. ⎭   J.C. 38.

25–09   See M. Wasik, "Partial Excuses in Criminal Law" (1982) 45 M.L.R. 516.

25–11   The idea of cumulative provocation was criticised in *Parr* v. *H.M. Advocate*, 1991 S.L.T 208, at least with reference to cases where there is an interval between the past provocation and the final incident, as such an interval negates the immediacy between the provocation and the blows struck which is an essential feature of the plea.

25–15   Any life that may have remained in the *Kizileviczius* confusion was destroyed by *Fenning* v. *H.M. Advocate*, 1985 J.C. 76. That case distinguished very sharply between self-defence and provocation, and laid down that a jury should first consider self-defence and that they should turn to provocation only after they had rejected self-defence, and that, having done so, they should consider the evidence on provocation afresh. The court's view was that not only were self-defence and provocation entirely different issues, but their

25–15 solution depended on quite distinct and distinguishable factual considerations: Lord Cameron at p. 544. The court did not give any illustrations of such distinct and distinguishable factual situations, and it is submitted that however the matter is to be legally analysed, in practice there will be very many cases where the evidence relied on for provocation is virtually indistinguishable from that relied on for self-defence, albeit the criteria for the two pleas are quite different: necessity for self-preservation in the one case, which might be quite rationally assessed by the accused, and in the other case loss of control.

25–19 Then proposition that cruel excess will defeat a plea of provocation was affirmed in *Lennon* v. *H.M. Advocate*, 1991 S.C.C.R. 611, an assault case.

25–24 *McDermott* was followed in *McKay* v. *H.M. Advocate*, 1991 S.C.C.R. 364, and the "adultery rule" was said to be applicable in any relationship which involved obligations of fidelity, if the killing was done in the heat of sudden and overwhelming indignation. Both these cases concerned heterosexual relationships, but there is no reason in principle for limiting the rule to such cases.

25–25 The scope for the operation of minor violence as provocation is, of course, limited by the requirement that any retaliation must bear a reasonable relation to the provocation offered: see *Thomson* v. *H.M.A.*, 1986 S.L.T. 281; P.W. Ferguson, *Crimes against the Person* (Edinburgh, 1990), para. 9.04.

25–26 to 25–30 These cases were criticised in *Thomson* v. *H.M. Advocate*, 1986 S.L.T. 281 as difficult to reconcile with Macdonald and the institutional writers: Lord Justice-Clerk at p. 284, and as of doubtful authority; Lord Hunter at pp. 285–286. The general impression given by *Thomson* is that the court were unhappy about the relaxation of the law in these cases. Lord Justice-General Emslie and Lord Justice-Clerk Ross suggest, however, in their evidence to the House of Lords Select Committee on Murder and Life Imprisonment that the law should be reconsidered, and that "there can be an event, not involving violence of such a gross character [as alarm by violence], that the ordinary reasonable man would say: 'This is enough to make any man see red and lose control of himself' ": Report of the Select Committee, 1989, H.L. Paper 78, Vol. III, para. 2072.

See also *Graham* v. *H.M.A.*, 1987 S.C.C.R. 20; *Cosgrove* v. *H.M.A.*, 1990 J.C. 333; *Parr* v. *H.M.A.*, 1991 S.L.T. 208.

25–29 Verbal provocation was left to the jury in *Stobbs* v. *H.M. Advocate*, 1983 S.C.C.R. 190.

25–33 Footnote 4a. *Brennan* v. *H.M.A.* is now reported at 1977 J.C. 38.

25–38 In *R.* v. *Camplin* [1978] A.C. 705 (see Celia Wells, "The Death Penalty for Provocation" [1978] Crim. L.R. 662), where the accused was a fifteen-year-old boy, the House of Lords preferred *McGregor* to *Bedder* v. *D.P.P.* [1954] 1 W.L.R. 1119. Lord Diplock said, "But to require old heads upon young shoulders is inconsistent with the law's compassion to human infirmity to which Sir Michael Foster [*Crown Cases and Crown Law* (1746), 315–316] ascribed the doctrine of provocation more than two centuries ago": [1978] A.C. at 717–718. His Lordship went on to suggest that juries should be directed that the reasonable man in terms of s.3 of the Homicide Act 1957 is "a person having the power of self-control to be expected of an ordinary person of the sex and age of the accused, but in other respects sharing such of the accused's characteristics as they think would affect the gravity of the provocation to him; and that the question is not merely whether such a person would in like circumstances be provoked to lose his self-control but also whether he would react to the provocation as the accused did": at 718E-F.

It was stressed in *R.* v. *Newell* (1980) 71 Cr.App.R. 331 that the relevant special characteristic must be one which is part of the accused's personality, and not something transitory like intoxication or grief, and that there must be a connection between that characteristic and the provocation offered. The conduct complained of must have been exclusively or particularly provocative to the accused because of a characteristic marking him off from the ordinary man, whether physically or mentally, or by reason of colour, race or creed. It is not enough that the accused belonged to an excitable or violent race.

In *R.* v. *Taaka* [1982] 2 N.Z.L.R. 198 it was held that psychiatric evidence that the accused, because of his personality and background, would brood for longer than normal, and that he had an obsessive personality which was directed towards his family, was relevant to a defence of provocation to a charge of murdering a cousin whose behaviour a fortnight before he had construed as an attempt to rape his (the accused's) wife.

The objective approach has also been rejected in Ireland as illogical. The court held that in considering provocation account should be taken of the accused's "temperament, character and circumstances": *People* v. *MacEoin* [1978] I.R. 27.

It seems to be generally agreed that drink is irrelevant, and that, as it was put in *Newell*, the jury must assume that the conduct in question was directed at a sober man: see, *e.g. R.* v. *O'Neill* [1982] V.R. 150. It has, however, been held in New Zealand that if there is evidence that a reasonable and sober man would have been provoked, the accused's intoxication may be taken into account in relation to the question of whether he was actually provoked: *R.* v. *Barton* [1977] 1 N.Z.L.R. 295.

CHAPTER 26

INVOLUNTARY CULPABLE HOMICIDE

26–12   The offences in sections 1 and 2 of what is now the Road Traffic Act 1988 now involve dangerous, and not reckless, driving: Road Traffic Act 1991, s.1; *infra*, paras. 26–13, 30–03.

26–13   The current provision is section 1 of the Road Traffic Act 1988 which, as substituted by section 1 of the Road Traffic Act 1991, provides:

> "1. A person who causes the death of another person by driving a mechanically propelled vehicle dangerously on a road or other public place is guilty of an offence."

Section 2 of the Road Traffic Act 1988 now also refers to dangerous and not to reckless driving, and dangerousness is defined by section 2A of that Act; see Road Traffic Act 1991, s.1.

Add new paragraph **26–13a**:

26–13a   *Causing death by careless driving when under the influence of drink or drugs*

Section 3A of the Road Traffic Act 1988, as inserted by section 3 of the Road Traffic Act 1991, provides:

> "(1) If a person causes the death of another person by driving a mechanically propelled vehicle on a road or other public place without due care and attention, or without reasonable consideration for other persons using the road or place, and—
> (a) he is, at the time when he is driving, unfit to drive through drink or drugs, or
> (b) he has consumed so much alcohol that the proportion of it in his breath, blood or urine at that time exceeds the prescribed limit, or
> (c) he is, within 18 hours after that time, required to provide a specimen in pursuance of section 7 of this Act, but without reasonable excuse fails to provide it,
> he is guilty of an offence.
> (2) For the purposes of this section a person shall be taken to be unfit to drive at any time when his ability to drive properly is impaired.
> (3) Subsection (1)(b) and (c) above shall not apply in relation to a person driving a mechanically propelled vehicle other than a motor vehicle."

Max. pen. 5 years' imprisonment and a fine on indictment: Road Traffic Offences Act 1988, Sched. 2, as amended by Road Traffic Act 1991, Sched. 2.

26–14   It was held in *Watson* v. *H.M. Advocate*, (1978), S.C.C.R. Supp. 192 that the accused's fault must be a material, *i.e.* more than a minimal, cause of the accident, but that it was wrong to direct the jury that they could acquit only if they were satisfied that the whole cause was the fault of another person.

26–20   It is homicide to cause a person's death by injecting him with a dangerous drug, given the necessary degree of recklessness, even where the injection was with the consent, or at the request, of the victim: see *Finlayson* v. *H.M.A.*, 1979 J.C. 33.

26–21   *Cf.* Lord Reid in *McKendrick* v. *Sinclair*, 1972 S.C. (H.L.) 25, 54: "But culpable homicide covers a very wide variety of cases from something not far short of murder, to cases deserving little punishment. In my own experience it was not very uncommon to direct that a charge of culpable homicide should be tried summarily."

26–24   In *H.M. Advocate* v. *Hartley*, 1989 S.L.T. 135 Lord Sutherland directed the jury that "Culpable homicide is simply the causing of death by any unlawful act. The unlawful act must be intentional, but it is quite immaterial whether death was the foreseeable result of that act."

The circumstances, however, were that the deceased had been assaulted by the accused who were convicted of murder.

26–25   Where a weapon is produced merely to deter a potential aggressor, and is not actively brandished at him, there may be no assault by the holder of the weapon, and therefore no culpable homicide if the aggressor runs on to the weapon and is fatally injured, and this apart from any question of self-defence: *Mackenzie* v. *H.M.A.*, 1983 S.L.T. 220.

26–26   In *Mathieson* v. *H.M. Advocate*, 1981 S.C.C.R. 196, where death was caused by culpable and reckless fire-raising, the High Court upheld a direction to the jury that if death results directly from the commission of an unlawful act, that is culpable homicide.

In *R.* v. *Dalby* [1982] 1 W.L.R. 425 A was charged with manslaughter by supplying V with a controlled drug. A and V had each injected himself before they parted company, and V then gave himself two further injections and died in the night. It was held that A was not guilty of manslaughter by an unlawful act since that type of manslaughter requires an act directed at the victim and involving direct physical injury. There may, of course, be manslaughter by gross negligence in certain cases of this kind, more especially where the drug is administered to V by A himself: see *H.M.A.* v. *Finlayson*, 1978 S.L.T. (Notes) 18; *Finlayson* v. *H.M.A.*, 1979 J.C. 33; *cf. Khaliq* v. *H.M.A.*, 1984 J.C. 23; *Ulhaq* v. *H.M.A.*, 1990 S.C.C.R. 593.

CHAPTER 28

ABORTION

28–05   The protection of the Act extends to abortions carried out by nurses and others acting under the direction of, and using methods prescribed by, a medical practitioner: *Royal College of Nursing* v. *D.H.S.S.* [1981] A.C. 800.

Section 37(1) of the Human Fertilisation and Embryology Act 1990 replaces section 1(1)(*a*) and (*b*) of the Abortion Act 1967 with the following:

> "(*a*) that the pregnancy has not exceeded its twenty-fourth week and that the continuance of the pregnancy would involve risk, greater than if the pregnancy were terminated, of injury to the physical or mental health of the pregnant woman or any existing children of her family; or
> (*b*) that the termination is necessary to prevent grave permanent injury to the physical or mental health of the pregnant woman; or

28–05   (c) that the continuance of the pregnancy would involve risk to the life of the pregnant woman, greater than if the pregnancy were terminated; or

   (d) that there is a substantial risk that if the child were born it would suffer from such physical or mental abnormalities as to be seriously handicapped."

Section 1(2) now applies to section 1(1)(b) as well as to section 1(1)(a): Human Fertilisation and Embryology Act 1990, s.37(2).

Section 37(3) of the Human Fertilisation and Embryology Act 1990 adds the following subsection to section 1:

   "(3A) The power under subsection (3) of this section to approve a place includes power, in relation to treatment consisting primarily in the use of such medicines as may be specified in the approval and carried out in such manner as may be so specified, to approve a class of places."

28–06   Add new paragraph **28–07**:

28–07   *Offences in relation to embryos.* The Human Fertilisation and Embryology Act 1990 creates the following offences:

   1. Creating, keeping or using an embryo outside the human body except in pursuance of a licence: ss.1, 3(1);
   2. Placing in a woman a live embryo or live gametes other than a human embryo or human gametes: s.3(2);
   3. Storing gametes except in pursuance of a licence: s.4(1)(a);
   4. In the course of providing treatment services (*i.e.* medical services provided to the public or a section of the public for the purpose of assisting women to carry children) using the sperm of any man unless the services are provided for the woman and the man together or using the eggs of any other woman, except in pursuance of a licence: ss.4(1)(b), 2(1);
   5. Mixing gametes with the live gametes of any animal except in pursuance of a licence: s.4(1)(c);
   6. Placing sperm and eggs in a woman in any circumstances specified in Regulations except in pursuance of a licence: s.4(3).

Max. pen. for contraventions of ss.3(2) or 4(1)(c), ten years and a fine on indictment, and for the other offences mentioned above two years and a fine on indictment, six months on summary conviction: s.41.

"Embryo" in the Act means a live fertilised human embryo, *i.e.* one in which a two cell zygote has appeared, and references to an embryo include an egg in the process of fertilisation: s.1.

CHAPTER 29

ASSAULT AND REAL INJURY

29–01   To commit an assault by setting a dog on a person one must cause the dog to move at the victim with the intention that the movement will at least frighten him: *Kay* v. *Allan* (1978) S.C.C.R. Supp. 188.

It was held in *Atkinson* v. *H.M. Advocate*, 1987 S.C.C.R. 534 that to enter a shop with one's face masked and jump over the counter towards the cashier can be an assault.

29–03 It may not be an assault to "present" a weapon at someone with intent to deter him from attaching the presenter, apart altogether from any question of self-defence: *Mackenzie* v. *H.M.A.*, 1983 S.L.T. 220.

29–06 Cases of assault to severe injury are now likely to be taken in the sheriff rather than the High Court: see P.W. Ferguson, *Crimes against the Person* (Edinburgh, 1990), para. 1.05.

Footnote 33. See also *Kerr (Stephen)* v. *H.M.A.*, 1986 S.C.C.R. 91.

29–12 The maximum penalty on any contravention of this section is nine months' imprisonment and a fine of level 5: 1975 Act, s.289E, as inserted by Criminal Justice Act 1982, s.54; Criminal Justice (Scotland) Act 1980, s.57. Contraventions of this section are now often tried on indictment as additional charges by virtue of s.457A(4) of the 1975 Act, as inserted by s.55(1) of the Criminal Justice Act 1982, despite the fact that the maximum penalty remains as on summary conviction.

In *Skeen* v. *Shaw and Anr.*, 1979 S.L.T. (Notes) 58 the High Court pointed out that the word "hinders" had been added to the definition of the offence subsequent to *Curlett* v. *McKechnie*. They reserved their opinion as to whether hindering can be committed without a physical element, but held that even if it can not the introduction of the term "demonstrates how small a degree any physical element must be in the act of persons who place a difficulty in the way of the police." In that case the accused were charged with standing in front of and threatening constables who had a prisoner in their custody, engaging in noisy altercation with them and making it difficult for them to get their prisoner into their van. There was, however, neither physical contact between the accused and the police nor any threat of physical violence.

See also *Carmichael* v. *Brannan*, 1986 S.L.T. 5.

For the position where the police officer is acting without warrant, see *Stirton* v. *MacPhail*, 1983 S.L.T. 34, and the commentary thereon at 1982 S.C.C.R. 307. See also *Stocks* v. *Hamilton*, 1991 S.C.C.R. 190: resistance to illegal detention. *Cf. Smith* v. *Hawkes* (1980) S.C.C.R. Supp. 261.

29–13 Section 10 of the Customs and Excise Act 1952 was repealed by the Customs and Excise Management Act 1979, and re-enacted by section 16 of that Act.

29–21 The need to prove the accused's knowledge of the character of the complainer in a charge under section 41 of the Police (Scotland) Act 1967 was upheld by the sheriff in *Annan* v. *Tait*, 1982 S.L.T. (Sh. Ct.) 108.

29–24 Certain cases of obtaining sexual intercourse with a woman without her consent are not rape but indecent assault: see *infra*, para. 33–21.

29–27   Section 72(2) of the Customs and Excise Act 1952 is repealed by the Customs and Excise Management Act 1979, and re-enacted by section 85(2) of that Act.

29–28   Max. pen. for section 7 offences is now six months and a fine of level 5: Public Order Act 1986, Sched. 2.

29–29   See now Representation of the People Act 1983, s.115(2).

29–30   It was held in *Roberts* v. *Hamilton*, 1989 S.L.T. 399 that if A intends to strike B and in fact strikes C who is standing nearby, he is guilty of assaulting C. This appears to be on the basis of "transferred intent," so that the likelihood of C being injured may not be relevant. It appears also, however, that there must be an intention to assault someone, and that it is still the law that assault cannot be committed recklessly, although there are suggestions to that effect in *Roberts* and in the earlier case of *Connor* v. *Jessop*, 1988 S.C.C.R. 624.

29–31   A police officer is justified in using reasonable force in order to subdue someone whom he reasonably but wrongly believes to be an escaping house-breaker: *McLean* v. *Jessop*, 1989 S.C.C.R. 13. A private citizen's power of arrest is limited, and so too is the degree of force he is entitled to use: *Codona* v. *Cardle*, 1989 S.L.T. 791; *Bryans* v. *Guild*, 1990 J.C. 51.

   For examples of excessive force by an arresting police officer, see *Bonar* v. *McLeod*, 1983 S.C.C.R. 161; *Marchbank* v. *Annan*, 1987 S.C.C.R. 718. For an example of resistance by someone detained illegally, see *Stocks* v. *Hamilton*, 1991 S.C.C.R. 190.

29–34   Cruel excess is a question of fact: *Moore* v. *MacDougall*, 1989 S.C.C.R. 659.

29–38   It has been held that section 107(1) of the Mental Health (Scotland) Act 1960 (now section 122 of the Mental Health (Scotland) Act 1984) which provides that no person shall be liable to criminal proceedings in respect of anything done in pursuance of the Act, applies to protect a nurse from a charge of assault by using such force as is reasonably necessary to control mentally handicapped children: *Skinner* v. *Robertson*, 1980 S.L.T. (Sh. Ct.) 43. For an example of the use of excessive force against a mental patient, in this case an adult, see *Norman* v. *Smith*, 1983 S.C.C.R. 100 in which the court made no reference to section 107, but did refer to a departmental circular on the control of patients.

   On the parent's right to prevent a teacher imposing corporal punishment, see *Campbell and Cosans* v. *United Kingdom*, Judgments and Decisions of European Court of Human Rights, Series A, Vol. 48, 25th February 1982.

   Although the accused in the odd case of *Stewart* v. *Thain*, 1981 J.C. 13 was a teacher, the incident complained of took place outwith school, and he appears to have acted as the specifically appointed agent of the child's parent who later complained about the propriety of the form of chastisement used: inducing a 15-year-old boy to remove his trousers and bend over some furniture, and then lifting the waistband of his pants and smacking him on the upper part of his buttocks. The accused was charged with indecent assault, although there was no suggestion of any sexual element, and was acquitted on the authority of *Gray* v. *Hawthorn*. It was said that humiliation might form part of a legitimate punishment.

In line with the court's approach to the problem of consent, the general position is that where the "chastisement" displays evil intent it constitutes an assault: *Guest* v. *Annan*, 1988 S.C.C.R. 275; *Peebles* v. *MacPhail*, 1989 S.C.C.R. 410: *B.* v. *Harris*, 1990 S.L.T. 208; *Byrd* v. *Wither*, 1991 S.L.T. 206.

29–39   The English Court of Appeal declined to follow the ratio of *Smart* in *Attorney-General's Reference (No. 6 of 1980)* [1981] Q.B. 715, but held that consent was not a defence to assault where there was an intention to do actual bodily harm. "Minor struggles" were said to be another matter. It was held to be irrelevant whether the assault took place in public or private. The court noted that this meant that most fights other than sporting events were illegal, but expressed the hope that their decision would not lead to unnecessary prosecutions.

29–40   Ritual female circumcision is prohibited by the Prohibition of Female Circumcision Act 1985: max. pen. five years' imprisonment and a fine on indictment, six months on summary conviction.

29–42   For an example of an assault between rugby players, see *R.* v. *Billinghurst* [1978] Crim. L.R. 553.

Footnote 36. *Cf. Butcher* v. *Jessop*, 1989 S.L.T. 593.

29–44   For an example of the application of the "due measure" rule to provocation in assault, see *Lennon* v. *H.M. Advocate*, 1991 S.C.C.R. 611.

29–49   Drugging may in certain circumstances be committed by supplying persons with drugs and the means for using them in the knowledge that they are to be used by the persons supplied to the danger of their health: *Khaliq* v. *H.M.A.*, 1984 J.C. 23; *Ulhaq* v. *H.M.A.*, 1991 S.L.T. 614; *supra*, para. 4–53.

29–51   Section 95 is now section 105 of the Mental Health (Scotland) Act 1984.

29–52   In *Jas. McLean*, Glasgow High Court, May 1980, unreported, where there was a charge of abducting a little girl, and also a charge of raping her, Lord Kincraig directed the jury on the abduction charge that (transcript of Judge's Charge, p. 7):

" . . . it is a crime to carry off or confine any person forcibly against their will without lawful authority. In the case of a child of six 'forcibly' is not a necessary element in the proof. It would be sufficient to constitute the crime of abducting a child if there was evidence of her

29–52   being led away by the accused or inducing her to follow. That would be sufficient to establish proof that she was taken away against her will. So far as any proper authority is concerned, a stranger has no proper authority to lead away a child."

See also *Elliot* v. *Tudhope*, 1987 S.C.C.R. 85, a charge of wrongful detention against a police officer.

For abduction in connection with elections, see now Representation of the People Act 1983, section 115(2)(*b*).

29–54   Add new paragraph **29–54a**:

29–54a   *Hostages*. The Taking of Hostages Act 1982, implementing the International Convention against the Taking of Hostages, provides by section 1:

> "(1) A person, whatever his nationality, who, in the United Kingdom or elsewhere,—
> (*a*) detains any other person ('the hostage'), and
> (*b*) in order to compel a State, international governmental organisation or person to do or abstain from doing any act, threatens to kill, injure or continue to detain the hostage,
> commits an offence."

Max. pen. life imprisonment.

See also the Internationally Protected Persons Act 1978, section 1(3), *infra*, para. 29–65.

29–56   In *W.* v. *H.M. Advocate*, 1982 S.C.C.R. 152 the accused was charged with culpable and reckless injury by throwing from a fifteenth-floor flat a bottle which hit someone on the ground below. He had been warned of the danger before he threw the bottle. The degree of recklessness required was said to be a total indifference to and disregard of the safety of the public.

29–58   Footnote 98. For road traffic see now Road Traffic Act 1988. The Burgh Police (Scotland) Act 1892 was repealed by the Civic Government (Scotland) Act 1982.

29–60   *Khaliq* v. *H.M. Advocate*, 1984 J.C. 23 and *Ulhaq* v. *H.M. Advocate*, 1991 S.L.T. 614, are authority for an offence of recklessly endangering the health of particular persons, in those cases by causing them to sniff glue: see *supra*, para. 4–53.

In *Gizzi and Anr.* v. *Tudhope*, 1982 S.C.C.R. 442, which was a case of reckless discharge of firearms, the accused were held to be reckless in firing towards a clump of trees without considering whether there might be anyone in range behind them. *Allan* v. *Patterson*, 1980 J.C. 57, *supra*, paras. 7–70 to 7–74, was applied.

Footnote 15. Section 1 of the Guard Dogs Act 1975 provides:

> "(1) A person shall not use or permit the use of a guard dog at any premises unless a person ('the handler') who is capable of controlling the dog is present on the premises and the dog is under the control of the handler at all times while it is being so used except while it is secured so that it is not at liberty to go freely about the premises.

(2) The handler of a guard dog shall keep the dog under his control at all times while it is being used as a guard dog at any premises except—

(*a*) while another handler has control over the dog; or

(*b*) while the dog is secured so that it is not at liberty to go freely about the premises.

(3) A person shall not use or permit the use of a guard dog at any premises unless a notice containing a warning that a guard dog is present is clearly exhibited at each entrance to the premises."

No offence is committed under s. 1(1) by the user of the dog where the handler is absent, provided the dog has been secured: *Rafferty* v. *Smith* (1978) S.C.C.R. Supp. 200, following *Hobson* v. *Gledhill* [1978] 1 W.L.R. 215.

The owner and the person in charge of a dog which is dangerously out of control in a public place are guilty of an offence, there being a defence for the owner if he was not in charge of the dog at the material time, and can prove it was in charge of someone he reasonably believed to be a fit and proper person: max. pen. if someone is injured, two years and a fine on indictment, six months on summary conviction, otherwise six months and a fine of the statutory maximum on summary conviction: Dangerous Dogs Act 1991, s.3.

The breeding or sale of fighting dogs is made an offence by section 1 of the Dangerous Dogs Act 1991; max. pen. six months and a fine of level 5.

The Cruelty to Animals Act 1876 is replaced by the Animals (Scientific Procedures) Act 1986.

29–64 See now Representation of the People Act 1983, section 115.

Add new paragraph **29–65**:

29–65 *Threats to internationally protected persons*. Section 1 of the Internationally Protected Persons Act 1978 provides, *inter alia:*

"(3) If a person in the United Kingdom or elsewhere, whether a citizen of the United Kingdom and Colonies or not—

(*a*) makes to another person a threat that any person will do an act which is an offence mentioned in paragraph (*a*) of the preceding subsection; or

(*b*) attempts to make or aids, abets, counsels or procures or is art and part in the making of such a threat to another person,

with the intention that the other person shall fear that the threat will be carried out, the person who makes the threat or, as the case may be, who attempts to make it or aids, abets, counsels or procures or is art and part in the making of it, shall in any part of the United Kingdom be guilty of an offence and liable on conviction on indictment to imprisonment for a term not exceeding ten years and not exceeding the term of imprisonment to which a person would be liable for the offence constituted by doing the act threatened at the place where the conviction occurs and at the time of the offence to which the conviction relates.

(4) For the purposes of the preceding subsections it is immaterial whether a person knows that another person is a protected person.

(5) In this section—

'act' includes omission;

29–65 'a protected person' means, in relation to an alleged offence, any of the following, namely—

(*a*) a person who at the time of the alleged offence is a Head of State, a member of a body which performs the functions of Head of State under the constitution of the State, a Head of Government or a Minister for Foreign Affairs and is outside the territory of the State in which he holds office;

(*b*) a person who at the time of the alleged offence is a representative or an official of a State or an official or agent of an international organisation of an intergovernmental character, is entitled under international law to special protection from attack on his person, freedom or dignity and does not fall within the preceding paragraph;

(*c*) a person who at the time of the alleged offence is a member of the family of another person mentioned in either of the preceding paragraphs and—

(i) if the other person is mentioned in paragraph (*a*) above, is accompanying him,

(ii) if the other person is mentioned in paragraph (*b*) above, is a member of his household;

'relevant premises' means premises at which a protected person resides or is staying or which a protected person uses for the purpose of carrying out his functions as such a person; and

'vehicle' includes any means of conveyance;

and if in any proceedings a question arises as to whether a person is or was a protected person, a certificate issued by or under the authority of the Secretary of State and stating any fact relating to the question shall be conclusive evidence of that fact."

Add new paragraphs **29–66** and **29–67**:

29–66 *Taking hostages.* Section 1 of the Taking of Hostages Act 1982 makes it an offence to detain any other person ("the hostage") and threaten to kill, injure or detain him in order to compel a State, international governmental organisation or person to do or abstain from doing any act: max. pen. life imprisonment: see *supra*, para. 29–54a.

29–67 *Torture.* Section 134 of the Criminal Justice Act 1988 provides:

"(1) A public official or person acting in an official capacity, whatever his nationality, commits the offence of torture if in the United Kingdom or elsewhere he intentionally inflicts severe pain or suffering on another in the performance or purported performance of his official duties.

(2) A person not falling within subsection (1) above commits the offence of torture, whatever his nationality, if—

(*a*) in the United Kingdom or elsewhere he intentionally inflicts severe pain or suffering on another at the instigation or with the consent or aquiescence—

(i) of a public official; or

(ii) of a person acting in an official capacity; and

(*b*) the official or other person is performing or purporting to perform his official duties when he instigates the commission of the offence or consents to or acquiesces in it.

(3) It is immaterial whether the pain or suffering is physical or mental and whether it is caused by an act or an omission.

(4) It shall be a defence for a person charged with an offence under this section in respect of any conduct of his to prove that he had lawful authority, justification or excuse for that conduct.

(5) For the purposes of this section "lawful authority, justification or excuse" means—

    (*a*) in relation to pain or suffering inflicted in the United Kingdom, lawful authority, justification or excuse under the law of the part of the United Kingdom where it was inflicted;

    (*b*) in relation to pain or suffering inflicted outside the United Kingdom—

        (i) if it was inflicted by a United Kingdom official acting under the law of the United Kingdom or by a person acting in an official capacity under that law, lawful authority, justification or excuse under that law;

        (ii) if it was inflicted by a United Kingdom official acting under the law of any part of the United Kingdom or by a person acting in an official capacity under such law, lawful authority, justification or excuse under the law of the part of the United Kingdom under whose law he was acting; and

        (iii) in any other case, lawful authority, justification or excuse under the law of the place where it was inflicted.

(6) A person who commits the offence of torture shall be liable on conviction on indictment to imprisonment for life."

CHAPTER 30

STATUTORY OFFENCES CONCERNED WITH PERSONAL INJURY

30–01   The current road traffic law is contained in the Road Traffic Act 1988, the Road Traffic Offenders Act 1988 and the Road Traffic (Consequential Provisions) Act 1988.

30–02   Most of the 1972 Act is now contained in the Road Traffic Act 1988. The current Regulations are the Road Vehicles (Construction and Use) Regulations 1986.

30–03   Section 2 of the Road Traffic Act 1972 (which became section 2 of the Road Traffic Act 1988) replaced the earlier offence of driving recklessly or in a dangerous manner with an offence of driving recklessly, in line with the movement away from strict liability offences. The courts, however, interpreted "recklessly" in such a way as to give it a largely objective meaning: *Allan* v. *Patterson*, 1980 J.C. 57; *R.* v. *Lawrence (Stephen)* [1982] A.C. 510. The result was that the offence of reckless driving could be proved by evidence of dangerous driving, with little or no reference to the driver's state of mind. At the same time, driving which was not dangerous *qua* driving, but involved taking a deliberate risk by driving an obviously faulty vehicle, could probably still be punished as reckless. Parliament has now replaced the offence of reckless driving with one of dangerous driving, in which dangerous driving is defined in terms which reflect the decisions in *Allan* v. *Patterson* and *Lawrence*.

Sections 2, 2A and 3 of the Road Traffic Act 1988, as substituted by sections 1 and 2 of the Road Traffic Act 1991, now read as follows:

103

30–03   "2. A person who drives a mechanically propelled vehicle dangerously on a road or other public place is guilty of an offence.

2A.—(1) For the purposes of sections 1 and 2 above a person is to be regarded as driving dangerously if (and, subject to subsection (2) below, only if)—

(a) the way he drives falls far below what would be expected of a competent and careful driver, and

(b) it would be obvious to a competent and careful driver that driving in that way would be dangerous.

(2) A person is also to be regarded as driving dangerously for the purposes of sections 1 and 2 above if it would be obvious to a competent and careful driver that driving the vehicle in its current state would be dangerous.

(3) In subsections (1) and (2) above 'dangerous' refers to danger either of injury to any person or of serious damage to property; and in determining for the purposes of those subsections what would be expected of, or obvious to, a competent and careful driver in a particular case, regard shall be had not only to the circumstances of which he could be expected to be aware but also to any circumstances shown to have been within the knowledge of the accused.

(4) In determining for the purposes of subsection (2) above the state of a vehicle, regard may be had to anything attached to or carried on or in it and to the manner in which it is attached or carried.

3. If a person drives a mechanically propelled vehicle on a road or other public place without due care and attention, or without reasonable consideration for other persons using the road or place, he is guilty of an offence."

Driving in public places other than roads is not penalised by sections 1 to 3 of the Road Traffic Act 1988 where it is in accordance with an authorisation given by the Secretary of State for a motoring event: Road Traffic Act 1988, s.13A, as inserted by Road Traffic Act 1991, s.5.

30–04   In *McQuaid* v. *Anderton* [1981] 1 W.L.R. 154 it was held that a person in the driver's seat of a towed vehicle was driving it, and *Wallace* v. *Major* was not followed.

Footnote 10. *Ames* v. *MacLeod* was approved by a full bench in *McArthur* v. *Valentine*, 1990 J.C. 146.

30–06   Sections 1 to 3 of the Road Traffic Act 1988 now apply to any mechanically propelled vehicle: Road Traffic Act 1991, ss.1 and 2.

30–07   In *Dunn* v. *Keane*, 1976 J.C. 39 it was held that the driveway from the public road to a hotel car park was a road to which the public had access, following *Harrison* v. *Hill*.

The current definition of "road" is contained in section 151 of the Roads (Scotland) Act 1984, which is incorporated by reference in section 192(2) of the Road Traffic Act 1988. A road is "any way (other than a waterway) over which there is a public right of passage (by whatever means) and includes the road's verge, and any bridge (whether permanent or temporary) over which, or tunnel through which, the road passes." That portion of *Harrison* v. *Hill* which extends the meaning of road to ways on which the public are permitted access but do not have access as of right is therefore no longer applicable: *Young* v. *Carmichael*, 1991 S.C.C.R. 332. For an example of the application of the current definition to a parking area near a public house, see *Beattie* v. *Scott*, 1990 S.C.C.R. 435.

30–09   It is careless driving to reverse when one cannot see clearly what is behind one, particularly in an area where children are likely to be playing: *McCrone* v. *Normand*, 1989 S.L.T. 332: *Farquhar* v. *MacKinnon*, 1986 S.C.C.R. 524.

30–10   In *Wilson* v. *MacPhail*, 1991 S.C.C.R. 170 the accused had overtaken a queue of traffic by going on to the wrong side of the road and had caused some inconvenience to oncoming traffic. The sheriff convicted him of a contravention of section 3 on the basis that he had failed to show reasonable consideration for other drivers, but the High Court, who upheld the conviction, held that the proper test was whether the accused had shown due care in regard to actual and potential inconvenience to other drivers: *cf.* *Price* v. *D.P.P.* [1990] R.T.R. 413.

30–11   Sections 5 and 6 of the 1972 Act are now sections 4 and 5 of the Road Traffic Act 1988. Section 4 applies to any mechanically propelled vehicle: Road Traffic Act 1991, s.4.

A drug in this context is "a substance which is taken into the human body by whatsoever means which does not fall within the description 'drink' . . . and which is not taken as a food, but which does affect the control of the human body": *Bradford* v. *Wilson* (1984) 78 Cr.App.R. 77, Robert Goff, L.J. at 120–121. A person suffering from the effects of glue-sniffing is therefore unfit through a drug: *ibid*; *Duffy* v. *Tudhope*, 1983 S.C.C.R. 440.

30–13   Section 4(4) of the Road Traffic Act 1988 provides:

> "The court may, in determining whether there was such a likelihood as is mentioned in subsection (3) above, disregard any injury to him and any damage to the vehicle."

30–14   Necessity has been held to be a defence to a charge of driving or attempting to drive with an excess of alcohol in one's blood: *Tudhope* v. *Grubb*, 1983 S.C.C.R. 350 (Sh.Ct.); but see also *McLeod* v. *MacDougall*, 1988 S.C.C.R. 519; *supra*, para. 13–18.

30–15   The much litigated section 6 was repealed by Schedule 8 to the Transport Act 1981 and replaced by the following (which is now section 5 of the Road Traffic Act 1988) which removes the peculiarity of the earlier provision which made the mode of proof part of the offence:

> "(1) If a person—
> (*a*) drives or attempts to drive a motor vehicle on a road or other public place; or
> (*b*) is in charge of a motor vehicle on a road or other public place;
> after consuming so much alcohol that the proportion of it in his breath, blood or urine exceeds the prescribed limit he is guilty of an offence.
> (2) It is a defence for a person charged with an offence under subsection (1)(*b*) above to prove that at the time he is alleged to have committed the offence the circumstances were such that there was no

30–15   likelihood of his driving the vehicle whilst the proportion of alcohol in his breath, blood or urine remained likely to exceed the prescribed limit.

(3) The court may, in determining whether there was such a likelihood as is mentioned in subsection (2) above, disregard any injury to him and any damage to the vehicle."

30–16   See also *Keane* v. *McSkimming*, 1983 S.C.C.R. 220.

Section 22 of the 1972 Act is now contained in sections 35 and 36 of the Road Traffic Act 1988.

Footnote 91. For penalties see now Road Traffic Offenders Act 1988. The current Regulations are the Traffic Signs, Regulations and General Directions 1981.

30–17   See now the "Zebra" Pedestrian Crossing Regulations 1971, the duty to accord precedence being in reg. 8; "Pelican" Pedestrian Crossing Regulations and General Directions 1987, where the relevant regulation is reg. 17.

30–19   The Stage Carriages Act 1832 was repealed by the Statute Law (Repeals) Act 1981. The Burgh Police (Scotland) Act 1892 is repealed by the Civic Government (Scotland) Act 1982.

30–20   Section 27 is now as substituted by section 32 of the Merchant Shipping Act 1988 and provides:

"(1) This section applies—
(*a*) to the master of, or any seaman employed in, a ship registered in the United Kingdom; and
(*b*) to the master of, or any seaman employed in, a ship which—
  (i) is registered under the law of any country outside the United Kingdom, and
  (ii) is in a port in the United Kingdom or within the seaward limits of the territorial sea of the United Kingdom while proceeding to or from any such port.
(2) If a person to whom this section applies, while on board his ship or in its immediate vicinity—
(*a*) does any act which causes or is likely to cause—
  (i) the loss or destruction of or serious damage to his ship or its machinery, navigational equipment or safety equipment, or
  (ii) the loss or destruction of or serious damage to any other ship or any structure, or
  (iii) the death of or serious injury to any person, or
(*b*) omits to do anything required—
  (i) to preserve his ship or its machinery, navigational equipment or safety equipment from being lost, destroyed or seriously damaged, or
  (ii) to preserve any person on board his ship from death or serious injury, or
  (iii) to prevent his ship from causing the loss or destruction of or serious damage to any other ship or any structure, or the death of or serious injury to any person not on board his ship,
and either of the conditions specified in subsection (3) of this section is satisfied with respect to that act or omission, he shall (subject to subsections (6) and (7) of this section) be guilty of an offence.

106

(3) Those conditions are—

(*a*) that the act or omission was deliberate or amounted to a breach or neglect of duty;

(*b*) that the master or seaman in question was under the influence of drink or a drug at the time of the act or omission.

(4) If a person to whom this section applies—

(*a*) discharges any of his duties, or performs any other function in relation to the operation of his ship or its machinery or equipment, in such a manner as to cause, or to be likely to cause, any such loss, destruction, death or injury as is mentioned in subsection (2)(*a*) of this section, or

(*b*) fails to discharge any of his duties, or to perform any such function, properly to such an extent as to cause, or to be likely to cause, any of those things,

he shall (subject to subsections (6) and (7) of this section) be guilty of an offence.

(5) A person guilty of an offence under this section shall be liable—

(*a*) on summary conviction, to a fine not exceeding the statutory maximum;

(*b*) on conviction on indictment, to imprisonment for a term not exceeding two years or a fine, or both.

(6) In proceedings for an offence under this section it shall be a defence to prove—

(*a*) in the case of an offence under subsection (2) of this section where the act or omission alleged against the defendant constituted a breach or neglect of duty, that the defendant took all reasonable steps to discharge that duty;

(*b*) in the case of an offence under subsection (4) of this section, that the defendant took all reasonable precautions and exercised all due diligence to avoid committing the offence; or

(*c*) in the case of an offence under either of those subsections—

    (i) that he could have avoided committing the offence only by disobeying a lawful command, or

    (ii) that in all the circumstances the loss, destruction, damage, death or injury in question, or (as the case may be) the likelihood of its being caused, either could not reasonably have been foreseen by the defendant or could not reasonably have been avoided by him."

Section 457 is now replaced by section 30 of the Merchant Shipping Act 1988 which provides:

"(1) If, having regard to the nature of the service for which it is intended—

(*a*) a ship in a port in the United Kingdom, or

(*b*) a ship registered in the United Kingdom which is in any other port,

is, by reason of any of the matters mentioned in subsection (3), not fit to go to sea without serious danger to human life, then, subject to subsections (5) and (6), the master and the owner of the ship shall each be guilty of an offence.

(2) Where, at the time when a ship is not fit to go to sea as mentioned in subsection (1), any responsibilities of the owner with respect to the particular matters by reason of which the ship is not fit to go to sea have been assumed (whether wholly or in part) by any person or persons other than the owner, and have been so assumed by that person or (as the case may be) by each of those persons either—

(*a*) directly, under the terms of a charter-party or management agreement made with the owner, or

107

(*b*) indirectly, under the terms of a series of charter-parties or management agreements,

the reference to the owner in subsection (1) shall be construed as including a reference to that other person or (as the case may be) to each of those other persons.

(3) The matters referred to in subsection (1) are—

(*a*) the condition, or the unsuitability for its purpose, of—
    (i) the ship or its machinery or equipment, or
    (ii) any part of the ship or its machinery or equipment;

(*b*) undermanning;

(*c*) overloading or unsafe or improper loading;

(*d*) any other matter relevant to the safety of the ship.

(4) A person guilty of an offence under this section shall be liable—

(*a*) on summary conviction to a fine not exceeding £50,000;

(*b*) on conviction on indictment, to imprisonment for a term not exceeding two years or a fine, or both.

(5) It shall be a defence in proceedings for an offence under this section to prove that at the time of the alleged offence—

(*a*) arrangements had been made which were appropriate to ensure that before the ship went to sea it was made fit to do so without serious danger to human life by reason of the matters falling within subsection (3) which are specified in the charge (or, in Scotland, which are libelled in the complaint, petition or indictment); or

(*b*) it was reasonable for such arrangements not to have been made . . . "

Section 30(6) and (7) provides additional defences where the relevant responsibilities had been assumed by other persons and the defender had exercised reasonable diligence to secure their proper discharge, having regard in particular to whether the defender should have been aware of any deficiency in the discharge of these responsibilities and to what he could have done to terminate a charter or intervene in the management of the ship.

Section 31 of the Merchant Shipping Act 1988 also places a general duty on shipowners to take all reasonable steps to secure that the ship is operated in a safe manner: max. pen. as above. "Owner" includes charterer and ship-manager.

Actual damage is not necessary for an offence against section 27(2)(*b*): *Foreman* v. *MacNeill* (1978) S.C.C.R. Supp. 210.

30–21   In order to obtain a conviction under this section, the Crown must show that a potential danger to persons passing along the railway existed as the result of the accused's negligence: *Rodger* v. *Smith*, 1981 S.L.T. (Notes) 31.

30–22   The current law is contained in the Air Navigation Order 1989, Articles 50 to 52, which replaces "wilfully" with "recklessly." It is an offence against Article 52(1) for anyone to be drunk on an aircraft.

Section 11 of the Civil Aviation Act 1949 is repealed by the Civil Aviation Act 1982, and re-enacted by section 81 of that Act.

30–23   The Protection of Aircraft Act 1973 was repealed by the Aviation Security Act 1982. Section 1 of the 1973 Act is now section 2 of the 1982 Act; the power to direct searches, etc. is now in section 13 of that Act. Section 16 of the 1973 Act is now section 4 of the 1982 Act.

Section 2 of the 1973 Act is now section 3 of the 1982 Act, subject to some insignificant verbal changes.

30–26   Section 1 of the Firearms Act 1982 applies the Firearms Act 1968 to any imitation firearm which has the appearance of being a firearm to which section 1 of the 1968 Act applies, if it is so constructed or adapted as to be readily convertible into a firearm to which that section applies, *i.e.* if it can be so converted without any special skill on the part of the person converting it in the construction or adaptation of any kind of firearm, and the conversion work involved does not require equipment or tools other than such as are in common use by persons carrying on works of construction and maintenance in their own homes. In the application of the 1982 Act, section 57(1) of the 1968 Act is to be read without paras. (*b*) and (*c*). The provisions of section 4(3) and (4) of the 1968 Act do not apply to imitation firearms to which the 1982 Act applies: 1982 Act, section 2(2). In addition, the 1982 Act does not operate to apply to imitation firearms the provisions of the 1968 Act relating to, or to the enforcement of control over, the manner in which a firearm is used or the circumstances in which it is carried, but this is without prejudice to the application of these provisions to imitation firearms independently of the 1982 Act.

Kelly v. *MacKinnon*, 1982 J.C. 94, which held that the fact that a replica revolver and a starting pistol which had been rendered incapable of firing were easily convertible so as to be capable of being fired did not make them firearms, must now be applied subject to the Firearms Act 1982.

Section 7(2) of the Firearms (Amendment) Act 1988 provides that any weapon to which section 1 of the Firearms Act 1968, as amended by section 2 of the 1988 Act, has or would have applied, shall remain a weapon to which it applies, if it had at any time a rifled barrel less than 24 inches long, notwithstanding anything done to convert it to a shotgun or air weapon. Section 2 of the 1988 Act redefines the class of shotguns exempted from section 1 of the 1968 Act.

Footnote 27. Add: *R.* v. *Burke* (1978) 67 Cr.App.R. 220; *cf.* *Walkingshaw* v. *Wallace*, 1990 S.C.C.R. 203 (Sh. Ct.). The view has been expressed that it is unlikely that any firearm made in this century will be regarded as an antique: *Bennett* v. *Brown* (1980) 71 Cr.App.R. 109. Provision is made for licensing museums to possess firearms: Firearms (Amendment) Act 1988, s.19, Sched.

30–27   The offence is one of strict liability, and it is immaterial that the accused does not know that what he has is a firearm: *R.* v. *Hussain* [1981] 1 W.L.R. 416.

A rifle whose rifling has been removed so as to make it a smooth bore gun does not require a firearms certificate: *R.* v. *Hucklebridge* [1980] 1 W.L.R. 1284.

Shotguns with more than a two-inch diameter bore, or with a magazine (other than a non-detachable magazine which can hold only two cartridges), or which are revolver guns, are not exempted from section 1: Firearms (Amendment) Act 1988, s.2.

30–27 An air weapon is one in which the propulsion is caused by air. Where the propulsion is caused by a gas, such as compressed carbon dioxide, the weapon is not an air weapon: *R.* v. *Thorpe* [1987] 1 W.L.R. 383.

Possession includes having control of: see *Argo* v. *Carmichael*, 1990 J.C. 210.

30–29 The transfer of shotguns in breach of any instructions in the transferee's certificate, or without intimation to the chief constable who issued the transferor's certificate, is penalised by section 4 of the Firearms (Amendment) Act 1988. The sale of ammunition for shotguns is governed by section 5 of that Act: max. pen. for breaches of sections 4 or 5, six months and a fine of level 5.

Footnote 32. Max. pen. now three years and a fine on indictment: Criminal Justice Act 1988, s.44(2).

30–31 Paragraphs (*a*) and (*c*) are substituted by section 1 of the Firearms (Amendment) Act 1988 as follows:

"(2) For paragraph (*a*) of subsection (1) there shall be substituted—
'(*a*) any firearm which is so designed or adapted that two or more missiles can be successively discharged without repeated pressure on the trigger;
(*ab*) any self-loading or pump-action rifle other than one which is chambered for .22 rim-fire cartridges;
(*ac*) any self-loading or pump-action smooth-bore gun which is not chambered for .22 rim-fire cartridges and either has a barrel less than 24 inches in length or (excluding any detachable, folding, retractable or other movable butt-stock) is less than 40 inches in length overall;
(*ad*) any smooth-bore revolver gun other than one which is chambered for 9mm. rim-fire cartridges or loaded at the muzzle end of each chamber;
(*ae*) any rocket launcher, or any mortar, for projecting a stabilised missile, other than a launcher or mortar designed for line-throwing or pyrotechnic purposes or as signalling apparatus;'.
(3) For paragraph (*c*) of subsection (1) there shall be substituted—
'(*c*) any cartridge with a bullet designed to explode on or immediately before impact, any ammunition containing or designed or adapted to contain any such noxious thing as is mentioned in paragraph (*b*) above and, if capable of being used with a firearm of any description, any grenade, bomb (or other like missile), or rocket or shell designed to explode as aforesaid.' "

In addition, section 1(4) of the 1988 Act empowers the Secretary of State to apply the provisions of the Firearms Act 1968 relating to prohibited weapons and ammunition to any other firearm (other than an air weapon) not lawfully on sale in Great Britain in substantial numbers before 1988 which appears to him to be especially dangerous or wholly or partly composed of material making it not readily detectable by a metal detector, as well as to any ammunition which appears to him to be specially dangerous.

Section 5 of the 1968 Act describes the kind of weapon which is prohibited, and the prohibition extends to any weapon so describable, even if it has been modified so as to be capable of firing only single shots: *Jessop* v. *Stevenson*, 1988 S.L.T. 223, where the modification could be reversed by a few minutes' work.

A harmless container is not "adapted" for the discharge of a noxious liquid merely by being filled with the liquid: *R.* v. *Formosa* [1991] 2 Q.B. 1.

An electric stunning device is a prohibited weapon, since it discharges a noxious thing, *i.e.* electricity: *Flack* v. *Baldry* [1988] 1 W.L.R. 393.

It has been held that section 5 creates an offence of strict liability, and that it is not a defence to a charge of possessing a CS gas canister that one was reasonably ignorant of the fact that it contained gas: *R.* v. *Bradish* [1990] 1 Q.B. 981.

Section 7(1) of the Firearms (Amendment) Act 1988 provides that a prohibited weapon (other than a smooth-bore gun (which is not a self-loading or pump action gun) which was prohibited only because of the shortness of its barrel) shall remain prohibited notwithstanding anything done to convert it to a different kind of weapon.

Possession of all the parts of a stripped down prohibited weapon is possession of the weapon: *R.* v. *Pannell* (1982) 76 Cr.App.R. 53.

30–32   The shortening to less than twenty-four inches of the barrel of a smooth bore gun which is a firearm in terms of section 1 of the 1968 Act, other than one with a bore exceeding two inches in diameter, is an offence under section 6(1) of the Firearms (Amendment) Act 1988. It is not an offence under that section, however, for a registered firearms dealer to shorten the barrel of a gun for the sole purpose of replacing a defective part of the barrel so as to produce a barrel of not less than twenty-four inches long: s.6(2); max. pen. for a contravention of s.6(1) five years and a fine on indictment, six months on summary conviction.

30–35   It has been held that it is not necessary to prove that at some time before its actual use the firearm was being carried with the intention of using it, and that the ratio of such cases as *R.* v. *Jura* [1954] 1 Q.B. 503 (para. 30–46 in the main work) does not apply to section 18: *R.* v. *Houghton (Andrew)* [1982] Crim. L.R. 112.

The English courts take the view that "have with him" is wider than "carry," and extends to all situations where there was a close physical link between A and the firearms and a degree of immediate control by him over it: *R.* v. *Kelt* [1977] 1 W.L.R. 1365; *cf. R.* v. *Jones (Keith)* [1987] 1 W.L.R. 692.

Footnote 41. Delete the references to the Vagrancy Act and the Prevention of Crimes Act and substitute Civic Government (Scotland) Act 1982, s.57. Section 175 of the Road Traffic Act 1972 is now s.178 of the Road Traffic Act 1988.

Footnote 42. Max. pen. now life imprisonment: Criminal Justice Act 1988, s.44(3).

30–36   The possession of a shotgun certificate is not lawful authority within s.19: *Ross* v. *Collins* [1982] Crim. L.R. 368; but it has been

30–36   held that the exercise of a public right of recreation on the foreshore is: *McLeod* v. *McLeod*, 1982 S.C.C.R. 130 (Sh. Ct.).

30–37   See *Ferguson* v. *MacPhail*, 1987 S.C.C.R. 52.

30–38   It has been held in England that the intention to endanger life must be for an unlawful purpose, so that where the purpose is self-defence, section 16 has not been contravened: *R.* v. *Georgiades* [1989] 1 W.L.R. 759. The court expressed the view that cases where such a defence could be raised would be rare: *cf. Grieve* v. *MacLeod*, 1967 J.C. 32; *Evans* v. *Hughes* [1972] 1 W.L.R. 1452.

30–39   Section 4 of the Vagrancy Act 1824 is repealed by the Civic Government (Scotland) Act 1982.

30–40   Where consecutive sentences are imposed, the relevant period under s.21 is that of their aggregate: *Davies* v. *Tomlinson* (1980) 71 Cr.App.R. 279.

30–41   Footnote 53. Max. pen. now life imprisonment: Criminal Justice Act 1988, s.44(3).

30–43   Footnote 58. Max. imprisonment now three years: Criminal Justice Act 1988, s.46(1).

30–44   A flick knife is a weapon made for use for causing personal injury: *Tudhope* v. *O'Neill*, 1982 S.C.C.R. 45; *cf. Gibson* v. *Wales* [1983] 1 W.L.R. 393: *R.* v. *Simpson (Calvin)* [1983] 1 W.L.R. 1494. So, too, are nunchaca sticks: *Hemming* v. *Annan*, 1982 S.C.C.R. 432.

Where an article such as a machete has both an offensive and an innocent use, it is not an offensive weapon per se: *Woods* v. *Heywood*, 1988 S.L.T. 849.

Intention to cause personal injury is a question of fact which can be inferred from the general circumstances of the accused's possession: *Lopez* v. *MacNab*, 1978 J.C. 41; *Miller* v. *Douglas*, 1988 S.C.C.R. 565; *Ralston* v. *Lockhart*, 1986 S.C.C.R. 400 (use for other illegal purpose); *Barr* v. *MacKinnon*, 1988 S.C.C.R. 561; *Kane* v. *H.M. Advocate*, 1988 S.C.C.R. 585. It has been held in England that intention to cause injury does not include an intention to intimidate unless it is accompanied by an intention to injure by shock: *R.* v. *Rapier* (1979) 70 Cr.App.R. 17. See also *R.* v. *Williamson* (1977) 67 Cr.App.R. 35.

Footnote 65. See *McLaughlin* v. *Tudhope*, 1987 S.C.C.R. 456.

Footnote 69. Add: *Coull* v. *Guild*, 1986 S.L.T. 184.

Footnote 70. See *Coull* v. *Guild, supra, Ralston* v. *Lockhart, supra*; *Kane* v. *H.M.A., supra*.

Footnote 74. Add: *Ralston* v. *Lockhart, supra*.

30–45   What constitutes a reasonable excuse is a question of fact for the trial court: compare *Hemming* v. *Annan*, 1982 S.C.C.R. 432 and *Kincaid* v. *Tudhope*, 1983 S.C.C.R. 389.

In *Glendinning* v. *Guild*, 1988 S.L.T. 252, a decision on reasonable excuse, the court stated that the Act was concerned with the possession and not the use of the weapon, so that a person carrying a weapon with a reasonable excuse does not become guilty of a contravention of the Act just by using it in an unreasonable way, such as waving it about. In *Miller* v. *Douglas*, 1988 S.C.C.R. 565 the weapon was carried for offensive purposes, although it was not actually used when the occasion arose, and the accused's conviction was upheld on appeal.

Footnote 78. *Cf. R.* v. *Georgiades* [1989] 1 W.L.R. 759.

30–46 *Ohlson* was applied in *Bates* v. *Bulman* [1979] 1 W.L.R. 1190 where the accused, after punching a man, requested and received from a friend a clasp knife which he opened and held against the victim's head. For the meaning of "has with him," see *supra*, para. 30–35.

Add new paragraph **30–46a**:

30–46a *Obstructing search for weapons.* Section 4(1) of the Criminal Justice (Scotland) Act 1980 gives a police constable power to search persons he has reasonable cause to suspect of having offensive weapons, and section 4(2) provides:

"Any person who—
(a) intentionally obstructs a constable in the exercise of the constable's powers under subsection (1) above; or
(b) conceals from a constable acting in the exercise of the said powers an offensive weapon,
shall be guilty of an offence and liable on summary conviction to a fine not exceeding [level 3 on the standard scale]."

It is not an offence under section 4(2)(*b*) for a person in possession of a weapon to hand it to a friend on the approach of the police: *Burke* v. *Mackinnon*, 1983 S.C.C.R. 23.

30–47 Section 4 of the Vagrancy Act was repealed by the Civic Government (Scotland) Act 1982. Section 73 of the Customs and Excise Act 1952 is now section 86 of the Customs and Excise Management Act 1979.

30–48 Footnote 1. Max. fine now level 5: Criminal Justice Act 1988, s.46(2).

Add new paragraph, **30–48a**:

30–48a It is an offence under section 141 of the Criminal Justice Act 1988 to manufacture, sell or hire or offer for sale or hire, expose or possess for sale or hire, or lend or give to anyone else, any weapon of a kind specified by the Secretary of State by order, other than a firearm or a crossbow. The importation of such weapons is also prohibited. It is a defence for the accused to prove that any conduct with which he is charged was for the purpose of the Crown or a

30–48a visiting force, or of making the weapon available to a non-profit making museum. It is also a defence for someone acting on behalf of a museum who is charged with hiring or lending a weapon to prove that he had reasonable grounds for believing that the hirer or lessee would use it only for cultural, artistic or educational purposes: max. pen. on summary conviction 6 months and a fine of level 5.

30–50 Although no cases or information have been prescribed under section 3(3), failure to give information may be an offence under section 3(1) where the information is necessary to prevent exposure to risk to health or safety: *Carmichael* v. *Rosehall Engineering Works Ltd.*, 1983 S.C.C.R. 353; *R.* v. *Swan Hunter Shipbuilders Ltd.* [1981] I.C.R. 831.

On the relationship between section 3 and section 4, see *Aitchison* v. *Howard Doris Ltd.*, 1979 S.L.T. (Notes) 22.

CHAPTER 31

OFFENCES AGAINST CHILDREN

31–02 Max. pen. is now ten years' imprisonment in all cases: Criminal Justice Act 1988, s.45.

31–04 It has been held in the House of Lords that the offence of wilful neglect requires intention or at least recklessness: *R.* v. *Sheppard* [1981] A.C. 394. Where what is in issue is failure to provide medical aid the prosecution must therefore show either that the parent was aware of the risk or that the parent's unawareness was due to his not caring whether the child's health was at risk or not: Lord Diplock at 403A.

The matter has not been reconsidered in Scotland since *Sheppard*, so that the law remains as laid down in *R.* v. *Senior* [1899] 1 Q.B. 283 and *Clark* v. *H.M. Advocate*, 1968 J.C. 53: *c.f.* Lord Fraser of Tullybelton's dissenting speech in *Sheppard* at 416 to 417.

31–13 Add new paragraph **31–14**:

31–14 *Indecent photographs.* It is an offence to take or permit to be taken or possess any indecent photograph of a person under the age of 16: Civic Government (Scotland) Act 1982, ss.52, 52A, see *infra*, para. 41–22a.

CHAPTER 32

CRUELTY TO ANIMALS

32–01 Section 2(3) of the Protection of Animals (Amendment) Act 1988 inserts a new section 1A into the 1912 Act, which makes it an offence to be present without reasonable excuse (proof of which lies on the accused) at an animal fight, and a new section 13 which makes it an offence to advertise such fights; max. pen. in each case a fine of level 4.

Footnote 3. See *Braid* v. *Brown*, 1990 J.C. 189.

Footnote 4. The Protection of Animals (Amendment) Act 1988 repeals s.3 of the Protection of Animals (Amendment) Act 1954 and the other Acts mentioned in this footnote. Section 1 of the 1988 Act amends the Protection of Animals (Amendment) Act 1954 so as to provide that anyone convicted of cruelty under the 1912 Act may be disqualified from having custody of an animal of any kind for a specified period. The 1988 Act also repeals the Protection of Animals (Cruelty to Dogs) (Scotland) Act 1934.

An order of disqualification which refers to having the custody of cattle is to be interpreted as extending to sheep: *Wastie* v. *Phillips* [1972] 1 W.L.R. 1293.

32–02   It was held in *Patchett* v. *MacDougall*, 1983 J.C. 63 that it is not necessarily cruelty to kill an animal by shooting it at point-blank range.

Footnote 7. See also *Tudhope* v. *Ross*, 1986 S.C.C.R. 467 (Sh.Ct.) which held, *inter alia*, that where the net result of the accused's cruelty was to reduce the pain of a hydrophobic dog by rendering it unconscious, it could not be said that unnecessary suffering had been caused.

32–04   Delete "Cruelty to Animals Act 1876" and substitute "Animals (Scientific Procedures) Act 1986."

32–06   The Cruelty to Animals Act 1876 was repealed by the Animals (Scientific Procedures) Act 1986, section 3 of which prohibits the use of any experimental or other scientific procedure on a vertebrate animal which may have the effect of causing the animal pain, suffering, distress or lasting harm, except by persons licensed to do so, and as part of an approved project in an approved place. Max. pen. two years' imprisonment and a fine: s.22(1).

Footnote 23. See now Animals (Scientific Procedures) Act 1986, s.16; exhibition includes showing live on television for general reception: max. pen. three months and a fine of level 4: s.22(3).

32–08   The slaughter of animals is now controlled by the Slaughter of Animals (Scotland) Act 1980, and the Slaughter of Poultry Act 1967 as amended by the Animal Health and Welfare Act 1984.

32–09   These Acts are repealed and replaced by the Wildlife and Countryside Act 1981.

CHAPTER 33

RAPE

33–03
33–04   There is English authority that a person who is born of a particular sex and remains biologically of that sex is a person of that sex even if he has undergone a sex-change operation: *R.* v. *Tan* [1983] Q.B. 1053.

33–06   It seems clear now that the crime here is indecent assault: *Sweeney and Anr.* v. *X*, 1982 S.C.C.R. 509.

33–09   Where the woman is under the influence of drink the degree of violence required may be less than in the case of a sober woman: *Sweeney and Anr.* v. *X*, 1982 S.C.C.R. 509; *Quinn* v. *H.M.A.*, 1990 S.L.T. 877.

Add new paragraph **33–09a**:

33–09a   *Error.* A mistaken but genuine belief that the woman is a consenting party is a defence to rape: *Meek and Ors.* v. *H.M.A.*, 1982 S.C.C.R. 613, and see commentary thereon; *R.* v. *Morgan* [1976] A.C. 182; *cf. Pappajohn* v. *The Queen* [1980] 2 S.C.R. 121. It is not necessary for the judge to direct the jury on this matter where the defence case is that the woman actively co-operated and the Crown case is that she struggled: *ibid.*; *Quinn* v. *H.M.A.*, 1990 S.L.T. 877; the point was not taken in *Sweeney and Anr.* v. *X*, 1982 S.C.C.R. 509. For recent English cases on recklessness in this matter, which apparently occupies a special position in English law (which, in view of *Meek, supra,* may also apply in Scotland), see *R.* v. *Pigg* [1983] 1 W.L.R. 6; *R.* v. *Satnam, S.* (1984) 78 Cr.App.R. 149.
It has been held in New Zealand that if the accused initially believes the woman is consenting, but realises after penetration that this is not the case and carries on nonetheless, he is guilty of rape: *Kaitamaki* v. *The Queen* [1985] A.C. 147.
An error resulting from intoxication has been held to be irrelevant: *R.* v. *Woods* (1981) 74 Cr.App.R. 312; *Leary* v. *The Queen* [1978] 1 S.C.R. 29.

33–10   "The important matter is not the amount of resistance put up but whether the woman remained an unwilling party throughout. The significance of resistance is only as evidence of unwillingness": *Barbour* v. *H.M.A.*, 1982 S.C.C.R. 195, Lord Stewart at 198; *cf. R.* v. *Olugboja* [1982] Q.B. 320.

33–12   A husband can be guilty of raping his wife, *S.* v. *H.M.A.*, 1989
33–13   S.L.T. 469; *H.M.A.* v. *Duffy*, 1983 S.L.T. 7; *H.M.A.* v. *Paxton*, 1985 S.L.T. 96.

33–16   Section 96 of the Mental Health (Scotland) Act 1960 is now
to   replaced by section 106 of the Mental Health (Scotland) Act 1984,
33–18   the word "defective" being replaced throughout by "a woman who is protected by the provisions of this section." In terms of section 106(6) a woman is so protected "if she is suffering from a state of arrested or incomplete development of mind which includes significant impairment of intelligence and social functioning."

33–19   Section 80(4) of the Criminal Justice (Scotland) Act 1980 applies what is now section 107 of the Mental Health (Scotland) Act 1984 to homosexual acts, *i.e.* sodomy or gross indecency between males.

Section 96, is now section 106 of the Mental Health (Scotland) Act 1984.

33–21 It seems to be clear from *Sweeney and Anr.* v. *X*, 1982 S.C.C.R. 509 that to have intercourse with a woman who has made herself so drunk as to be incapable of consent is indecent assault, and the position should be the same where the woman is asleep: See also *Quinn* v. *H.M.A.*, 1990 S.L.T. 877. Clandestine injury is thus just another name for an indecent assault involving penetration.

CHAPTER 34

SODOMY AND BESTIALITY

34–01 Sodomy in private between consenting men over the age of twenty-one was legalised by section 80 of the Criminal Justice (Scotland) Act 1980: see *infra*, para. 36–17.

CHAPTER 35

INCEST

Delete Chapter 35 and substitute the following:

35–01 The law of incest is now contained in the Incest and Related Offences (Scotland) Act 1986, which repeals the Incest Act 1567, and inserts four new sections (sections 2A to 2D) in the Sexual Offences (Scotland) Act 1976.

In terms of section 2A sexual intercourse between the following persons is incestuous: parent and child, grandparent and grandchild, siblings, aunt and nephew, uncle and niece, great-grandparents and great-grandchildren, where in each case the parties are of different sexes. Incest is committed whether the relationship is of the full blood or of the half blood and whether or not it is traced through or to any person whose parents were not married to each other. The relationship must, however, be consanguineous, except in the case of adoptive parents and children.

It is a defence for the accused to prove that he did not know and had no reason to suspect that his partner was related to him in one of the degrees specified, or that he did not consent to the intercourse, or that he was married to his partner by virtue of a marriage entered into abroad but recognised as valid in Scotland.

Section 2A(3) specifically provides that incest is limited to the relationships listed above.

35–02 One result of the 1986 Act is that intercourse between step-relations is no longer incestuous. Section 2B of the Sexual Offences (Scotland) Act 1967, however, makes it an offence for a

35–02 step-parent or former step-parent to have intercourse with a step-child who is either under the age of 21, or who, although of or over that age, has at any time before becoming 18, lived in the same household and been treated as a child of the step-parent's family. The same defences are available as in the case of incest, with an additional defence of reasonable belief that the child was of or over the age of 21. Although that defence appears as an independent alternative defence in section 2B(*b*), it will of course be irrelevant where the basis of the charge is that the child lived in family with the accused when she was under 18.

35–03 The 1986 Act also creates a new offence for a person over the age of 16 to have intercourse with a child under that age who is a member of the same household as the accused and in relation to whom the accused is in a position of trust or authority. It is a defence for the accused to prove that: (1) he believed on reasonable grounds that the other person was 16 or over; or (2) that he, the accused, did not consent to the intercourse; or (3) that the parties were married by a foreign marriage recognised as valid in Scotland: Sexual Offences (Scotland) Act 1967, s.2C.

35–04 The maximum penalty for any of the above offences is life imprisonment: *ibid.*, s.2D.

CHAPTER 36

OTHER SEXUAL OFFENCES

36–13 *Quaere* whether mere awareness of the presence of children is enough to constitute indecent exposure to them where they were not the object of the exercise: *cf. West* v. *McNaughtan*, 1990 S.C.C.R. 439 where this point was not taken.

36–14 Section 4 of the Vagrancy Act 1824 was repealed by the Civic Government (Scotland) Act 1982.

36–15 *Cf. Niven* v. *Tudhope*, 1982 S.C.C.R. 365.

36–17
36–18 Homosexual offences are now governed by section 80 of the Criminal Justice (Scotland) Act 1980 whose general effect is that homosexual conduct between consenting males over the age of 21 in private is not criminal; it does not even constitute the common law crime of shameless indecency. Section 7 of the Sexual Offences (Scotland) Act 1976 is repealed by the Act of 1980. Section 80 of the Act of 1980 provides, *inter alia:*

> "(1) Subject to the provisions of this section, a homosexual act in private shall not be an offence provided that the parties consent thereto and have attained the age of twenty-one years.
> (2) An act which would otherwise be treated for the purposes of this Act as being done in private shall not be so treated if done—

118

(*a*) when more than two persons take part or are present or

(*b*) in a lavatory to which the public have, or are permitted to have, access whether on payment or otherwise . . .

(5) Subsection (1) above shall not prevent a homosexual act from being an offence under any provision of the Army Act 1955, the Air Force Act 1955 or the Naval Discipline Act 1957.

(6) In this section, 'a homosexual act' means sodomy or an act of gross indecency by one male person with another male person."

The effect of these provisions is that homosexual behaviour which is not protected by them remains a crime at common law, whether it is sodomy or some lesser form of gross indecency between males which would be prosecuted as shameless indecency or, in cases involving young boys, as lewd practices: see para. 36–09 in the main work.

It is also an offence, under section 80(7), to commit or be party to, or to procure or attempt to procure, the commission of a homosexual act in any of the following cases:

"(*a*) otherwise than in private;

(*b*) without the consent of both parties to the act;

(*c*) with a person under the age of twenty-one years; or

(*d*) where the act is committed on board a United Kingdom merchant ship, wherever it may be, by a male person who is a member of the crew of that ship with another male person who is a member of the crew of that ship or any other United Kingdom merchant ship."

"Member of the crew" includes the master of the ship, and a "United Kingdom merchant ship" is one registered in the United Kingdom and habitually used or used at the time of the offence for carrying passengers or goods for reward: s.80(8).

The maximum penalty where the charge is brought under section 80(7) is two years' imprisonment and a fine on indictment, three months or a fine on summary conviction: s.80(10). Proceedings must be commenced not later than twelve months after the offence: s.80(14).

It is a defence to a charge under section 80(7)(*c*), where the accused is under 24 years of age and has not been previously charged with a like offence, that he had reasonable cause to believe the other person was aged 21 or over: s.80(11); *cf.* paras. 36–03 *et seq.* in the main work.

Male persons who are mentally handicapped are protected by section 80(3) which provides:

"A male person who is suffering from mental [handicap] which is of such a nature or degree that he is incapable of living an independent life or of guarding himself against serious exploitation cannot in law give any consent which, by virtue of subsection (1) above, would prevent a homosexual act from being an offence; but a person shall not be convicted on account of the incapacity of such a male person to consent, of an offence consisting of such an act if he proves that he did not know and had no reason to suspect that male person to be suffering from such mental [handicap]."

In addition section 107 of the Mental Health (Scotland) Act 1984 applies to sodomy or gross indecency between males: Criminal Justice (Scotland) Act 1980, s.80(4).

36–20 Shameless indecency has recently been revived and extended to the sale or display of obscene articles: see *infra*, para. 41–16.

36–21 It was held in *Lockhart* v. *Stephen*, 1987 S.C.C.R. 642 (Sh.Ct.) that vulgar and offensive public performances likely to encourage only normal adult sexual activity were not shamelessly indecent, but other judges might take a different view.

36–22 To present a show of obscene films to a group of men constitutes shameless indecency, provided that more than two men in all are present: see *supra*, para. 36–17; *Watt* v. *Annan*, 1978 J.C. 84.

36–23 Sexual activities short of intercourse between persons so related that intercourse between them would be incest constitutes shameless indecency, at least in the case of parent and child: *R.* v. *H.M.A.*, 1988 S.L.T. 623.

36–24 Section 380 of the Burgh Police (Scotland) Act 1892 was repealed by the Civic Government (Scotland) Act 1982.

36–25 For an example of brothel keeping, see *Milne* v. *McNicol* (1965) S.C.C.R. Supp. 8.
    Premises to which people resort for sodomy or other acts of gross indecency between males in circumstances in which resort thereto for heterosexual acts would make them a brothel are to be treated as a brothel for the purposes of section 13: Criminal Justice (Scotland) Act 1980, s.80(13).

36–26 See Leno, "De Lustis," 1979 S.L.T. (News) 73.
    In *Kelly* v. *Purvis* [1983] Q.B. 663, where the premises in question were a massage parlour in which the masseuses offered an extra masturbation service for fees payable directly to them, it was held that any premises where more than one woman offered to participate in physical acts of indecency for the sexual gratification of men was a brothel. It does not matter that sexual intercourse is not provided, and it was said that it would also not matter if no charge was made by the women concerned: *cf. Winter* v. *Woolfe* [1931] 1 K.B. 549.

36–28 Section 403 of the Burgh Police (Scotland) Act 1892 was repealed by the Civic Government (Scotland) Act 1982.

36–29 Including a male brothel: Criminal Justice (Scotland) Act 1980, s.80(13); *supra*, para. 36–25.

36–32 Section 96(1)(*b*) of the Mental Health (Scotland) Act 1960 is now replaced by s.106(1)(*b*) of the Mental Health (Scotland) Act 1984, and applies to procuring or encouraging women protected by the section (see *supra*, paras. 33–16 to 33–18) to have unlawful sexual intercourse.

Add new paragraph **36–32a:**

36–32a *Procuring males*. It is an offence to procure or attempt to procure the commission of a homosexual act contrary to section 80(7) of the Criminal Justice (Scotland) Act 1980: *supra*, para. 36–17.

It is also an offence contrary to section 80(9) of that Act to procure or attempt to procure the commission of a homosexual act between two other male persons: maximum penalty as for s.80(7); *supra*, para. 36–17.

36–38 Section 96(1)(*c*) of the Mental Health (Scotland) Act 1960 is now replaced by section 106(1)(*c*) of the Mental Health (Scotland) Act 1984, and applies to women protected by the section (see *supra*, paras. 33–16 to 33–18).

36–39 It has been held in England that, to procure a woman for a single act of lewdness with oneself is not to procure her to become a common prostitute: *R.* v. *Morris-Lowe* [1985] 1 W.L.R. 29.

It has also been held that one cannot attempt to procure for prostitution someone whom one reasonably believes to be a prostitute already: *R.* v. *Brown (R.A.)* [1984] 1 W.L.R. 1211.

36–40 The 1989 Draft Code defines "prostitute" as meaning a person who, for gain, offers his body to others or offers to do sexual acts to their bodies, whether or not he selects those to whom he makes his services available: s.122. The absence of selection may make a person a "common" prostitute, as against just a prostitute, but the definition seems very wide.

Footnote 10. Add: *Smith* v. *Sellers*, 1978 J.C. 79.

36–41 Section 381(22) and (23) of the Burgh Police (Scotland) Act 1892 was repealed as a result of being replaced by section 46 of the Civic Government (Scotland) Act 1982 which provides:

"(1) A prostitute (whether male of female) who for the purposes of prostitution—
(*a*) loiters in a public place:
(*b*) solicits in a public place or in any other place so as to be seen from a public place; or
(*c*) importunes any person who is in a public place,
shall be guilty of an offence and liable, on summary conviction, to a fine not exceeding [level 2 on the standard scale].

(2) In subsection (1) above, 'public place' has the same meaning as in section 133 of this Act but includes—
(*a*) any place to which at the material time the public are permitted to have access, whether on payment or otherwise; and
(*b*) any public conveyance other than a taxi or hire car within the meaning of section 23 of this Act."

"Public place" is defined in section 133 as follows:

" 'public place' means any place (whether a thoroughfare or not) to which the public have unrestricted access and includes—
(*a*) the doorways or entrances of premises abutting on any such place; and
(*b*) any common passage, close, court, stair, garden or yard pertinent to any tenement or group of separately owned houses."

36–41   Section 23 provides, *inter alia*:

"(1) . . .

'taxi' means a hire car which is engaged, by arrangements made in a public place between the person to be conveyed in it (or a person acting on his behalf) and its driver for a journey beginning there and then; and

'private hire car' means a hire car other than a taxi within the meaning of this subsection.

(2) In subsection (1) above, 'hire car' means a motor vehicle with a driver (other than a vehicle being a public service vehicle within the meaning of section 1(1)(*a*) of the Public Passenger Vehicles Act 1981) which is, with a view to profit, available for hire by the public for personal conveyance."

A prostitute cannot be convicted of importuning without evidence of her "status" as a prostitute independent of and prior to the occasion of importuning which is the subject of the charge: *White* v. *Allan*, 1985 S.L.T. 396.

Section 80(12) of the Criminal Justice (Scotland) Act 1980 provides:

"A person who knowingly lives wholly or in part on the earnings of another from male prostitution or who solicits or importunes any male person for the purpose of procuring the commission of a homosexual act within the meaning of subsection (6) above shall be liable:

(*a*) on summary conviction to imprisonment for a term not exceeding six months; or

(*b*) on conviction on indictment to imprisonment for a term not exceeding two years."

For the meaning of "a homosexual act," see *supra*, para. 36–17.

See also C. Gane, "Soliciting for Immoral Purposes," 1978 S.L.T. (News) 181.

36–43   Max. pen. for a contravention of s.12(1)(*a*) of the Sexual Offences (Scotland) Act 1976 is the same as for s.12(1)(*b*): para. 36–41 in the main work.

36–46   In *R.* v. *Farrugia (Francis)* (1979) 69 Cr.App.R. 108 taxi drivers waited at an escort agency where they also collected prostitutes and took them to hotels and there introduced them to the agency's clients. They were paid only their normal fare but they collected an agency fee from the client which they delivered to the agency, £5 of which was received by some of the girls. The girls did not pay any of their own earnings to the agency. The drivers, as well as the persons running the agency, were convicted of living on the earnings of prostitution.

36–48   See also *R.* v. *Calderhead* (1979) Cr.App.R. 37.

CHAPTER 37

TREASON AND ALLIED OFFENCES

37–47   Section 2 of the Official Secrets Act 1911 is replaced by the Official Secrets Act 1989 ("the 1989 Act") which creates a number of offences relating to the disclosure of information.

Add new paragraphs **37–47a** to **37–47h**:

37–47a *Disclosure of information by Crown servants and contractors*
Sections 1 to 4 of the 1989 act create a number of offences consisting in the disclosure (or in some cases the damaging disclosure) without lawful authority by persons who are or have been Crown servants or government contractors, of information, documents or other articles which have come into their possession by virtue of their positions as such. In the case of sections 1 to 3 it is a defence for the accused to prove that he did not know and had no reasonable cause to believe that the information was covered by the section or, where relevant, that its disclosure would be damaging. Max. pen. in each case two years and a fine on indictment, six months on summary conviction: s.10(1).

37–47b Section 1(1) relates to disclosure by present or former members of the security and intelligence services, or persons whose work is connected with these services and who have received written notification that they are subject to section 1(1). Section 1(3) relates to damaging disclosure by other present or former Crown servants or government contractors of intelligence or security information. A disclosure is damaging if it damages, or is such that its unauthorised disclosure is likely to damage, the security and intelligence services, or if it falls within a class of information, etc., whose unauthorised disclosure is likely to have such an effect.

37–47c Section 2 relates to damaging disclosure by Crown servants or government contractors of defence information, etc., disclosure being damaging if it (*a*) damages the capability of the armed forces, or leads to loss of life or injury to their members or serious damage to their equipment or installations, or (*b*) endangers the interests of the United Kingdom abroad, or seriously obstructs the promotion or protection of these interests by the United Kingdom or endangers the safety of British citizens abroad, or (*c*) is likely to have any of these effects.

37–47d Section 3 applies to the damaging disclosure of information, etc., relating to international relations or any confidential information, etc., obtained from a foreign state. A disclosure is damaging if it endangers the interests of the United Kingdom abroad, seriously obstructs the promotion or protection of these interests or endangers the safety of British citizens abroad, or is likely to have any of these effects.

37–47e Section 4 applies to information, etc., whose disclosure (*a*) results in the commission of an offence, or facilitates an escape from legal custody or the doing of anything prejudicial to the safe keeping of persons in custody, or impedes the prevention or detection of offences or the arrest or prosecution of suspected offenders; or (*b*) is likely to have any of these effects. It also applies to information obtained as the result of a warrant under section 2 of the Interception of Communications Act 1985 or the Security Services Act 1989.

37–47e It is a defence for the accused to prove, in the case of information, etc., under (*a*), that he did not know and had no reasonable cause to believe that the disclosure would have any of the effects listed, and in the case of any information under the section that he did not know that the section applied to the information, etc.

37–47f *Disclosure by other persons*
Section 5 of the 1989 Act provides:

"(1) Subsection (2) below applies where—
(*a*) any information, document or other article protected against disclosure by the foregoing provisions of this Act has come into a person's possession as a result of having been—
    (i) disclosed (whether to him or another) by a Crown servant or government contractor without lawful authority; or
    (ii) entrusted to him by a Crown servant or government contractor on terms requiring it to be held in confidence or in circumstances in which the Crown servant or government contractor could reasonably expect that it would be so held; or
    (iii) disclosed (whether to him or another) without lawful authority by a person to whom it was entrusted as mentioned in sub-paragraph (ii) above; and
(*b*) the disclosure without lawful authority of the information, document or article by the person into whose possession it has come is not an offence under any of those provisions.
(2) Subject to subsections (3) and (4) below, the person into whose possession the information, document or article has come is guilty of an offence if he discloses it without lawful authority knowing, or having reasonable cause to believe, that it is protected against disclosure by the foregoing provisions of this Act and that it has come into his possession as mentioned in subsection (1) above.
(3) in the case of information or a document or article protected against disclosure by sections 1 to 3 above, a person does not commit an offence under subsection (2) above unless—
(*a*) the disclosure by him is damaging; and
(*b*) he makes it knowing, or having reasonable cause to believe, that it would be damaging;
and the question whether a disclosure is damaging shall be determined for the purposes of this subsection as it would be in relation to a disclosure of that information, document or article by a Crown servant in contravention of section 1(3), 2(1) or 3(1) above.
(4) A person does not commit an offence under subsection (2) above in respect of information or a document or other article which has come into his possession as a result of having been disclosed—
(*a*) as mentioned in subsection (1)(*a*)(i) above by a government contractor; or
(*b*) as mentioned in subsection (1)(*a*)(iii) above,
unless that disclosure was by a British citizen or took place in the United Kingdom, in any of the Channel Islands or in the Isle of Man or a colony.
(5) For the purposes of this section information or a document or article is protected against disclosure by the foregoing provisions of this Act if—
(*a*) it relates to security or intelligence, defence or international relations within the meaning of section 1, 2 or 3 above or is such as is mentioned in section 3(1)(*b*) above; or

124

(*b*) it is information or a document or article to which section 4 above applies;

and information or a document or article is protected against disclosure by sections 1 to 3 above if it falls within paragraph (*a*) above.

(6) A person is guilty of an offence if without lawful authority he discloses any information, document or other article which he knows, or has reasonable cause to believe, to have come into his possession as a result of a contravention of section 1 of the Official Secrets Act 1911."

37–47g   Section 6 of the 1989 Act provides:

"(1) This section applies where—
(*a*) any information, document or other article which—
   (i) relates to security or intelligence, defence or international relations; and
   (ii) has been communicated in confidence by or on behalf of the United Kingdom to another State or to an international organisation,

has come into a person's possession as a result of having been disclosed (whether to him or another) without the authority of that State or organisation or, in the case of an organisation, of a member of it; and
(*b*) the disclosure without lawful authority of the information, document or article by the person into whose possession it has come is not an offence under any of the foregoing provisions of this Act.

(2) Subject to subsection (3) below, the person into whose possession the information, document or article has come is guilty of an offence if he makes a damaging disclosure of it knowing, or having reasonable cause to believe, that it is such as is mentioned in subsection (1) above, that it has come into his possession as there mentioned and that its disclosure would be damaging.

(3) A person does not commit an offence under subsection (2) above if the information, document or article is disclosed by him with lawful authority or has previously been made available to the public with the authority of the State or organisation concerned or, in the case of an organisation, of a member of it.

(4) For the purposes of this section 'security or intelligence,' 'defence' and 'international relations' have the same meaning as in section 1, 2 and 3 above and the question whether a disclosure is damaging shall be determined as it would be in relation to a disclosure of the information, document or article in question by a Crown servant in contravention of sections 1(3), 2(1) and 3(1) above.

(5) For the purposes of this section information or a document or article is communicated in confidence if it is communicated on terms requiring it to be held in confidence or in circumstances in which the person communicating it could reasonably expect that it would be so held."

37–47h *Safeguarding information*

Section 8 of the 1989 Act provides:

"(1) Where a Crown servant or government contractor, by virtue of his position as such, has in his possession or under his control any document or other article which it would be an offence under any of the foregoing provisions of this Act for him to disclose without lawful authority he is guilty of an offence if—
(*a*) being a Crown servant, he retains the document or article contrary to his official duty; or
(*b*) being a government contractor, he fails to comply with an official direction for the return or disposal of the document or article,

　or if he fails to take such care to prevent the authorised disclosure of the document or article as a person in his position may reasonably be expected to take.

(2) It is a defence for a Crown servant charged with an offence under subsection (1)(*a*) above to prove that at the time of the alleged offence he believed that he was acting in accordance with his official duty and had no reasonable cause to believe otherwise.

(3) In subsections (1) and (2) above references to a Crown servant include any person, not being a Crown servant or government contractor, in whose case a notification for the purposes of section 1(1) above is in force.

(4) Where a person has in his possession or under his control any document or other article which it would be an offence under section 5 above for him to disclose without lawful authority, he is guilty of an offence if—

(*a*) he fails to comply with an official direction for its return or disposal; or

(*b*) where be obtained it from a Crown servant or government contractor on terms requiring it to be held in confidence or in circumstances in which that servant or contractor could reasonably expect that it would be so held, he fails to take such care to prevent its unauthorised disclosure as a person in his position may reasonably be expected to take.

(5) Where a person has in his possession or under his control any document or other article which it would be an offence under section 6 above for him to disclose without lawful authority, he is guilty of an offence if he fails to comply with an official direction for its return or disposal.

(6) A person is guilty of an offence if he discloses any official information, document or other article which can be used for the purpose of obtaining access to any information, document or other article protected against disclosure by the foregoing provisions of this Act and the circumstances in which it is disclosed are such that it would be reasonable to expect that it might be used for that purpose without authority.

(7) For the purposes of subsection (6) above a person discloses information or a document or article which is official if—

(*a*) he has or has had it in his possession by virtue of his position as a Crown servant or government contractor; or

(*b*) he knows or has reasonable cause to believe that a Crown servant or government contractor has or has had it in his possession by virtue of his position as such.

(8) Subsection (5) of section 5 above applies for the purposes of subsection (6) above as it applies for the purposes of that section.

(9) In this section 'official direction' means a direction duly given by a Crown servant or government contractor or by or on behalf of a prescribed body of a prescribed class.''

37–50　Section 2 of the 1911 Act was repealed by the 1989 Act: *supra*, para. 37–47.

37–53　The death penalty was removed by the Armed Forces Act 1981, Sched. 5, Pt. II.

37–56　For the current form of section 5 of the Designs Act 1949, see Copyright, Designs and Patents Act 1988, Schedule 4.

37–57　Section 18 of the 1967 Act is replaced by section 34 of the Legal Aid (Scotland) Act 1986 which applies to information furnished to the Scottish Legal Aid Board for the purposes of the Act which applies both to legal aid and to legal advice and assistance: max. pen. a fine of level 4.

37–58 Footnote 8. Section 17 of the Ministry of Supply Act 1939 was repealed by the Supply Powers Act 1975 and replaced by s.5 of that Act; s.80 of the Agriculture Act 1947 was repealed by the Agricultural Statistics Act 1979 and replaced by s.3 of that Act; the Cinematograph Films Act 1957 was repealed by the Film Levy Finance Act 1981, and s.5 is replaced by s.8 of that Act.

CHAPTER 38

OFFENCES OF DISHONESTY AGAINST THE STATE

38–01 The Customs and Excise Act 1952 has been largely repealed by and re-enacted in the Customs and Excise Management Act 1979, "the 1979 Act."

38–02 Section 304 is now replaced by section 170 of the 1979 Act which, as amended by section 23 of the Forgery and Counterfeiting Act 1981 and section 12(1)(*a*) of the Finance Act 1988, provides:

"(1) Without prejudice to any other provision of the Customs and Excise Acts 1979, if any person—
(*a*) knowingly acquires possession of any of the following goods, that is to say—
  (i) goods which have been unlawfully removed from a warehouse or Queen's warehouse;
  (ii) goods which are chargeable with a duty which has not been paid;
  (iii) goods with respect to the importation or exportation of which any prohibition or restriction is for the time being in force under or by virtue of any enactment; or
(*b*) is in any way knowingly concerned in carrying, removing, depositing, harbouring, keeping or concealing or in any manner dealing with any such goods
and does so with intent to defraud Her Majesty of any duty payable on the goods or to evade any such prohibition or restriction with respect to the goods he shall be guilty of an offence under this section and may be detained.
(2) Without prejudice to any other provision of the Customs and Excise Acts 1979, if any person is, in relation to any goods, in any way knowingly concerned in any fraudulent evasion or attempt at evasion—
(*a*) of any duty chargeable on the goods;
(*b*) of any prohibition or restriction for the time being in force with respect to the goods under or by virtue of any enactment; or
(*c*) of any provision of the Customs and Excise Acts 1979 applicable to the goods,
he shall be guilty of an offence under this section and may be detained.
(3) Subject to subsection (4) or (4A) below, a person guilty of an offence under this section shall be liable—
(*a*) on summary conviction, to a penalty of the prescribed sum or of three times the value of the goods, whichever is the greater, or to imprisonment for a term not exceeding 6 months, or to both; or

(b) on conviction on indictment, to a penalty of any amount, or to imprisonment for a term not exceeding 7 years, or to both.

(4) In the case of an offence under this section in connection with a prohibition or restriction on importation or exportation having effect by virtue of section 3 of the Misuse of Drugs Act 1971, subsection (3) above shall have effect subject to the modifications specified in Schedule 1 to this Act. [Max. pen. life imprisonment for Class A drugs, 14 years for Class B: Controlled Drugs (Penalties) Act 1985.]

(4A) In the case of an offence under this section in connection with the prohibition contained in sections 20 and 21 of the Forgery and Counterfeiting Act 1981, subsection (3)(b) above shall have effect as if for the words '2 years' there were substituted the words '10 years.'

(5) In any case where a person would, apart from this subsection, be guilty of—

(a) an offence under this section in connection with a prohibition or restriction; and

(b) a corresponding offence under the enactment or other instrument imposing the prohibition or restriction, being an offence for which a fine or other penalty is expressly provided by that enactment or other instrument,

he shall not be guilty of the offence mentioned in paragraph (a) of this subsection."

Cf. R. v. Whitehead [1982] Q.B. 1272.

Sections 20 and 21 of the Forgery and Counterfeiting Act 1981 refer to the importation and exportation of counterfeit notes and coins.

"Fraudulently" in section 170(2) requires proof of dishonest conduct deliberately intended to evade the prohibition, restriction or duty, but does not require proof of an act of deceit in presence of a customs officer. A failure to stop a car when signalled to do so by a police officer is therefore sufficient if done with the necessary intent: Att.-Gen.'s Reference (No. 1 of 1981) [1982] Q.B. 848; see also R. v. Jakeman (1982) 76 Cr.App.R. 223.

Merely to deal in prohibited goods, such as drugs, which must at some time have been illegally imported does not in itself show an intent to evade the prohibition—there must be a nexus between the dealing and the importation: R. v. Watts and Stack (1979) 70 Cr.App.R. 187.

An insurance company which pays out on a policy for the theft of goods where the goods are known to be uncustomed is not guilty of a breach of section 170, but such a payment is contra bonos mores and there is no obligation on the company to make it: Geismar v. Sun Alliance Ltd. [1978] 1 Q.B. 383.

"Evade" means only "avoid or get round," and a person who believes he is acting legally can act with intent to evade a prohibition: R. v. Hurford-Jones (1977) 65 Cr.App.R. 263, a case under what is now section 68(2) of the 1979 Act—being knowingly concerned in that export of goods with intent to evade a prohibition.

In R. v. Taaffe [1984] A.C. 539 it was held that the prosecution must show that the accused knew the goods were subject to a prohibition; and that where he believed that what were in fact drugs was currency, and also mistakenly believed that currency was subject to a prohibition, he had committed no offence. See also R. v. Hennessey (Timothy) (1978) 68 Cr.App.R. 419.

Footnote 9. Section 290(2) is now s.154(2) of the 1979 Act.

38–03   Section 70 is now replaced by section 83 of the 1979 Act which provides:

"(1) Where, in pursuance of any power conferred by the customs and excise Acts or of any requirement imposed by or under those Acts, a seal, lock or mark is used to secure or identify any goods for any of the purposes of those Acts and—

(*a*) at any time while the goods are in the United Kingdom or within the limits of any port or on passage between ports in the United Kingdom, the seal, lock or mark is wilfully and prematurely removed or tampered with by any person; or

(*b*) at any time before the seal, lock or mark is lawfully removed, any of the goods are wilfully removed by any person,

that person and the person then in charge of the goods shall each be liable on summary conviction to a penalty of [level 5 on the standard scale].

(2) For the purposes of subsection (1) above, goods in a ship or aircraft shall be deemed to be in the charge of the master of the ship or commander of the aircraft.

(3) Where, in pursuance of any Community requirement or practice which relates to the movement of goods between countries or of any international agreement to which the United Kingdom is a party and which so relates,—

(*a*) a seal, lock or mark is used (whether in the United Kingdom or elsewhere) to secure or identify any goods for customs or excise purposes; and

(*b*) at any time while the goods are in the United Kingdom, the seal, lock or mark is wilfully and prematurely removed or tampered with by any person, that person and the person then in charge of the goods shall each be liable on summary conviction to a penalty of [level 5 of the standard scale]."

Footnote 10. The definition is now in s.1(1) of the 1979 Act.

38–04   Section 71 is re-enacted by section 84 of the 1979 Act with some verbal amendments. The offence is committed whether or not the intended recipient is in a position to receive the message or is actually engaged in smuggling at the time: s.84(3). It is for the accused to prove that any signal was not connected with smuggling: s.84(4). The offence is specifically made a summary offence.

38–05   Section 72 is now section 85 of the 1979 Act. Breach of subs. (1) is made a summary offence punishable by a fine of level 1.

Footnotes 12, 14. The definition is now in s.1(1) of the 1979 Act.

38–06   Section 73 is now re-enacted by section 86 of the 1979 Act, with the replacement of "customs Acts" by "any provision of the customs and excise Acts relating to imported goods or prohibited or restricted goods." The "customs and excise Acts" are the 1979 Act, the other Acts of 1979 relating to duties (cc. 3 to 7 inclusive), and any other enactment for the time being in force relating to customs and excise.

It has been held that a person can be "armed" even when he is not carrying a weapon, provided that he has arms "readily available": *R.* v. *Jones (Keith)* [1987] 1 W.L.R. 692. In that case the captain of a boat had the arms in a locker in the wheelhouse.

38–07 Section 74 is now section 87 of the 1979 Act. A contravention of the section is a summary offence: max. pen. a fine of level 3.

38–08 The relevant provisions are now sections 167 to 169 of the 1979 Act.

38–09 Section 301 is replaced by section 167 of the 1979 Act, which, as applied to Scotland by section 175(1)(*b*) of that Act, provides:

"(1) If any person either knowingly or recklessly—
(*a*) makes or signs, or causes to be made or signed, or delivers or causes to be delivered to the Commissioners or an officer, any declaration, notice, certificate or other document whatsoever; or
(*b*) makes any statement in answer to any question put to him by an officer which he is required by or under any enactment to answer, being a document or statement produced or made for any purpose of any assigned matter, which is untrue in any material particular, he shall be guilty of an offence under this subsection and may be detained; and any goods in relation to which the document or statement was made shall be liable to forfeiture.
(2) Without prejudice to subsection (4) below, a person who commits an offence under subsection (1) above shall be liable—
(*a*) on summary conviction, to a penalty of the prescribed sum, or to imprisonment for a term not exceeding 6 months, or to both; or
(*b*) on conviction on indictment, to a penalty of any amount, or to imprisonment for a term not exceeding 2 years, or to both.
(3) If any person—
(*a*) makes or signs, or causes to be made or signed, or delivers or causes to be delivered to the Commissioners or an officer, any declaration, notice, certificate or other document whatsoever; or
(*b*) makes any statement in answer to any question put to him by an officer which he is required by or under any enactment to answer, being a document or statement produced or made for any purpose of any assigned matter, which is untrue in any material particular, then, without prejudice to subsection (4) below, he shall be liable on summary conviction to a penalty of [level 4 on the standard scale].
(4) Where by reason of any such document or statement as is mentioned in subsection (1) or (3) above the full amount of any duty payable is not paid or any overpayment is made in respect of any drawback, allowance, rebate or repayment of duty, the amount of the duty unpaid or of the overpayment shall be recoverable as a debt due to the Crown or may be recovered as a civil debt."

Footnote 15. See now s.170; *supra*, para. 38–02.

38–10 Section 302 is now section 168 of the 1979 Act: max. pen. two years and a fine on indictment, six months on summary conviction.

38–11 Section 303 is now section 169 of the 1979 Act. Breach of section 169 is specifically made a summary offence. The offence of hindering or deceiving an officer may be committed before, during or after the weighing, etc.

Footnote 16. Section 271 is now s.136 of the 1979 Act.

38–12 Footnote 17. Section 44 is now s.49 of the 1979 Act.

Section 45 is re-enacted with some verbal alterations in section 50 of the 1979 Act: max. pen. seven years and a fine on indictment, six months and the prescribed sum or three times the value of the goods, whichever is the greater, on summary conviction, for offences under what was formerly s.45(1) of the Act of 1952 and is now s.50(2) or (3) of the 1979 Act: see Finance Act 1988, s.12(1)(a). Where the offence relates to a prohibition or restriction having effect by virtue of s.3 of the Misuse of Drugs Act 1971 penalties are as for contraventions of the latter Act. Max. pen. for offences under what was formerly s.45(2) of the Act of 1952 and is now s.50(6) of the 1979 Act is a fine of level 3 or three times the value of the goods, whichever is the greater. Where an offence under s.50(2) or (3) relates to counterfeit currency or coin, the maximum penalty is ten years' imprisonment: Forgery and Counterfeiting Act 1981, s.20.

Section 50(7) provides:

> "In any case where a person would, apart from this subsection, be guilty of—
>
> (a) an offence under this section in connection with the importation of goods contrary to a prohibition or restriction; and
>
> (b) a corresponding offence under the enactment or other instrument imposing the prohibition or restriction, being an offence for which a fine or other penalty is expressly provided by that enactment or other instrument,
>
> he shall not be guilty of the offence mentioned in paragraph (a) of this subsection."

Importation is not limited to the first port entered, but occurs at the port where the goods are discovered and at any port in the U.K. entered en route thereto. The only *mens rea* required is the knowledge that one is engaged in importing prohibited goods: *MacNeil* v. *H.M.A.*, 1986 S.C.C.R. 288. On the meaning of being concerned in, see *infra*, para. 43–07; and *MacNeil, supra*. It has been held that where goods are intercepted by the customs and replaced by harmless substances before being left to go to the originally intended recipient, the latter is guilty of being concerned in their unlawful importation even if he took no part in the enterprise prior to the replacement; *R.* v. *Ciappara* [1988] Crim.L.R. 172.

Cf. R. v. *Whitehead* [1982] Q.B. 1272, a case under s.304 of the Act of 1952.

Section 55 is re-enacted with some verbal alterations in section 67 of the 1979 Act. Breach of section 67 is specifically made a summary offence.

Section 7 is replaced by section 13 of the 1979 Act. The new section gives a specific power of detention.

Section 9 is replaced by section 15 of the 1979 Act, breach of which is specifically made a summary offence, for which the offender may be detained.

Section 10 is replaced by section 16 of the 1979 Act. Section 16(3) provides that any person committing or aiding or abetting the commission of an offence under the section may be detained.

38–17   Footnote 21. Section 56 of the Pipe-lines Act 1962 is repealed by the 1979 Act and re-enacted by s.162 of that Act.

38–18   Section 92 is now section 100 of the 1979 Act. Breach of subsection (1) is specifically made a summary offence.

Removal, etc., of goods liable to forfeiture is now an indictable offence with a maximum penalty of any amount and seven years' imprisonment: max. pen. on summary conviction six months and a fine of the prescribed sum or three times the value of the goods, whichever is the greater: see Finance Act 1988, s.12(1)(*a*).

Footnote 22. See now s.100 of the 1979 Act, as amended by Finance Act 1988, s.9.

38–19   Section 98 is now section 17 of the Alcoholic Liquor Duties Act 1979, breach of which is an indictable offence with a maximum penalty of any amount and two years' imprisonment: max. pen. on summary conviction is six months and the prescribed sum or three times the value of the goods, whichever is the greater.

38–21   Section 38 of the Finance Act 1972 was repealed by the Value Added Tax Act 1983 and replaced by section 39 of that Act, which, as amended by the Finance Act 1985, Schedule 6, provides, *inter alia*:

> "(1) If any person is knowingly concerned in, or in the taking of steps with a view to, the fraudulent evasion of tax by him or any other person, he shall be liable—
> (*a*) on summary conviction, to a penalty of the statutory maximum or of three times the amount of the tax, whichever is the greater, or to imprisonment for a term not exceeding 6 months or to both; or
> (*b*) on conviction on indictment, to a penalty of any amount or to imprisonment for a term not exceeding 7 years or to both.
> (1A) Any reference in subsection (1) above or subsection (3) below to the evasion of tax includes a reference to the obtaining of—
> (*a*) a payment under section 14(5) above; or
> (*b*) a refund under section 21 or section 22 above; or
> (*c*) a repayment under section 23 above;
> and any reference in those subsections to the amount of the tax shall be construed,—
> > (i) in relation to tax itself or a payment falling within paragraph (*a*) above, as a reference to the aggregate of the amount (if any) falsely claimed by way of credit for input tax and the amount (if any) by which output tax was falsely understated; and
> > (ii) in relation to a refund or repayment falling within paragraph (*b*) or paragraph (*c*) above, as a reference to the amount falsely claimed by way of refund or repayment.
> (2) If any person—
> (*a*) with intent to deceive produces, furnishes or sends for the purposes of this Act or otherwise makes use for those purposes of any document which is false in a material particular; or
> (*b*) in furnishing any information for the purposes of this Act makes any statement which he knows to be false in a material particular or recklessly makes a statement which is false in a material particular,

he shall be liable—

      (i) on summary conviction, to a penalty of the statutory maximum or, where subsection (2A) or subsection (2B) below applies, to the alternative penalty specified in that subsection if it is greater, or to imprisonment for a term not exceeding 6 months or to both; or

      (ii) on conviction on indictment, to a penalty of any amount or to imprisonment for a term not exceeding 7 years or to both.

(2A) In any case where—

(a) the document referred to in subsection (2)(a) above is a return required under this Act, or

(b) the information referred to in subsection (2)(b) above is contained in or otherwise relevant to such a return.

the alternative penalty referred to in subsection (2)(i) above is a penalty equal to three times the aggregate of the amount (if any) falsely claimed by way of credit for input tax and the amount (if any) by which output tax was falsely understated.

(2B) In any case where—

(a) the document referred to in subsection (2)(a) above is a claim for a refund under section 21 or section 22 above or for a repayment under section 23 above, or

(b) the information referred to in subsection (2)(b) above is contained in or otherwise relevant to such a claim.

the alternative penalty referred to in subsection (2)(i) above is a penalty equal to three times the amount falsely claimed.

(2C) The reference in subsection (2)(a) above to furnishing, sending or otherwise making use of a document which is false in a material particular, with intent to deceive, includes a reference to furnishing, sending or otherwise making use of such a document, with intent to secure that a machine will respond to the document as if it were a true document.

(2D) Any reference in subsection (2)(a) or subsection (2C) above to producing, furnishing or sending a document includes a reference to causing a document to be produced, furnished or sent.

(3) Where a person's conduct during any specified period must have involved the commission by him of one or more offences under the preceding provisions of this section, then, whether or not the particulars of that offence or those offences are known, he shall, by virtue of this subsection, be guilty of an offence and liable—

(a) on a summary conviction, to a penalty of the statutory maximum or, if greater, three times the amount of any tax that was or was intended to be evaded by his conduct, or to imprisonment for a term not exceeding 6 months or to both; or

(b) on conviction on indictment, to a penalty of any amount or to imprisonment for a term not exceeding 7 years or to both.

(3A) Where an authorised person has reasonable grounds for suspecting that an offence has been committed under the preceding provisions of this section, he may arrest anyone whom he has reasonable grounds for suspecting to be guilty of the offence.

(4) If any person acquires possession of or deals with any goods, or accepts the supply of any services, having reason to believe that tax on the supply of the goods or services or on the importation of the goods has been or will be evaded, he shall be liable on summary conviction to a penalty of level 5 on the standard scale or three times the amount of tax, whichever is the greater.

(5) If any person supplies goods or services in contravention of paragraph 5(2) of Schedule 7 to this Act, he shall be liable on summary conviction to a penalty of level 5 on the standard scale."

38–22   The Representation of the People Act 1949 is repealed and re-enacted by the Representation of the People Act 1983, "the 1983 Act," which is amended by the Representation of the People Act 1985, "the 1985 Act."

38–23   Corrupt practices other than personation are punishable on indictment by one year's imprisonment or a fine, and on conviction in a summary court by six months: 1983 Act, s.168, as amended by the 1985 Act, Sched. 3.
The procedure for prosecutions following a report from an election court was abolished by the 1985 Act: Sched. 4, para. 59.

38–24   Section 140(3) is now s.160(4) of the 1983 Act. Section 139 is now section 159 of that Act. The limitation to conviction on indictment was removed by the 1985 Act, Schedule 4, paragraph 60.

Footnote 26. Section 151(*a*) is now s.173(*a*) of the 1983 Act.
Footnote 27. Section 152 is now s.174 of the 1983 Act.

38–25   Reports are now made by the court itself, and in the case of justices of the peace are made to the Secretary of State: 1983 Act, ss.161 and 162 as amended by the 1985 Act, Sched. 4.

Footnote 28. Section 141(1) is now s.161 of the 1983 Act. The Election Commissioners Act was repealed by the Representation of the People Act 1969.
Footnote 29. Section 141(2) is now s.162 of the 1983 Act.

38–26   Section 47 is now section 60 of the 1983 Act.

Footnote 30. Section 168(2) became s.190 of the 1983 Act, which was repealed by the 1985 Act.

38–27   Section 63 is now section 75 of the 1983 Act, which was amended by Schedule 20 to the Broadcasting Act 1990 so as to apply to programmes included in any service licensed under Part I or Part III of the Broadcasting Act 1990, and by section 14(3) of the 1985 Act to substitute £5 for 50p in section 75(1)(*c*)(ii).

Footnote 34. *D.P.P.* v. *Luft* is now reported at [1977] A.C. 962.

38–28   Section 70 is now section 82 of the 1983 Act.

Footnote 35. Section 73(1) is now s.85(1) of the 1983 Act.

38–29   Section 99 is now section 113 of the 1983 Act.

38–30   Section 100 is now section 114 of the 1983 Act.

38–31   Section 101 is now section 115 of the 1983 Act. Section 138(3) is now section 158(3) of that Act, and section 139 is now section 159 of that Act.

38–32   The max. fine is now level 5: 1985 Act. Sched. 3.

Footnote 43. Section 147 is now s.169 of the 1983 Act; s.149(1) became s.172(3) of that Act, and was repealed by the 1985 Act, Sched. 4.

38–33   Section 140(4) is now section 160(4) of the 1983 Act. Section 139(1) to (3) is now section 159(1) to (3) of that Act.

Footnote 44. Section 152 is now s.174 of the 1983 Act; s.145 is now s.167 of that Act.

38–34   Section 99(1) and (2) is now section 93(1) and (2) of the 1983 Act, which was amended by Schedule 20 to the Broadcasting Act 1990 to apply to programmes included in any service licensed under Part I or Part III of the Broadcasting Act 1990. Paragraph 35 of Schedule 4 to the 1985 Act provides that an ordinary election is deemed to commence with the last date on which notice of the election may be published in accordance with the rules made under section 42 of the 1983 Act. Notification of a parliamentary vacancy arising during a recess is now made in the *London Gazette* in accordance with the Recess Elections Act 1975.

38–35   Sections 69 and 70 are now sections 81 and 82 of the 1983 Act.

Footnote 45. Section 61(6) is now s.73(6) of the 1983 Act.
Footnote 46. Section 72 is now s.84 of the 1983 Act, and s.73(1) is now s.85(1) of the 1983 Act as amended by the 1985 Act, Sched. 4.
Footnote 47. Section 66(3) is now s.78(3) of the 1983 Act; s.80 is now s.92 of that Act; s.95(3) is now s.110(3) of that Act.

38–36   The relevant parts of section 48 are now section 61 of the 1983 Act. Section 168(2) was re-enacted with some verbal alterations by section 190 of the 1983 Act, which was repealed by the 1985 Act.

38–37   Section 153(2) is now section 175(2) of the 1983 Act.

Footnote 49. Section 96 is now s.111 of the 1983 Act.
Footnote 50. Section 153(1) is now s.175(1) of the 1983 Act.

38–38   Section 91(1) is now section 106(1), (2), (5) and (6) of the 1983 Act with some verbal alterations. Section 106(1) and (2) apply to the election of councillors in Scotland: 1985 Act, Sched. 4, para. 41. Section 81 is now section 94 of the 1983 Act, and applies also to local government elections: 1985 Act, Sched. 4, para. 36.

38–39   Section 92 is now section 107 of the 1983 Act.

38–40   Section 84 is re-enacted by section 97 of the Representation of the People Act 1983. Section 97(3) provides:

"(3) If a constable reasonably suspects any person of committing an offence under subsection (1) above, he may if requested so to do by the

135

38–40 chairman of the meeting require that person to declare to him immediately his name and address and, if that person refuses or fails so to declare his name and address or gives a false name and address, he shall be liable on summary conviction to a fine not exceeding level 1 on the standard scale, and—
(a) if he refuses or fails so to declare his name and address or
(b) if the constable reasonably suspects him of giving a false name and address,
the constable may without warrant arrest him."

38–41 Section 52 is now section 65 of the 1983 Act: max. pen. for officials two years and a fine on indictment, six months on summary conviction; six months and a fine of level 5 on summary conviction for other persons: 1985 Act, Sched. 3.

38–42 Section 49 is now section 62 of the 1983 Act, and extends to a patient's declaration: see 1983 Act, s.7, as well as to a service declaration. Breach of section 62 is a summary offence; max. pen. six months and a fine of level 5: see 1985 Act, Sched. 3.

38–43 Sections 50 and 51 are now section 63 of the 1983 Act (as substituted by the 1985 Act, Sched. 4, para. 19) which applies to both parliamentary and local government elections. Section 63(2) provides that no person to whom section 63 applies shall be liable to any common law penalty or to an action of damages in respect of breach of his official duty.
Section 53 is now section 66 of the 1983 Act.
Section 86 is now section 99 of the 1983 Act: max. pen. a fine of level 4. The references to sheriff clerks, etc., were originally removed by the Returning Officers (Scotland) Act 1977.
Section 87 is now section 100 of the 1983 Act.
Footnote 53. Max. pen. now a fine of level 5: 1985 Act, Sched. 3.
Footnote 55. Max. pen. now a fine of level 3: *ibid.*

38–44 Section 129 is now section 149 of the 1983 Act: max. pen. one year and a fine on indictment, six months on summary conviction: 1985 Act, Sched. 3. The affidavits are those referred to in s.148 of that Act.

38–45 Section 155(1) is now section 178(1) of the 1983 Act as substituted by the 1985 Act, Schedule 4, paragraph 62, and concludes after "taken" with the words, "and the offence may for all incidental purposes be treated as having been committed, in any place in the United Kingdom." The term "British subject" is replaced by "Commonwealth citizen": see British Nationality Act 1981, s.37.

38–46 Section 156 is now section 179 of the 1983 Act; section 95 is now section 110 of the 1983 Act.
Footnote 58. Sections 63(6), 91 and 80(3) are now respectively ss.75(6), 106 and 92(3) of the 1983 Act.

CHAPTER 39

SEDITION AND ALLIED OFFENCES

39–09 The Unlawful Oaths Act 1797 and the Unlawful Oaths Act 1812 are repealed by the Statute Law (Repeals) Act 1981.

39–10   The current law is in the Prevention of Terrorism (Temporary Provisions) Act 1989, which makes the following provisions regarding proscribed organisations:

> "**2.**—(1) Subject to subsection (3) below, a person is guilty of an offence if he—
> (a) belongs or professes to belong to a proscribed organisation;
> (b) solicits or invites support for a proscribed organisation other than support with money or other property; or
> (c) arranges or assists in the arrangement or management of, or addresses, any meeting of three or more persons (whether or not it is a meeting to which the public are admitted) knowing that the meeting is—
> > (i) to support a proscribed organisation;
> > (ii) to further the activities of such an organisation; or
> > (iii) to be addressed by a person belonging or professing to belong to such an organisation.
>
> (2) A person guilty of an offence under subsection (1) above is liable—
> (a) on conviction on indictment, to imprisonment for a term not exceeding ten years or a fine or both;
> (b) on summary conviction, to imprisonment for a term not exceeding six months or a fine not exceeding the statutory maximum or both.
>
> (3) A person belonging to a proscribed organisation is not guilty of an offence under this section by reason of belonging to the organisation if he shows—
> (a) that he became a member when it was not a proscribed organisation under the current legislation; and
> (b) that he has not since he became a member taken part in any of its activities at any time while it was a proscribed organisation under that legislation.
>
> (4) In subsection (3) above 'the current legislation,' in relation to any time, means whichever of the following was in force at that time—
> (a) the Prevention of Terrorism (Temporary Provisions) Act 1974;
> (b) the Prevention of Terrorism (Temporary Provisions) Act 1976;
> (c) the Prevention of Terrorism (Temporary Provisions) Act 1984; or
> (d) this Act.
>
> (5) The reference in subsection (3) above to a person becoming a member of an organisation is a reference to the only or last occasion on which he became a member.
>
> **3.**—(1) Any person who in a public place—
> (a) wears any item of dress; or
> (b) wears, carries or displays any article,
> in such a way or in such circumstances as to arouse reasonable apprehension that he is a member or supporter of a proscribed organisation, is guilty of an offence, and liable on summary conviction to imprisonment for a term not exceeding six months or a fine not exceeding level 5 on the standard scale, or both.
>
> (2) In Scotland a constable may arrest without warrant anyone whom he has reasonable grounds to suspect of being a person guilty of an offence under this section.
>
> (3) In this section 'public place' includes any highway or, in Scotland, any road within the meaning of the Roads (Scotland) Act 1984 and any premises to which at the material time the public have, or are permitted to have, access, whether on payment or otherwise."

The proscribed organisations are the Irish Republican Army and the Irish National Liberation Army: *ibid.*, Sched. 1.

39–10   Section 9 of the Act prohibits the collection of money for terrorist activities, and provides:

"(1) A person is guilty of an offence if he—

(*a*) solicits or invites any other person to give, lend or otherwise make available, whether for consideration or not, any money or other property; or

(*b*) receives or accepts from any other person, whether for consideration or not, any money or other property,

intending that it shall be applied or used for the commission of, or in furtherance of or in connection with, acts of terrorism to which this section applies or having reasonable cause to suspect that it may be so used or applied.

(2) A person is guilty of an offence if he—

(*a*) gives, lends or otherwise makes available to any other person, whether for consideration or not, any money or other property; or

(*b*) enters into or is otherwise concerned in an arrangement whereby money or other property is or is to be made available to another person,

knowing or having reasonable cause to suspect that it will or may be applied or used as mentioned in subsection (1) above.

(3) The acts of terrorism to which this section applies are—

(*a*) acts of terrorism connected with the affairs of Northern Ireland; and

(*b*) subject to subsection (4) below, acts of terrorism of any other description except acts connected solely with the affairs of the United Kingdom or any part of the United Kingdom other than Northern Ireland.

(4) Subsection (3)(*b*) above does not apply to an act done or to be done outside the United Kingdom unless it constitutes or would constitute an offence triable in the United Kingdom.

(5) In proceedings against a person for an offence under this section in relation to an act within subsection (3)(*b*) above done or to be done outside the United Kingdom—

(*a*) the prosecution need not prove that that person knew or had reasonable cause to suspect that the act constituted or would constitute such an offence as is mentioned in subsection (4) above; but

(*b*) it shall be a defence to prove that he did not know and had no reasonable cause to suspect that the facts were such that the act constituted or would constitute such an offence."

Max. pen. 14 years and a fine on indictment, six months on summary conviction, and forfeiture of any property which the offender had at the time of the offence and intended to use for terrorist purposes: s.13(1), (2).

Section 18, which requires disclosure of information regarding terrorism (*cf. H.M. Advocate* v. *Von*, 1979 S.L.T. (Notes) 62), provides:

"(1) A person is guilty of an offence if he has information which he knows or believes might be of material assistance—

(*a*) in preventing the commission by any other person of an act of terrorism connected with the affairs of Northern Ireland; or

(*b*) in securing the apprehension, prosecution or conviction of any other person for an offence involving the commission, preparation or instigation of such an act,

and fails without reasonable excuse to disclose that information as soon as reasonably practicable—

138

(i) in England and Wales, to a constable;

(ii) in Scotland, to a constable or the procurator fiscal; or

(iii) in Northern Ireland, to a constable or a member of Her Majesty's forces. . . .

(3) Proceedings for an offence under this section may be taken, and the offence may for the purposes of those proceedings be treated as having been committed, in any place where the person to be charged is or has at any time been since he first knew or believed that the information might be of material assistance as mentioned in subsection (1) above."

Max. pen. five years and a fine on indictment, six months on summary conviction.

Section 7 of the Act empowers the Secretary of State to exclude from the United Kingdom persons, other than British citizens, who have been concerned anywhere with terrorism connected with the affairs of Northern Ireland or are or may be attempting to enter Great Britain or Northern Ireland in connection with such acts of terrorism. Failure to comply with an exclusion order is an offence, and it is also an offence to harbour, or be knowingly concerned in the entry to the United Kingdom of, a person subject to such an order: s.8; maximum penalty as for s.18, *supra*.

Section 10 of the Act penalises the soliciting or making of contributions for the benefit of a proscribed organisation: max. pen. as for a contravention of s.9.

"Terrorism" means the use of violence for political ends, and includes any use of violence for the purpose of putting the public or any section of the public in fear: s.20(1).

For hijacking, see *supra*, para. 16–19.

For the offence of taking hostages, see *supra*, para. 29–54a.

For the offence of threatening protected persons, see *supra*, para. 29–65.

39–12 Section 84 of the Representation of the People Act 1949 is re-enacted by section 97 of the Representation of the People Act 1983.

39–13 See now section 2(1)(*c*) of the Prevention of Terrorism (Temporary Provisions) Act 1989, *supra*, para. 39–10.

39–15 to 39–17 Sections 3 to 5A of the Public Order Act 1936 were repealed by the Public Order Act 1986.

On processions, see sections 12 and 14–16 of that Act.

39–19 Racial incitement is now dealt with in the Public Order Act 1986, section 17 of which defines "racial hatred" as "hatred against a group of persons in Great Britain defined by reference to colour, race, nationality (including citizenship) or ethnic or national origins." Sections 18 to 23, as amended by section 164 of the Broadcasting Act 1990, create a number of offences dealing with different ways of using or publishing "threatening, abusive or insulting words or behaviour intended or likely to stir up racial hatred" ("racial incitement"). A "programme service" may be a television or sound broadcasting service, and includes advertisements and any item included in the service: Broadcasting Act 1990,

39–19   s.202(1). For more detailed definitions, see the Broadcasting Act 1990.

Add new paragraphs **39–19a** to **39–19f**:

39–19a   Section 18 provides:

"(1) A person who uses threatening, abusive or insulting words or behaviour, or displays any written material which is threatening, abusive or insulting, is guilty of an offence if—

(*a*) he intends thereby to stir up racial hatred, or

(*b*) having regard to all the circumstances racial hatred is likely to be stirred up thereby.

(2) An offence under this section may be committed in a public or a private place, except that no offence is committed where the words or behaviour are used, or the written material is displayed, by a person inside a dwelling and are not heard or seen except by other persons in that or another dwelling.

(3) A constable may arrest without warrant anyone he reasonably suspects is committing an offence under this section.

(4) In proceedings for an offence under this section it is a defence for the accused to prove that he was inside a dwelling and had no reason to believe that the words or behaviour used, or the written material displayed, would be heard or seen by a person outside that or any other dwelling.

(5) A person who is not shown to have intended to stir up racial hatred is not guilty of an offence under this section if he did not intend his words or behaviour, or the written material, to be, and was not aware that it might be, threatening, abusive or insulting.

(6) This section does not apply to words or behaviour used, or written material displayed, solely for the purpose of being included in a programme included in a programme service."

39–19b   Section 19 provides:

"(1) A person who publishes or distributes written material which is threatening, abusive or insulting is guilty of an offence if—

(*a*) he intends thereby to stir up racial hatred, or

(*b*) having regard to all the circumstances racial hatred is likely to be stirred up thereby.

(2) In proceedings for an offence under this section it is a defence for an accused who is not shown to have intended to stir up racial hatred to prove that he was not aware of the content of the material and did not suspect, and had no reason to suspect, that it was threatening, abusive or insulting.

(3) References in this Part to the publication or distribution of written material are to its publication or distribution to the public or a section of the public."

39–19c   Section 20 penalises the presenter or director of a play in similar terms, excluding rehearsals, recordings or broadcasts unless these are attended by persons not directly connected with the rehearsal, etc. A performer is not a director unless he performs other than as directed, without reasonable excuse. It is a defence for a presenter or director who is not shown to have intended to stir up racial hatred to prove that he did not know and had no reason to suspect that the performance would involve the use of the offending words or behaviour, or that they were threatening, abusive or insulting, or that the circumstances of the performance would be such as were likely to stir up racial hatred.

39–19d Section 21 penalises the distribution or playing of a recording of visual images or sounds which are threatening, abusive or insulting, where these are intended or likely to stir up racial hatred. There is a defence in similar terms to that in section 18(5), *supra.*

39–19e Section 22 creates a similar offence in relation to broadcasting programme services, and penalises persons who provide the programme, or produce or direct it, or actually use offending words or behaviour. The section contains the following statutory defences:

> "(3) If the person providing the service, or a person by whom the programme was produced or directed, is not shown to have intended to stir up racial hatred, it is a defence for him to prove that—
> (*a*) he did not know and had no reason to suspect that the programme would involve the offending material, and
> (*b*) having regard to the circumstances in which the programme was included in a programme service, it was not reasonably practicable for him to secure the removal of the material.
> (4) It is a defence for a person by whom the programme was produced or directed who is not shown to have intended to stir up racial hatred to prove that he did not know and had no reason to suspect—
> (*a*) that the programme would be included in a programme service, or
> (*b*) that the circumstances in which the programme would be so included would be such that racial hatred would be likely to be stirred up.
> (5) It is a defence for a person by whom offending words or behaviour were used and who is not shown to have intended to stir up racial hatred to prove that he did not know and had no reason to suspect—
> (*a*) that a programme involving the use of the offending material would be included in a programme service, or
> (*b*) that the circumstances in which a programme involving the use of the offending material would be so included, or in which a programme so included would involve the use of the offending material, would be such that racial hatred would be likely to be stirred up.
> (6) A person who is not shown to have intended to stir up racial hatred is not guilty of an offence under this section if he did not know, and had no reason to suspect, that the offending material was threatening, abusive or insulting."

39–19f The possession of racially inflammatory material is dealt with by section 23 of the Act which provides:

> "(1) A person who has in his possession written material which is threatening, abusive or insulting, or a recording of visual images or sounds which are threatening, abusive or insulting, with a view to—
> (*a*) in the case of written material, its being displayed, published, distributed, or included in a programme service, whether by himself or another, or
> (*b*) in the case of a recording, its being distributed, shown, played, or included in a programme service, whether by himself or another,
> is guilty of an offence if he intends racial hatred to be stirred up thereby or, having regard to all the circumstances, racial hatred is likely to be stirred up thereby.

39–19f
(2) For this purpose regard shall be had to such display, publication, distribution, showing, playing, or inclusion in a programme service as he has, or it may reasonably be inferred that he has, in view.

(3) In proceedings for an offence under this section it is a defence for an accused who is not shown to have intended to stir up racial hatred to prove that he was not aware of the content of the written material or recording and did not suspect, and had no reason to suspect, that it was threatening, abusive or insulting."

39–23
For the meaning of "persistently follows" and "following in a disorderly manner," see *Elsey* v. *Smith*, 1982 S.C.C.R. 218, where the following was done by a car on a motorway "in order to follow somebody else, and . . . in order to achieve that object, . . . persistently [driving] near to that other person, in company with two other vehicles similarly engaged, and on occasions [altering] one's speed so as to require that other person to overtake": at 229. One determined effort to follow over a substantial distance may constitute persistent following: *ibid.* Following of a kind which is calculated to, and does, distress and harass, and which could have been restrained by interdict, is wrongful: *Elsey* v. *Smith* (*supra*).

"Wrongful" means contrary to the law, and an act which is protected from civil proceedings because it is carried out in an industrial dispute does not thereby cease to be wrongful for the purposes of a prosecution under section 7: *Galt* v. *Philp*, 1983 J.C. 51.

Watching and besetting may be carried out from inside the premises in question: *ibid.*

39–26
Section 15 of the Trade Union and Labour Relations Act 1974, as substituted by section 16 of the Employment Act 1980 and amended by Schedule 3 to the Employment Act 1982, is in the following terms:

"(1) It shall be lawful for a person in contemplation or furtherance of a trade dispute to attend—
(*a*) at or near his own place of work, or
(*b*) if he is an official of a trade union, at or near the place of work of a member of that union whom he is accompanying and whom he represents.
for the purpose only of peacefully obtaining or communicating information, or peacefully persuading any person to work or abstain from working.
(2) If a person works or normally works—
(*a*) otherwise than at any one place, or
(*b*) at a place the location of which is such that attendance there for a purpose mentioned in subsection (1) above is impracticable,
his place of work for the purposes of that subsection shall be any premises of his employer from which he works or from which his work is administered.
(3) In the case of a worker who is not in employment where—
(*a*) his last employment was terminated in connection with a trade dispute, or
(*b*) the termination of his employment was one of the circumstances giving rise to a trade dispute, subsection (1) above shall in relation to that dispute have effect as if any reference to his place of work were a reference to his former place of work.

(4) A person who is an official of a trade union by virtue only of having been elected or appointed to be a representative of some of the members of the union shall be regarded for the purposes of subsection (1) above as representing only those members; but otherwise an official of a trade union shall be regarded for those purposes as representing all its members."

39–28   Section 29 of the Trade Union and Labour Relations Act 1974, as amended by the Employment Act 1982, section 18, is in the following terms:

"(1) In this Act 'trade dispute' means a dispute between workers and their employer, which relates wholly or mainly to one or more of the following, that is to say—

(a) terms and conditions of employment, or the physical conditions in which any workers are required to work;

(b) engagement or non-engagement, or termination or suspension of employment or the duties of employment, of one or more workers;

(c) allocation of work or the duties of employment as between workers or groups of workers;

(d) matters of discipline;

(e) the membership or non-membership of a trade union on the part of a worker;

(f) facilities for officials of trade unions; and

(g) machinery for negotiation or consultation, and other procedures, relating to any of the foregoing matters, including the recognition by employers or employers' associations of the right of a trade union to represent workers in any such negotiation or consultation or in the carrying out of such procedures.

(2) A dispute between a Minister of the Crown and any workers shall, notwithstanding that he is not the employer of those workers, be treated for the purposes of this Act as a dispute between those workers and their employer if the dispute relates—

(a) to matters which have been referred for consideration by a joint body on which, by virtue of any provision made by or under any enactment, that Minister is represented; or

(b) to matters which cannot be settled without that Minister exercising a power conferred on him by or under an enactment.

(3) There is a trade dispute for the purposes of this Act even though it relates to matters occurring outside the United Kingdom, so long as the person or persons whose actions in the United Kingdom are said to be in contemplation or furtherance of a trade dispute relating to matters occurring outside the United Kingdom are likely to be affected in respect of one or more of the matters specified in subsection (1) of this section by the outcome of that dispute.

(5) An act, threat or demand done or made by one person or organisation against another which, if resisted, would have led to a trade dispute with that other, shall, notwithstanding that because that other submits to the act or threat or accedes to the demand no dispute arises, be treated for the purposes of this Act as being done or made in contemplation of a trade dispute with that other.

(6) In this section—

'employment' includes any relationship whereby one person personally does work or performs services for another;

'worker,' in relation to a dispute with an employer, means—

(a) a worker employed by that employer; or

(b) a person who has ceased to be employed by that employer where—

39–28

(i) his employment was terminated in connection with the dispute; or

(ii) the termination of his employment was one of the circumstances giving rise to the dispute.

(6) In the Conspiracy, and Protection of Property Act 1875 'trade dispute' has the same meaning as in this Act."

CHAPTER 40

MOBBING

40–03   Footnote 5. See also *Hancock* v. *H.M.A.*, 1981 J.C. 74.

40–13   In *Hancock* v. *H.M. Advocate*, 1981 J.C. 74, Lord Justice-General Emslie said, at page 86:

"I agree. A mob is essentially a combination of persons, sharing a common criminal purpose, which proceeds to carry out that purpose by violence, or by intimidation by sheer force of numbers. A mob has, therefore, a will and a purpose of its own, and all members of the mob contribute by their presence to the achievement of the mob's purpose, and to the terror of its victims, even where only a few directly engage in the commission of the specific unlawful acts which it is the mob's common purpose to commit. Where there has assembled a mob which proceeds to behave as a mob a question may arise whether all those present when it acts to achieve its common purpose are truly members of the mob or mere spectators. Membership of a mob is not to be inferred from proof of mere presence at the scene of its activities. The inference of membership is, however, legitimate if there is evidence that an individual's presence is a 'countenancing' or contributory presence, i.e., if his presence is for the purpose of countenancing or contributing to the achievement of the mob's unlawful objectives."

CHAPTER 41

BREACH OF THE PEACE, OBSCENE PUBLICATIONS AND BLASPHEMY

For a detailed discussion of breach of the peace, see Michael Christie, *Breach of the Peace* (Edinburgh, 1990).

41–01   It is not a breach of the peace or any other crime merely to form part of a disorderly crowd in circumstances not amounting to mobbing: *MacNeill* v. *Robertson and Ors.*, 1982 S.C.C.R. 468. It is necessary to aver that the accused himself behaved in a disorderly manner, either directly, or impliedly, by averring that each member of the crowd so behaved: *Tudhope* v. *Morrison*, 1983 S.C.C.R. 262 (Sh.Ct.); *cf. Tudhope* v. *O'Neill*, 1984 S.L.T. 424.

41–02   See also *Elsey* v. *Smith*, 1982 J.C. 107; *supra*, para. 39–23.

41–04 It has been held to be a breach of the peace to shout pro-I.R.A. slogans outside Celtic Football Park, on the ground that many spectators would have found them highly provocative and inflammatory: *Duffield and Anr.* v. *Skeen*, 1981 S.C.C.R. 66; *cf. Alexander* v. *Smith*, 1984 S.L.T. 176. It has also been held to be a breach of the peace to direct offensive remarks and gestures towards rival supporters inside a football ground: *Wilson* v. *Brown*, 1982 S.C.C.R. 49. It can even be a breach of the peace to cause embarrassment: *Sinclair* v. *Annan*, 1980 S.L.T. (Notes) 55, where the accused addressed indecent remarks to a woman. On the other hand, it has been held not to be a breach of the peace merely to sniff glue when in a state of apparent oblivion to one's surroundings: *Fisher* v. *Keane*, 1981 J.C. 50. But glue sniffing in the sight of someone who became sufficiently apprehensive to call the police was held to be a breach of the peace in *Taylor* v. *Hamilton*, 1984 S.C.C.R. 393.

In one case, *Logan* v. *Jessop*, 1987 S.C.C.R. 604, the High Court quashed a conviction for breach of the peace where the conduct complained of was shouting and swearing at police officers, the ostensible ground of the decision being the absence of any finding that words complained of "had been uttered in the presence of other members of the public who might have been expected to react to them in one way or another." *Logan* v. *Jessop*, however, was followed by a rash of cases in which convictions were sustained on the basis of *Wilson* v. *Brown, supra*, as involving conduct which might reasonably be expected to cause alarm, upset or annoyance to any person. *Logan* v. *Jessop* was virtually overruled and treated as limited to its own facts which included no finding that anyone at all was affected by what was said, and the police were said to be in the same position as anyone else so far as being sworn at was concerned: see *Saltman* v. *Allan*, 1989 S.L.T. 262; *Norris* v. *McLeod*, 1988 S.C.C.R. 572; *Stewart* v. *Jessop*, 1988 S.C.C.R. 492; *Boyle* v. *Wilson*, 1988 S.C.C.R 485. The zenith, or nadir, of this line of cases, depending on how one looks at them, was reached in *McMillan* v. *Normand*, 1989 S.C.C.R. 269 in which a man's conviction of breach of the peace for swearing at police officers in his own house was upheld on the basis of a finding that the officers "were concerned by his language."

Other interesting examples of breach of the peace can be found in *Butcher* v. *Jessop*, 1989 S.L.T. 593 (a fight between players during a football match); *McAvoy* v. *Jessop*, 1989 S.C.C.R. 301 (ordering an Orange Band to continue playing as the procession passed a chapel while worshippers were about to enter it); and *Stewart* v. *Lockhart*, 1990 S.C.C.R. 390 (transvestism in a red light district). In *Thompson* v. *MacPhail*, 1989 S.L.T. 637 it was held that to inject oneself in a locked cubicle of a public toilet was not a breach of the peace in the circumstances of that case.

The vague nature of the crime was explicitly accepted in *Carey* v. *Tudhope*, 1984 S.C.C.R. 157 (where a police officer was convicted of breach of the peace by threatening violence in crude language to a person whose friend had just been placed in a police van) in which the High Court said, "In many cases it becomes a matter of judgment for the judge to decide whether in the context and atmosphere of what occurred the facts did constitute the offence of breach of the peace in Scotland."

41–04   Subject to certain exceptions it is an offence under section 54 of the Civic Government (Scotland) Act 1982 for any person who plays an instrument, sings or performs or operates a sound producing device, so as to give other persons reasonable cause for annoyance to fail to desist on being required to do so by a uniformed constable: maximum penalty a fine of level 2; see also para. 47–11 in the main work.

41–09   See also *Ralston* v. *H.M. Advocate*, 1989 S.L.T. 474; *Butcher* v. *Jessop*, 1989 S.L.T. 593.

41–11   The High Court held in *Derrett* v. *Lockhart*, 1991 S.C.C.R. 109 that where the charge is one of breach of the peace by fighting it is appropriate for the court to approach the question of guilt by asking whether the accused was acting in self-defence.

41–14   Section 78 of the 1969 Act is replaced by section 43 of the Telecommunications Act 1984: max. pen. a fine of level 3. The offence does not extend to things done in the course of providing a programme service within the meaning of the Broadcasting Act 1990, these being dealt with in section 51(2A) of the Civic Government (Scotland) Act 1982, *infra*, para. 41–17.

41–15   Footnote 36a. Max. imprisonment now six months on summary conviction, seven years on indictment: Criminal Justice Act 1991, s.26(4).

41–16   It has been held in a number of cases that the common law crime of shameless indecency is committed by selling or exposing for sale (and perhaps even having for sale where there is also a charge of exposing for sale) articles which are obscene and "likely to deprave and corrupt the morals of the lieges and to create in their minds inordinate and lustful desires": *Robertson* v. *Smith*, 1980 J.C. 1; see *supra*, para. 1–32.

It is necessary for the Crown to show that the accused was aware of the obscene character of the article, and that his conduct was directed towards some person or persons with an intention or in the knowledge that it should corrupt or be calculated to corrupt them: *Dean* v. *John Menzies (Holdings) Ltd.*, 1981 J.C. 23, Lord Cameron at 32; *Tudhope* v. *Barlow*, 1981 S.L.T. (Sh.Ct.) 94. Nevertheless, the fact that the exposure is restricted to persons not under 18 years old, far from being a defence, is evidence of the accused's awareness of the obscene character of the material: *Robertson* v. *Smith, supra*; *Tudhope* v. *Taylor*, 1980 S.L.T. (Notes) 54; *Centrewall Ltd.* v. *MacNeill*, 1983 S.L.T. 326; *Smith* v. *Downie*, 1982 S.L.T. (Sh.Ct.) 23.

Books held as a reserve stock in a back shop or kept in drawers are "exposed for sale" if they are kept in immediate readiness for sale: *Scott* v. *Smith*, 1981 J.C. 46.

An averment that an article is "indecent and obscene" is tantamount to an averment that it is liable to corrupt and deprave, that being the common law meaning of "indecent and obscene": *Ingram* v. *Macari*, 1982 J.C. 1. Its tendency to corrupt and deprave is a matter of fact for the court, and not a matter for expert evidence: *Ingram* v. *Macari*, 1983 J.C. 1

It is not an offence at common law for a wholesaler to have obscene articles in his possession for circulation to retailers: *Sommerville* v. *Tudhope*, 1981 J.C. 58; the premises in which the articles were kept in that case were not premises to which the public were invited to resort, and there was therefore "no affront to public decency or morals nor any action which of itself is designed or calculated to corrupt the morals of the lieges": Lord Cameron at 63.

It may, however, be a crime to distribute obscene material to retailers with intent that it be sold to the public, the crime being describable as "trafficking in obscene publications," although there is no example of such a crime, only a reference by Lord Cooper in *Galletly* v. *Laird*, 1953 J.C. 16 to traffic in pornography as an evil which obscenity legislation is designed to prevent: see *Sommerville* v. *Tudhope, supra*. Such distribution might constitute a conspiracy to commit shameless indecency, or make the wholesaler art and part in the retailer's shameless indecency once the latter had exposed the articles for sale.

Section 45 of the Civic Government (Scotland) Act 1982 allows local authorities to apply Schedule 2 to the Act, which empowers them to license sex shops, *i.e.* premises used for dealing in, or displaying or demonstrating, what are called sex articles: Sched. 2, para. 2(1). Such articles specifically include reading matter and vision or sound recordings portraying sexual activity or genital organs or intended to stimulate or encourage sexual activity: *ibid.*, para. 2(4). Local authorities are thus empowered to license the sale of pornography, but such licences are of no avail in a prosecution for shameless indecency or obscenity, since paragraph 1 of Schedule 2 provides that nothing in the Schedule shall afford a defence to any charge except one under the Schedule itself (*e.g.* for breach of the licensing conditions) or be taken into account in any way in the trial of any such charge.

41–17 to 41–20   The relevant provisions of the Burgh Police (Scotland) Act 1892 and the corresponding provisions in local Acts are replaced by section 51 of the Civic Government (Scotland) Act 1982, as amended by section 163 of the Broadcasting Act 1990, which provides, *inter alia*:

> "(2) Subject to subsection (4) below, any person who publishes, sells or distributes or, with a view to its eventual sale or distribution, makes, prints, or keeps any obscene material shall be guilty of an offence under this section.
> (2A) Subject to subsection (4) below, any person who—
> (a) is responsible for the inclusion of any obscene material included in a programme service; or
> (b) with a view to its eventual inclusion in a programme so included, makes, prints, has or keeps any obscene material,
> shall be guilty of an offence under this section.
> (4) A person shall not be convicted of an offence under this section if he proves that he had used all due diligence to avoid committing the offence."

Max. pen. two years and a fine on indictment, three months on summary conviction: s.51(3). For a discussion of the law, see Keith

41–17   Ewing, "Obscene Publications. Effect of the Civic Government
to   (Scotland) Bill," 1982 S.L.T. (News) 55. For indecent displays, see
41–20   *infra*, para. 41–25.

     "Material" includes any book, magazine, bill, paper, print, film, tape, disc, or other kind of recording (whether of sound or visual images or both), photograph (positive or negative), drawing, painting, representation, model or figure: s.51(8). A programme service may be a television or sound broadcasting service, and includes advertisements and any item included in the service: Broadcasting Act 1990, ss.201(1), 202(1). For more detailed definitions, see the Broadcasting Act 1990.

     "Publishing" includes playing, projecting or otherwise reproducing: s.51(8).

     Section 51 does not apply to anything included in a play within the meaning of the Theatres Act 1968: s.51(6).

41–21   Section 2(4)(*b*) of the Theatres Act 1968 was repealed by the Indecent Displays (Control) Act 1981. Section 380 of the Burgh Police (Scotland) Act 1892 was replaced by s.51 of the Civic Government (Scotland) Act 1982, but no provision is made for a corresponding alteration in s.2(4)(*c*) of the Theatres Act, which was simply repealed by Sched. 8 to the Civic Government (Scotland) Act.

41–22   Section 1 of the Cinemas Act 1985 prohibits the use of premises for film exhibitions unless they are licensed for the purpose under the Act. "Film exhibition" means any exhibition of moving pictures produced other than in a programme included in a programme service within the meaning of the Broadcasting Act 1990 (*supra*, para. 41–17): Cinemas Act 1985, s.21(1), as amended by Broadcasting Act 1990.

     The use of unlicensed premises for an exhibition requiring a licence is made an offence by section 10(1)(*a*) of the Cinemas Act 1985: max. pen. a fine of £20,000: Cinemas Act 1985, s.11(1)(*a*).

     Presentation of an obscene film may constitute shameless indecency: *Watt* v. *Annan*, 1978 J.C. 84; *supra*, para. 1–32. Films are also covered by s.51 of the Civic Government (Scotland) Act 1982: *supra*, para. 41–17, *infra*, para. 41–25, which replaces earlier public and local legislation on obscenity.

     Add new paragraphs **41–22a** and **41–22b**:

41–22a   *Indecent Photographs of Children.* Section 52 of the Civic Government (Scotland) Act 1982 provides:

> "(1) Any person who—
> (*a*) takes, or permits to be taken, any indecent photograph of a child (meaning, in this section a person under the age of 16);
> (*b*) distributes or shows such an indecent photograph;
> (*c*) has in his possession such an indecent photograph with a view to its being distributed or shown by himself or others; or
> (*d*) publishes or causes to be published any advertisement likely to be understood as conveying that the advertiser distributes or shows such an indecent photograph, or intends to do so
> shall be guilty of an offence under this section.

(2) In proceedings under this section a person is to be taken as having been a child at any material time if it appears from the evidence as a whole that he was then under the age of 16. . ..

(4) For the purpose of this section, a person is to be regarded as distributing an indecent photograph if he parts with possession of it to, or exposes or offers it for acquisition by, another person."

Max. pen. two years' imprisonment on indictment: s.52(3).

It has been held that under the corresponding English legislation the circumstances in which the photograph is taken and the taker's motivation are irrelevant: *R.* v. *Graham-Kerr* [1988] 1 W.L.R. 1098, but that the age of the child may be relevant in considering whether the photograph is indecent: *R.* v. *Owen (Charles)* [1988] 1 W.L.R. 134.

41–22b Section 52A of the Civic Government (Scotland) Act 1982, as inserted by section 161 of the Criminal Justice Act 1988, provides:

"52A.—(1) It is an offence for a person to have any indecent photograph of a child (meaning in this section a person under the age of 16) in his possession.

(2) Where a person is charged with an offence under subsection (1), it shall be a defence for him to prove—

(*a*) that he had a legitimate reason for having the photograph in his possession; or

(*b*) that he had not himself seen the photograph and did not know, nor had any cause to suspect, it to be indecent; or

(*c*) that the photograph was sent to him without any prior request made by him or on his behalf and that he did not keep it for an unreasonable time.

(3) A person shall be liable on summary conviction of an offence under this section to a fine not exceeding level 5 on the standard scale.

(4) Subsections (2) and (8) of section 52 of this Act shall have effect for the purposes of this section as they have for the purposes of that section."

41–23 See also *Ingram* v. *Macari*, 1983 J.C. 1.

41–25 Delete original paragraph and substitute the following:

Indecent displays. The Indecent Advertisements Act 1889 was repealed by the Indecent Displays (Control) Act 1981, section 1 of which, as amended by Schedule 1 to the Cinematograph (Amendment) Act 1982, Schedule 2 to the Cinemas Act 1985 and Schedule 20 to the Broadcasting Act 1990, provides:

"(1) If any indecent matter is publicly displayed the person making the display and any person causing or permitting the display to be made shall be guilty of an offence.

(2) Any matter which is displayed in or so as to be visible from any public place shall, for the purposes of this section, be deemed to be publicly displayed.

(3) In subsection (2) above, 'public place,' in relation to the display of any matter, means any place to which the public have or are permitted to have access (whether on payment or otherwise) while that matter is displayed except—

149

    (*a*) a place to which the public are permitted to have access only on payment which is or includes payment for that display; or

    (*b*) a shop or any part of a shop to which the public can only gain access by passing beyond an adequate warning notice;

but the exclusions contained in paragraphs (*a*) and (*b*) above shall only apply where persons under the age of 18 years are not permitted to enter while the display in question is continuing.

    (4) Nothing in this section applies in relation to any matter—

    (*a*) included by any person in a television broadcasting service or other television programme service (within the meaning of Part I of the Broadcasting Act 1990); or

    (*b*) included in the display of an art gallery or museum and visible only from within the gallery or museum; or

    (*c*) displayed by or with the authority of, and visible only from within a building occupied by, the Crown or any local authority; or

    (*d*) included in a performance of a play (within the meaning of the Theatres Act 1968); or

    (*e*) included in a film exhibition as defined in the Cinemas Act 1985—

        (i) given in a place which as regards that exhibition is required to be licensed under section 1 of that Act or by virtue only of section 5, 7 or 8 of that Act, is not required to be so licensed; or

        (ii) which is an exhibition to which section 6 of that Act applies, given by an exempted organisation as defined in subsection (6) of that section.

    (5) In this section 'matter' includes anything capable of being displayed, except that it does not include an actual human body or any part thereof; and in determining for the purpose of this section whether any displayed matter is indecent—

    (*a*) there shall be disregarded any part of that matter which is not exposed to view; and

    (*b*) account may be taken of the effect of juxtaposing one thing with another.

    (6) A warning notice shall not be adequate for the purposes of this section unless it complies with the following requirements—

    (*a*) The warning notice must contain the following words, and no others—

'WARNING

Persons passing beyond this notice will find material on display which they may consider indecent. No admittance to persons under 18 years of age.'

    (*b*) The word 'WARNING' must appear as a heading.

    (*c*) No pictures or other matter shall appear on the notice.

    (*d*) The notice must be so situated that no one could reasonably gain access to the shop or part of the shop in question without being aware of the notice and it must be easily legible by any person gaining such access."

Max. pen. two years and a fine on indictment, on summary conviction the prescribed sum in the sheriff court and a fine of level 3 in the district court: s.4(2).

Nothing in this Act (except to the extent provided for by it) affects the law relating to shameless indecency or obscenity at common law or under section 51 of the Civic Government (Scotland) Act 1982: Indecent Displays (Control) Act 1981, s.5(4).

It is also an offence under section 51(1) of the Civic Government (Scotland) Act 1982 to display any obscene material in any public place or in any other place where it can be seen by the public:

maximum penalty three months' imprisonment and a fine on summary conviction, two years and a fine on indictment: s.51(3). It is a defence to show due diligence to avoid the offence: s.51(4). It remains to be seen whether publishing warnings or restricting entry to premises will constitute due diligence, or simply be seen as evidence of the accused's knowledge that the material is obscene: *cf.* P. W. Ferguson, "The Limits of Statutory Obscenity," 1983 S.L.T. (News) 249; *Centrewall Ltd.* v. *MacNeill*, 1983 S.L.T. 326. It should be noted that any place to which the public are permitted to have access, whether on payment or otherwise, is a public place for the purpose of s.51(1), so that that subsection can be contravened in circumstances which would not contravene the Indecent Displays (Control) Act 1981: Civic Government (Scotland) Act 1982, s.51(8); *cf.* s.133, *supra*, para. 36–41.

The Indecent Displays (Control) Act 1981 does not affect s.51 of the Civic Government (Scotland) Act 1982: Indecent Displays (Control) Act 1981, s.5(4)(*b*), as substituted by Civic Government (Scotland) Act 1982, s.51(7), but a person charged under s.51(1) may be convicted of a breach of the Indecent Displays (Control) Act 1981: Civic Government (Scotland) Act 1982, s.51(5).

Section 51(1) does not apply to any matter included in a performance of a play within the meaning of the Theatres Act 1968: Civic Government (Scotland) Act 1982, s.51(6).

'Material' has the same meaning in relation to offences under section 51(1) as it has in relation to offences under s.51(2); *supra*, para. 41–17.

41–28 Section 4 of the Vagrancy Act 1824 was repealed by the Civic Government (Scotland) Act 1982.

41–29 For a modern English case of blasphemy, see *R.* v. *Lemon* [1979] A.C. 617.

CHAPTER 43

DANGEROUS DRUGS

(See Keith S. Bovey, *Misuse of Drugs: A Handbook for Lawyers* (Edinburgh, 1986).)

Insert new paragraph **43–00**:

43–00 The provisions relating to penalties in this chapter have to be read subject to section 44 of the Criminal Justice (Scotland) Act 1987, which provides that where a person convicted on indictment of a contravention of section 4(2), 4(3) or 5(3) of the Misuse of Drugs Act 1971 is sentenced to imprisonment but no confiscation order is made against him, he must also be fined an amount determined by reference to his likely profits unless the court is satisfied that a fine is inappropriate. The court is also empowered to impose both a confiscation order and a fine as well as imprisonment.

43–05   A controlled drug is any "substance or product" specified in the Schedules to the Act.

The descriptions in the Schedules are generic terms and include derivative forms of the drug named, so that, *e.g.* "cocaine" includes both the direct extracts of the coca-leaf and whatever results from a chemical transformation thereof: *R.* v. *Greensmith* [1983] 1 W.L.R. 1124, and "amphetamine" includes salt of amphetamine: *Heywood* v. *Macrae*, 1988 S.L.T. 218.

Where the prohibited drug is defined as a preparation or product containing a drug, the prohibition does not extend to material which is in its natural state, although it contains the drug when it is in that state: *Murray* v. *McNaughton*, 1985 J.C. 3.

Synthetically produced cannabis resin is not included in the prohibition, but the Crown do not have to prove that any cannabis resin produced was not synthetically produced: *Guild* v. *Ogilvie*, 1986 S.L.T. 343.

Class C drugs now include buprenorphine ("Temgesic"): Misuse of Drugs Act 1971 (Modification) Order 1989. Class C drugs also include diazepam, nitrazepam and temazepam, but these drugs are exempted from the prohibition on importation and exportation, and, when in the form of a medicinal product, from the prohibition on simple possession: Misuse of Drugs Regulations 1985, reg. 4, Sched. 4.

Footnote 7. *Cf. R.* v. *Hunt* [1987] A.C. 532.
Footnote 11. See now Misuse of Drugs Regulations 1985, reg. 4(3).
Footnote 13. See now Misuse of Drugs Regulations 1985, reg. 4.

43–06   The relevant sections of the Customs and Excise Act are now section 50(1), 68(2) and 170 of the Customs and Excise Management Act 1979: *cf. R.* v. *Whitehead* [1982] Q.B. 1272.

43–07   Being concerned in the supply of drugs covers more than art and part guilt in supply, and extends to a great variety of activities both at the centre and at the fringes of drug-dealing, including the activities of couriers, go-betweens, lookouts, financiers, advertisers, and any person who was a link in a chain of distribution or took part in breaking up or adulterating quantities of drugs and weighing and packing drug deals: *Kerr (D.A.)* v. *H.M. Advocate*, 1986 S.C.C.R. 81, Lord Hunter at p. 87. A person may be convicted of being concerned in the supply of drugs, even if no actual supply takes place: *Kerr, supra*, and the offence can relate to drugs supplied or to be supplied by the accused himself. For a discussion of the *mens rea* required for the offence of being concerned in supply, see *Tudhope* v. *McKee*, 1988 S.L.T. 153. As to jurisdiction, see *Clements* v. *H.M.A.*, 1991 S.C.C.R. 266; *supra*, para. 3–51.

"Supply" means "transfer physical control": *Donnelly* v. *H.M.A.*, 1985 S.L.T. 243; *R.* v. *Maginnis* [1987] A.C. 303. Where, therefore, X gives A a drug to keep for him, A supplies the drug to X when he returns it to him, although it has remained in X's ownership throughout: *R.* v. *Delgado* [1984] 1 W.L.R. 89; *Murray* v. *Mac-Phail*, 1991 S.C.C.R. 245.

Regulations 8 and 9 of the Misuse of Drugs Regulations 1985 permit the manufacture or compounding of drugs by a medical, dental or veterinary practitioner or pharmacist acting in his capacity as such, and the supply of certain drugs by such persons and other specified persons such as nursing sisters and laboratory analysts to persons lawfully entitled to possess them.

Footnote 14. Max. pen. for Class A drugs is now life imprisonment: Controlled Drugs (Penalties) Act 1985.

43–08   Regulation 6 of the 1973 Regulations is now regulation 6 of the Misuse of Drugs Regulations 1985.

Regulation 10 of the Misuse of Drugs Regulations 1985 permits the persons specified in regulations 8 and 9 thereof (*supra*, para. 43–07) to possess certain drugs for the purpose of acting in their capacity as such persons. Whether a doctor who administers drugs to himself is doing so in his capacity as a practitioner is a question of fact: *R. v. Dunbar* [1981] 1 W.L.R. 1536.

Footnote 17. Max. pen. for Class A drugs is now life imprisonment: Controlled Drugs (Penalties) Act 1985.

43–09   The law now is that the only quantitative limitation is that of identifiability. It is an offence to be in possession of an identifiable quantity of a drug, whether or not it is so minute as to be unusable: *Keane v. Gallacher*, 1980 J.C. 77. The same view is now taken in England: *R. v. Boyesen* [1982] A.C. 768.

Footnote 18. Add after the reference to *McAttee v. Hogg*: *McRae v. H.M.A.*, 1975 J.C. 34: see also *Mingay v. MacKinnon*, 1980 J.C. 33.

A may be in possession of goods which are in the custody of another, provided they are subject to his control: Misuse of Drugs Act 1971, s.37(3). He may also be in possession of drugs which are in the hands of an innocent agent, provided that he was responsible for the agent having them, or must have known that his dealing with them would involve their being in the agent's hands: *Amato v. Walkingshaw*, 1990 J.C. 45.

43–10   A plant is cultivated when it is grown, and the term "cultivate" does not require that any particular care or labour be bestowed on it: *Tudhope v. Robertson*, 1980 J.C. 62. The evidence of cultivation in that case was "the positioning of the plants to secure the light necessary to growth, the condition of the plants, the presence of the seeds, and the objective which the respondents had in mind in having the plants in their house at all.": L.J.-G. at 65–66.

43–11   It has been held in England that in view of the definition of cannabis as any part of any plant of the genus cannabis: para. 43–05, in the main work, to grow a cannabis plant is to produce the drug cannabis: *Taylor v. Chief Constable of Kent* [1981] 1 W.L.R. 606.

Footnote 31. Add: *R. v. Josephs and Christie* (1977) 65 Cr.App.R. 253.

43–11   Add new paragraphs **43–11a** and **43–11b**:

43–11a   *Manufacture and supply of substances used to produce drugs*
Section 12 of the Criminal Justice (International Co-operation) Act 1990 makes it an offence to manufacture or supply to another a substance listed in Schedule 2 to the Act, knowing or suspecting that it is to be used for the unlawful production of a controlled drug: max. pen. 14 years' imprisonment and a fine on indictment, six months on summary conviction.

43–11b   *Concealing or dealing in the proceeds of drug trafficking*
Section 14 of the Criminal Justice (International Co-operation) Act 1990 provides:

"(1) A person is guilty of an offence if he—
(*a*) conceals or disguises any property which is, or in whole or in part directly or indirectly represents, his proceeds of drug trafficking; or
(*b*) converts or transfers that property or removes it from the jurisdiction,
for the purpose of avoiding prosecution for a drug offence or the making or enforcement in his case of a confiscation order.
(2) A person is guilty of an offence if, knowing or having reasonable grounds to suspect that any property is, or in whole or in part directly or indirectly represents, another person's proceeds of drug trafficking, he—
(*a*) conceals or disguises that property; or
(*b*) converts or transfers that property or removes it from the jurisdiction,
for the purpose of assisting any person to avoid prosecution for a drug trafficking offence or the making or enforcement of a confiscation order.
(3) A person is guilty of an offence if, knowing or having reasonable grounds to suspect that any property is, or in whole or in part directly or indirectly represents, another person's proceeds of drug trafficking, he acquires that property for no, or for inadequate, consideration.
(4) In subsections (1)(*a*) and (2)(*a*) above the references to concealing or disguising any property include references to concealing or disguising its nature, source, location, disposition, movement or ownership or any rights with respect to it.
(5) For the purposes of subsection (3) above consideration given for any property is inadequate if its value is significantly less than the value of that property, and there shall not be treated as consideration the provision for any person of services or goods which are of assistance to him in drug trafficking.
(6) A person guilty of an offence under this section is liable—
(*a*) on summary conviction, to imprisonment for a term not exceeding six months or a fine not exceeding the statutory maximum or both;
(*b*) on conviction on indictment, to imprisonment for a term not exceeding fourteen years or a fine or both."

A "drug trafficking offence" is defined in the Drug Trafficking Offences Act 1986, section 38.
It is also an offence to do anything to prejudice an investigation into drug trafficking which one knows or suspects is taking place,

subject to a defence of lack of knowledge or suspicion, or of reasonable grounds for suspicion that ones actings were likely to prejudice the investigation, and to a defence of lawful authority or reasonable excuse for ones actings: Criminal Justice (Scotland) Act 1987, s.42; max. pen. five years and a fine on indictment, six months on summary conviction.

It is also an offence to enter into an arrangement with a person one knows or suspects to be a drug trafficker whereby that person is helped to retain control of the proceeds of drug trafficking: *ibid.*, s.43: max. pen. 14 years and a fine on indictment, six months on summary conviction. It is a defence for the accused to prove that he did not know or suspect that the arrangement related to the proceeds of drug trafficking, or that the arrangement had the prohibited effect: *ibid.* s.43(4)(*b*), (*c*). No offence is committed if the accused discloses the arrangement to the authorities before it is entered into, or as soon as reasonable thereafter if the disclosure is made on his own initiative, or if he proves that he intended to make such disclosure but there is a reasonable excuse for his failure to have done so: *ibid.* s.43(3), (4)(*c*).

43–13 The existence of section 28 of the Misuse of Drugs Act 1971 does not affect the onus on the Crown to prove that the accused had possession of the drug, in the sense in which possession is defined in *R. v. Warner* [1969] A.C. 256: see para. 3–38 in the main work; *Mackenzie v. Skeen*, 1983 S.L.T. 121; *R. v. Ashton-Rickardt* [1978] 1 W.L.R. 37. But once it is proved that cannabis has been cultivated it is for the accused to show that he did not know it was cannabis: *R. v. Champ* (1981) 73 Cr.App.R. 367. So, where A is carrying a box which he knows contains something, and the Crown prove that that something was a drug, A is in possession of the drug, and it is up to him to make out a section 28 defence: *R. v. McNamara* (1988) 87 Cr.App.R. 246, L.C.J. at pp. 251–252.

The position with regard to the offence of being concerned in supply is unclear: see *Tudhope v. McKee*, 1988 S.L.T. 153.

43–14 See now Misuse of Drugs (Designation) Order 1986.

Footnote 36. See now Misuse of Drugs Regulations 1985, regs. 8–11.

CHAPTER 44

OFFENCES IN CONNECTION WITH OFFICIALS

44–01 Footnote 5. See now Customs and Excise Management Act 1979, s.15; Representation of the People Act 1983, ss.63–66, 99 and 100.

44–05 The maximum period of imprisonment is now seven years in all cases: Criminal Justice Act 1988, s.47.

44–08 Where it is proved that any money, gift or other consideration has been paid or given to or received by a person in public employment by or from a person seeking a contract from the public body

44–08 concerned, there is a presumption of corruption: Prevention of Corruption Act 1916, s.2; see, *e.g. R.* v. *Braithwaite* [1983] 1 W.L.R. 385.

It was said in *R.* v. *Mills* (1978) 68 Cr.App.R. 154 that to receive money only with the intention of entrapping the giver was not to receive it with any intention of keeping it, and such money was therefore not received in breach of s.2 of the Prevention of Corruption Act 1916.

It is no defence that while the accused knew that what he was given was intended as a bribe he did not accept it as such but as a reward for work done in the past: *R.* v. *Mills, supra.*

44–09 See now Customs and Excise Management Act 1979, section 15.

44–12 See now Representation of the People Act 1983, as amended by Representation of the People Act 1985.

CHAPTER 46

BETTING, GAMING AND LOTTERIES

Note: The financial limits set by various provisions of the legislation are regularly updated by statutory instrument.

46–04 Section 10 of the Betting and Gaming Duties Act 1972 is repealed by the Betting and Gaming Duties Act 1981, and re-enacted by section 10 of that Act.

46–22 See *Poole Stadium Ltd.* v. *Squires* [1982] 1 W.L.R. 235.

46–32 An advertisement placed inside a betting office window but readable only from outside is published outside: *Windsors Ltd.* v. *Oldfield* [1981] 1 W.L.R. 1176. An advertisement which draws attention to the facilities available in a betting office is in breach of the section even if it does not say that the premises to which it is affixed are a betting office: *ibid.*

Section 10(5) is amended by section 2 of the Betting, Gaming and Lotteries (Amendment) Act 1984 so as to apply to any advertisement other than one to which section 10(6) applies. Section 10(6), as inserted by section 2 of the 1984 Act, applies to advertisements published inside a licensed betting office, or which comply with prescribed restrictions and are published outside a licensed betting office from a place inside such an office or in premises giving access thereto, or which are painted on or otherwise attached to the outside of premises in which such an office is situated.

46–34 Footnote 74. The Burgh Police (Scotland) Act 1892 was repealed by the Civic Government (Scotland) Act 1982.

46–39 See *Brown* v. *Plant*, 1985 S.L.T. 371.

46–43   The section extends to inclusion in other programme services: Broadcasting Act 1990, Sched. 20.

46–47   Subsections (2) to (4) are replaced by the following provisions:

"(2) Where a machine to which this Part of this Act applies is used for gaming as an incident of any such entertainment, the whole proceeds of the entertainment, after deducting the expenses of the entertainment, shall be devoted to purposes other than private gain.

(2A) Where a machine to which this Part of this Act applies is used for gaming as an incident of an entertainment to which this section applies, the opportunity to win prizes by means of the machine, or that opportunity together with any other facilities for participating in lotteries or gaming shall not be the only, or the only substantial, inducement to persons to attend the entertainment." (Lotteries Act 1975, Sched. 4).

46–49   Section 41(11) is repealed by the Lotteries and Amusements Act 1976, Sched. 5.

46–64   Section 1 of the Lotteries (Amendment) Act 1984 inserts a new subsection (2A) into section 2, makes it a defence in proceedings related to tickets, advertisements or other documents to prove that the accused believed on reasonable grounds that the lottery was being promoted and conducted wholly outside Great Britain.

46–69   It is not necessary for there to be a lottery that the prizes are provided out of money contributed by the participants; it is enough that chances in the lottery are secured by some payment by the participants, such as the purchase of a packet of cigarettes which contains a lottery ticket: *Imperial Tobacco Ltd.* v. *Att.-Gen.* [1981] A.C. 718.

46–73   See *Brown* v. *Plant*, 1985 S.L.T. 371.

CHAPTER 47

POLLUTION

47–01   Part I of the Control of Pollution Act 1974 is replaced by Part II
47–02   of the Environmental Protection Act 1990.

Add new paragraph **47–02a**:

47–02a   *Transporting controlled waste.* Section 1 of the Control of Pollution Amendment Act 1989 makes it an offence for a person other than a registered carrier of controlled waste to transport such waste in the course of anyone's business or with a view to profit: max. pen. a fine of level 5.

47–03   Section 31(1) to (3) of the Control of Pollution Act 1974 was amended by Schedule 23 to the Water Act 1989 , Schedule 15 to the Environmental Protection Act 1990 and the Water Consolidation (Consequential Provisions) Act 1991 and now reads as follows:

157

"(1) Subject to subsections (2) and (3) of this section, a person shall be guilty of an offence if he causes or knowingly permits—

(*a*) any poisonous, noxious or polluting matter to enter controlled waters; or

(*b*) any matter to enter any inland waters so as to tend (either directly or in combination with other matter which he or another person causes or permits to enter those waters) to impede the proper flow of the waters in a manner leading or likely to lead to a substantial aggravation of pollution due to other causes or of the consequences of such pollution; or

(*c*) any solid waste matter to enter controlled waters.

(2) A person shall not be guilty of an offence by virtue of the preceding subsection if—

(*a*) the entry in question is authorised by, or is a consequence of an act authorised by, a disposal licence or a consent given by the Secretary of State or a river purification authority in pursuance of this Act and the entry or act is in accordance with the conditions, if any, to which the licence or consent is subject; or

(*b*) the entry in question is authorised by, or is a consequence of an act authorised by—

   (i) section 33 of the Water (Scotland) Act 1980 (which among other things relates to temporary discharges by water authorities in connection with the construction of works) or any prescribed enactment, or

   (ii) any provision of a local Act or statutory order which expressly confers power to discharge effluent into water, or

   (iii) any licence granted under Part II of the Food and Environment Protection Act 1985; or

   (iv) any consent given under Chapter II of Part III of the Water Resources Act 1991; or

   (v) an authorisation granted under Part I of the Environmental Protection Act 1990 for a prescribed process designated for central control; or

   (vi) a waste management licence granted under Part II of the Environmental Protection Act 1990; or

(*c*) the entry in question is caused or permitted in an emergency in order to avoid danger to life or health and—

   (i) he takes all such steps as are reasonably practicable in the circumstances for minimising the extent of the entry in question and of its polluting effects; and

   (ii) as soon as reasonably practicable after the entry occurs, particulars of the entry are furnished to the river purification authority in whose area it occurs; or

(*d*) the matter in question is trade or sewage effluent discharged as mentioned in paragraph (*a*) of subsection (1) of section 32 or matter discharged as mentioned in paragraph (*b*) or (*c*) of that subsection and the entry in question is not from a vessel;

and a person shall not be guilty of an offence by virtue of the preceding subsection by reason only of his permitting water from an abandoned mine to enter controlled waters.

(3) A person shall not by virtue of paragraph (*b*) or (*c*) of subsection (1) of this section be guilty of an offence by reason of his depositing the solid refuse of a mine or quarry on any land so that it falls or is carried into inland waters if—

(*a*) he deposits the refuse on the land with the consent (which shall not be unreasonably withheld) of the river purification authority in whose area the land is situated; and

(*b*) no other site for the deposit is reasonably practicable; and
(*c*) he takes all reasonably practicable steps to prevent the refuse from entering those inland waters."

Section 31(5) is now section 31(4): max. pen. now two years and a fine on indictment, three months on summary conviction.

The relevant definitions are now contained in sections 30A and 56 of the 1974 Act as substituted by Schedule 23 to the Water Act 1989.

7–04 Section 32, as amended by Schedule 23 to the Water Act 1989, and Schedule 15 to the Environmental Protection Act 1990 reads as follows:

"(1) Subject to subsections (3) to (5) of this section, a person shall be guilty of an offence if he causes or knowingly permits—

(*a*) any trade effluent or sewage effluent to be discharged—
    (i) into any controlled waters, or
    (ii) from land in Scotland through a pipe into the sea outside the seaward limits of controlled waters, or
    (iii) from a building or from plant on to or into any land or into any waters of a loch or pond which are not inland waters; or
(*b*) any matter other than trade or sewage effluent to be discharged into controlled waters from a sewer as defined by section 59(1) of the Sewerage (Scotland) Act 1968 or from a drain as so defined; or
(*c*) any matter other than trade or sewage effluent to be discharged into controlled waters from a drain which a roads authority is obliged or entitled to keep open by virtue of section 31 of the Roads (Scotland) Act 1984, and in respect of which the river purification authority in whose area the discharge occurs has, not later than the beginning of the period of three months ending with the date of the discharge, served on the roads authority a notice stating that this paragraph is to apply to the drain,

unless the discharge is made with the consent in pursuance of section 34 of this Act of the river purification authority in whose area the discharge occurs (or, in a case falling within paragraph (*a*)(ii) of this subsection, of the river purification authority whose area includes the point at which the pipe passes or first passes into or under controlled waters from the sea outside them) and is in accordance with the conditions, if any, to which the consent is subject.

(2) Where any sewage effluent is discharged as mentioned in paragraph (*a*) of the preceding subsection from any works or sewer vested in a local authority and the authority did not cause or knowingly permit the discharge but was bound to receive into the works or sewer, either unconditionally or subject to conditions which were observed, matter included in the discharge, the authority shall be deemed for the purposes of that subsection to have caused the discharge.

(3) The Secretary of State may—

(*a*) by an order made before subsection (1) of this section comes into force provide that that subsection shall not, while the order is in force, apply to discharges which are of a kind or in an area specified in the order and for which, if this Act had not been passed, consent in pursuance of the Rivers (Prevention of Pollution) (Scotland) Acts 1951 and 1965 would not have been required;
(*b*) by order vary or revoke any order in force by virtue of the preceding paragraph;

and an order made by virtue of this subsection may require any river purification authority specified in the order to publish in a manner so specified such information about the order as is so specified.

159

47–04   (4) Subsection (1) of this section shall not apply to any discharge which—

(*a*) is from a vessel; or

(*b*) is authorised by a licence granted under Part II of the Food and Environment Protection Act 1985; or

(*c*) is authorised by an authorisation granted under Part I of the Environmental Protection Act 1990 for a prescribed process designated for central control,

and a person shall not be guilty of an offence under subsection (1) if—

(i) the discharge is caused or permitted in an emergency in order to avoid danger to life or health;

(ii) he takes all such steps as are reasonably practicable in the circumstances for minimising the extent of the discharge and of its polluting effects; and

(iii) as soon as reasonably practicable after the discharge occurs, particulars of the discharge are furnished to the river purification authority in whose area it occurs.

(5) A local authority shall not be guilty of an offence by virtue of subsection (1) of this section by reason only of the fact that a discharge from a sewer or works vested in the authority contravenes conditions of a consent relating to the discharge if—

(*a*) the contravention is attributable to a discharge which another person caused or permitted to be made into the sewer or works; and

(*b*) the authority either was not bound to receive the discharge into the sewer or works or was bound to receive it there subject to conditions but the conditions were not observed; and

(*c*) the authority could not reasonably have been expected to prevent the discharge into the sewer or works;

and a person shall not be guilty of such an offence in consequence of a discharge which he caused or permitted to be made into a sewer or works vested in a local authority if the authority was bound to receive the discharge there either unconditionally or subject to conditions which were observed.

(6) In subsection (2) of this section and the preceding subsection, 'local authority' means a local authority within the meaning of the Sewerage (Scotland) Act 1968.

(7) A person who is guilty of an offence by virtue of subsection (1) of this section shall be liable—

(*a*) on summary conviction, to imprisonment for a term not exceeding three months or a fine not exceeding the statutory maximum or both;

(*b*) on conviction on indictment, to imprisonment for a term not exceeding two years or a fine or both."

47–05   The Dumping at Sea Act 1974 was repealed by the Food and Environment Protection Act 1985 which sets up a licensing system for the depositing of things in the sea or under the sea bed. Section 9 makes it an offence to carry out these activities except in accordance with a licence. It is a defence to prove that the dumping was necessary in order to secure the safety of a vessel or marine structure or to save life, provided that the necessity was not due to the accused's own fault, and that the incident is notified within a reasonable time to the Minister of Agriculture, Fisheries and Food or the Secretary of State.

47–06   The Prevention of Oil Pollution Act 1986 inserts the following subsections into section 2 of the 1971 Act:

160

"(2A) If any oil or mixture containing oil is discharged as mentioned in paragraph (i) or (ii) below into waters (including inland waters) which—

(a) are landward of the line which for the time being is the baseline for measuring the breadth of the territorial waters of the United Kingdom; and

(b) are navigable by sea-going ships,

then, subject to the provisions of this Act, the following shall be guilty of an offence, that is to say—

(i) if the discharge is from a vessel, the owner or master of the vessel, unless he proves that the discharge took place and was caused as mentioned in paragraph (ii) below;

(ii) if the discharge is from a vessel but takes place in the course of a transfer of oil to or from another vessel or a place on land and is caused by the act or omission of any person in charge of any apparatus in that other vessel or that place, the owner or master of that other vessel or, as the case may be, the occupier of that place.

(2B) Subsection (2A) above shall not apply to any discharge which—

(a) is made into the sea; and

(b) is of a kind or is made in circumstances for the time being prescribed by regulations made by the Secretary of State."

Sections 1(1), (3) and (4) and 2(1)(a) and (b) were repealed by the Merchant Shipping (Prevention of Oil Pollution) Order 1983. Section 2(1)(a) and (b) is replaced by the relevant parts of the Merchant Shipping (Prevention of Oil Pollution) Regulations 1983, regulation 8 of which places an obligation on the owner or master of a vessel to obey the regulations: max. pen. a fine on indictment, £1,000 on summary conviction: reg. 34.

Both owner and master are liable to prosecution for breach of s.2(1): *Davies* v. *Smith*, 1983 S.C.C.R. 232.

47–11 Sched. 9 to the Roads (Scotland) Act 1984 amends section 62(1) by substituting "road" for "street" and removing the definition of "street." It also amends section 62(2)(e) by substituting "public road (within the meaning of the Roads (Scotland) Act 1984" for "highway."

CHAPTER 48

PERJURY AND ALLIED OFFENCES

48–08 Footnote 17. See now Act of Adjournal (Consolidation) 1988, Form 33. The forms are directive and not mandatory, and it is sufficient that the witness acknowledges his obligation to tell the truth: *McAvoy* v. *H.M.A.*, 1991 S.C.C.R. 123.

48–09 The earlier Oaths Acts are repealed and re-enacted in the Oaths Act 1978, s.5 of which provides:

"(1) Any person who objects to being sworn shall be permitted to make his solemn affirmation instead of taking an oath.

48–09
(2) Subsection (1) above shall apply in relation to a person to whom it is not reasonably practicable without inconvenience or delay to administer an oath in the manner appropriate to his religious belief as it applies in relation to a person objecting to be sworn.

(3) A person who may be permitted under subsection (2) above to make his solemn affirmation may also be required to do so.

(4) A solemn affirmation shall be of the same force and effect as an oath."

48–11
It has been held to be perjury for a witness to make a statement when he does not know whether it is true or not: *Simpson* v. *Tudhope*, 1988 S.L.T. 297.

48–14
It has now been held that materiality means no more than relevance, and is to be determined by the judge as a question of law. Any evidence which is competent and relevant either to proof of the charge or to the credibility of the witness can found a charge of perjury. The fact that the false evidence was trivial or insignificant is relevant only if it shows that the perjury was not wilful: *Lord Advocate's Reference (No. 1 of 1985)*, 1987 S.L.T. 187, disapproving paragraph 48–14 in the main work.

48–15
See also *Aitchison* v. *Simon*, 1976 S.L.T. (Sh.Ct.) 73.

48–16
48–17
Whether a statement was a precognition may be a question for the jury in the perjury trial: *Low* v. *H.M.A.*, 1988 S.L.T. 97.

A statement taken by a police officer on his own initiative may not be a precognition even if it is taken after the subsequent accused has appeared on petition: *H.M.A.* v. *McGachy,* 1991 S.C.C.R. 884.

48–17
See also *Aitchison* v. *Simon*, 1976 S.L.T. (Sh.Ct.) 73.

48–18
It was held by the Judicial Committee in *Tsang Ping-Nam* v. *The Queen* [1981] 1 W.L.R. 1462 that it is not an attempt to pervert the course of justice for a witness giving "Queen's Evidence" to resile from his original witness statement which had not been on oath.

48–25
Section 11 applies both to the European Court itself, and to "any court attached thereto": European Communities (Amendment) Act 1986, s.2.

48–27
The words "by a person . . . declare" were removed by the Administration of Justice Act 1977, Sched. 5.

48–34
It has been held in England that to give a person one knows to be a suspected criminal the registration numbers of unmarked police cars in order to assist his escape is an attempt to pervert the course of justice even where the giver does not know of the suspect's guilt, and does not act corruptly, dishonestly or threateningly: *R.* v. *Thomas (Derek)* [1979] Q.B. 326.

48–36
It has been held in England to be an attempt to pervert the course of justice for an accused to interfere with his portion of a blood specimen before sending it for analysis, with intent to pervert the

162

course of justice, but without doing anything further. This was on the view that the resultant false analysis would be bound to be communicated to the accused's solicitor or the police, so that there was risk of injustice, and that that risk was sufficient to constitute the offence: *R.* v. *Murray (Gordon)* [1982] 1 W.L.R. 475.

48–38 It is an offence to induce one's solicitor to provide a court with false information in a plea in mitigation: *H.M.A.* v. *Murphy*, 1978 J.C. 1.

48–39 It has been held to be a crime to make a false report of the loss of an article without any element of accusation, and also to make a false complaint about the behaviour of a police dog: *Bowers* v. *Tudhope*, 1987 S.L.T. 748; *Robertson* v. *Hamilton*, 1987 S.C.C.R. 477.

In *Walkingshaw* v. *Coid*, 1988 S.C.C.R. 454 the sheriff held that a charge that the accused had reported an assault on one of them to the police, and that at the subsequent trial they had all claimed that they could not recall the incident, was not a relevant charge of wasting police time in the absence of any averment that the original report was false.

48–40 Once investigations have begun with a view to identifying the culprit in an offence which is known to have been committed, the giving of any false information to the police may constitute an attempt to pervert the course of justice, as in *Dean* v. *Stewart*, 1980 S.L.T. (Notes) 85 where the driver of a car (which had failed to stop after an accident) and another man pretended that the other man had been driving the car. It seems, therefore, that to tell lies to the police when interviewed by them in the course of criminal investigation is a crime.

It has been held in England that it is not an attempt to pervert the course of justice to have endorsements removed from the DVLC records where this is not done with intent to interfere with any pending or imminent proceedings or investigations which might lead to proceedings: *R.* v. *Selvage* [1982] Q.B. 372.

There is still no general rule that telling lies to the police is a crime, but see *Waddell* v. *MacPhail*, 1986 S.C.C.R. 593; *infra*, para. 48–45.

48–41 For examples of wilfulness, see *Orr* v. *Annan*, 1988 S.L.T. 251.

48–42 The Road Traffic Act 1972 is replaced by the Road Traffic Act 1988, section 25 of the 1972 Act being now section 170 of the 1988 Act, as amended by Schedule 4 to the Road Traffic Act 1991.

48–43 Sections 161 and 162 are now sections 164 and 165 of the Road Traffic Act 1988, as amended by Schedule 4 to the Road Traffic Act 1991, which gives vehicle examiners some of the same powers as police constables.

48–44 Section 164 is now section 168 of the Road Traffic Act 1988. Sections 165 and 15 are now sections 169 and 37 respectively of the 1988 Act.

48–45 Sections 167 and 168 are now sections 171 and 172 respectively of the Road Traffic Act 1988.

Section 172, as substituted by section 21 of the Road Traffic Act 1991, provides:

"(1) This section applies—
(a) to any offence under the preceding provisions of this Act except—
    (i) an offence under Part V, or
    (ii) an offence under section 13, 16, 51(2), 61(4), 67(9), 68(4), 96 or 120,
and to an offence under section 178 of this Act,
(b) to any offence under sections 25, 26 or 27 of the Road Traffic Offenders Act 1988,
(c) to any offence against any other enactment relating to the use of vehicles on roads, except an offence under paragraph 8 of Schedule 1 to the Road Traffic (Driver Licensing and Information Systems) Act 1989, and
(d) to manslaughter, or in Scotland culpable homicide, by the driver of a motor vehicle.
(2) Where the driver of a vehicle is alleged to be guilty of an offence to which this section applies—
(a) the person keeping the vehicle shall give such information as to the identity of the driver as he may be required to give by or on behalf of a chief officer of police, and
(b) any other person shall if required as stated above give any information which it is in his power to give and may lead to identification of the driver.
(3) Subject to the following provision, a person who fails to comply with a requirement under subsection (2) above shall be guilty of an offence.
(4) A person shall not be guilty of an offence by virtue of paragraph (a) of subsection (2) above if he shows that he did not know and could not with reasonable diligence have ascertained who the driver of the vehicle was.
(5) Where a body corporate is guilty of an offence under this section and the offence is proved to have been committed with the consent or connivance of, or to be attributable to neglect on the part of, a director, manager, secretary or other similar officer of the body corporate, or a person who was purporting to act in any such capacity, he, as well as the body corporate, is guilty of that offence and liable to be proceeded against and punished accordingly.
(6) Where the alleged offender is a body corporate, or in Scotland a partnership or an unincorporated association, or the proceedings are brought against him by virtue of subsection (5) above or subsection (11) below, subsection (4) above shall not apply unless, in addition to the matters there mentioned, the alleged offender shows that no record was kept of the persons who drove the vehicle and that the failure to keep a record was reasonable.
(7) A requirement under subsection (2) may be made by written notice served by post; and where it is so made—
(a) it shall have effect as a requirement to give the information within the period of 28 days beginning with the day on which the notice is served, and
(b) the person on whom the notice is served shall not be guilty of an offence under this section if he shows either that he gave the information as soon as reasonably practicable after the end of that period or that it has not been reasonably practicable for him to give it.

(8) Where the person on whom a notice under subsection (7) above is to be served is a body corporate, the notice is duly served if it is served on the secretary or clerk of that body.

(9) For the purposes of section 7 of the Interpretation Act 1978 as it applies for the purposes of this section the proper address of any person in relation to the service on him of a notice under subsection (7) above is—

(*a*) in the case of the secretary or clerk of a body corporate, that of the registered or principal office of that body or (if the body corporate is the registered keeper of the vehicle concerned) the registered address, and

(*b*) in any other case, his last known address at the time of service.

(10) In this section—

'registered address,' in relation to the registered keeper of a vehicle, means the address recorded in the record kept under the Vehicles (Excise) Act 1971 with respect to that vehicle as being that person's address, and

'registered keeper,' in relation to a vehicle, means the person in whose name the vehicle is registered under that Act;

and references to the driver of a vehicle include references to the rider of a cycle.

(11) Where, in Scotland, an offence under this section is committed by a partnership or by an unincorporated association other than a partnership and is proved to have been committed with the consent or connivance or in consequence of the negligence of a partner in the partnership or, as the case may be, a person concerned in the management or control of the association, he (as well as the partnership or association) shall be guilty of the offence."

The right to require information depends on the officer being in possession of information which supports an allegation made by him of an offence which is ultimately charged: *Hingston* v. *Pollock*, 1990 J.C. 138; *Galt* v. *Goodsir*, 1982 J.C. 4.

Where the person asked for information goes beyond declining to provide it, and gives false information, he is guilty of attempting to pervert the course of justice: *Waddell* v. *MacPhail*, 1986 S.C.C.R. 593.

Footnote 17. See now Weights and Measures Act 1985, s.81(3).

CHAPTER 49

ESCAPES FROM LAWFUL CUSTODY

49–08   In *Fletcher* v. *Tudhope*, 1984 S.C.C.R. 267, it was held to be an attempt to pervert the course of justice to warn a person that he was about to be arrested, where the intention was to enable him to escape the police who were looking for him.

49–09   See, *e.g. Allan James Cairns Peden*, Criminal Appeal Court, March 1978, unreported, where someone who was under arrest tried to run away from the arresting officer; he was convicted of

49–09   attempting to pervert the course of justice. In *McAllister* v. *H.M. Advocate*, 1987 S.L.T. 552, the escape was from a hospital where the accused was in the custody of prison officers.

49–10   Section 12 is now section 13 of the Prisons (Scotland) Act 1989.

49–11   Borstal was abolished by section 45(3) of the Criminal Justice (Scotland) Act 1980.

49–12   Section 105 of the 1960 Act is now section 120 of the Mental Health (Scotland) Act 1984, section 61(5) of the 1960 Act now being section 68(5) of the 1984 Act.

Footnote 27. Section 72 of the 1967 Act was amended by Sched. 3 to the 1984 Act and applies to patients liable to be retaken under sections 28, 44 or 121 of the 1984 Act.

49–13   The 1960 Act was repealed and re-enacted as amended in the consolidating Mental Health (Scotland) Act 1984.

Footnote 28. See now Mental Health (Scotland) Act 1984, ss.28 and 62(1)(*c*).

49–14   Section 98 of the 1960 Act is now section 108 of the Mental Health (Scotland) Act 1984, section 103 of the 1960 Act now being section 120 of the 1984 Act.

49–15   Footnote 31. Max. pen. now nine months' imprisonment and a fine of the prescribed sum on summary conviction: Criminal Justice (Scotland) Act 1980, s.57.

49–16   In *Miln* v. *Stirton*, 1982 S.L.T. (Sh.Ct.) 11 it was held that a charge against a wife of attempting to defeat the ends of justice by harbouring her husband against whom, as she knew, there was an outstanding extract conviction warrant for his arrest, was incompetent; the sheriff followed Hume, i.49 and Alison, i.669. See now, however, *Smith* v. *Watson*, 1982 J.C. 34, *supra*, para. 20–05.

49–18   Section 98(2) of the 1960 Act is now section 108(2) of the Mental Health (Scotland) Act 1984.

49–19   Section 31 of the Merchant Shipping Act 1970 was repealed by section 19 of the Merchant Shipping Act 1974.

CHAPTER 50

OFFENCES IN CONNECTION WITH JUDICIAL OFFICIALS

50–02   Footnote 3: Max. pen. now nine months' imprisonment and a fine of the prescribed sum on summary conviction: Criminal Justice (Scotland) Act 1980, s.57.

50–04   See also *Maxwell* v. *H.M. Advocate*, 1980 J.C. 40.

CHAPTER 51

CONTEMPT OF COURT

51–01   Footnote 2. *H.M.A.* v. *Airs* is now reported at 1975 J.C. 64.

51–04   For a witness to be guilty of prevarication he must be shown to be deliberately refusing to give evidence it is proved he was able to give: *Childs* v. *McLeod*, 1981 S.L.T. (Notes) 27. For the procedure in dealing with such a witness, see *Hutchison* v. *H.M.A.*, 1984 S.L.T. 233.

Footnote 24. See also *Bacon, Petr.*, 1986 S.C.C.R. 265; *Smith, Petr.*, 1987 S.C.C.R. 726.

Add new paragraph **51–04a**:

51–04a   Section 10 of the Contempt of Court Act 1981, which affects the decision in *H.M. Advocate* v. *Airs*, 1975 J.C. 64, provides:

> "No court may require a person to disclose, nor is any person guilty of contempt of court for refusing to disclose, the source of information contained in a publication for which he is responsible, unless it be established to the satisfaction of the court that disclosure is necessary in the interests of justice or national security or for the prevention of disorder or crime."

51–05   An accused who refuses to appear in court and insists on remaining in the court cells is in contempt of the court: *Dawes* v. *Cardle*, 1987 S.C.C.R. 135.

51–06   The maximum penalty under section 344 is now a fine of level 3 or twenty-one days' imprisonment: Criminal Justice Act 1982, Sched. 7. Presumably conduct covered by the section should be prosecuted under the section, and not under the general law of contempt which provides for greater penalties: see Contempt of Court Act 1981, s.15(2).

51–10   It has been held in England that where documents are made available by a party under an order to produce them in proceedings it is a contempt of court for them to be made publicly available by the other party: *Home Office* v. *Harman* [1983] 1 A.C. 280.

51–11   To introduce references to an immediately pending trial for assaulting a patient with severe brain damage by trying to block her air supply into a television programme dealing with the issue of maintaining life-support systems for such patients may be a contempt of court, and will certainly be so if the

51–11 references are such as to suggest that the accused was carrying out a policy of withdrawing such support: *Atkins* v. *London Weekend Television Ltd.*, 1978 J.C. 48, a rare case where the prosecution was abandoned because of the contempt. Where prosecutions have continued after contempt by prejudicial publicity they have been held to be competent on the ground that the contempt occurred some time before the trial so that its continuing effect, if any, could be countered by appropriate directions to the jury: *Stuurman* v. *H.M.A.*, 1980 J.C. 111; *X.* v. *Sweeney*, 1982 J.C. 70. For cases in summary procedure, see *Tudhope* v. *Glass*, 1981 S.C.C.R. 336; *Aitchison* v. *Bernardi*, 1984 S.L.T. 343.

The court in *Atkins, supra,* recognised it as part of the common law that prejudice which is an incidental and unintended by-product of a discussion of public affairs is not contempt, and s.5 of the Contempt of Court Act 1981 now provides that a publication made as part of a discussion in good faith of public affairs or other matters of general public interest is not to be treated as contempt under the strict liability rule if the risk of impediment or prejudice to particular legal proceedings is merely incidental to the discussion. This defence would not have succeeded in *Atkins*, since the reference to the particular case was specific and deliberate. The court might also have held that in any event in the circumstances responsibility did not depend on the strict liability rule but on recklessness, since they described the respondents as having "undoubtedly chose[n] to sail very close to the wind and [taken] what they must have recognised was a calculated risk": at 56. Section 5 is at least in part a consequence of the decision of the European Court of Human Rights in *Sunday Times Ltd.* v. *United Kingdom* [1979] 2 E.H.R.R. 245 in which the decision of the House of Lords in *Att.-Gen.* v. *Times Newspapers Ltd.* [1974] A.C. 273 was criticised. On the interpretation of s.5 see *Att.-Gen.* v. *English* [1983] 1 A.C. 116.

Merely to report that a witness has been given police protection and is being kept during a trial at a secret address where this is in fact so, is not a contempt: *Kemp, Petr.*; *The Scotsman Publications Ltd., Petrs.*, 1982 J.C. 29.

Footnote 37. Add: *Atkins* v. *London Weekend Television Ltd.*, 1978 J.C. 48; *H.M.A.* v. *George Outram & Co. Ltd.*, 1980 J.C. 51; *H.M.A.* v. *News Group Newspapers Ltd.*, 1989 S.C.C.R. 156.

51–12 It was held in the Full Bench case of *Hall* v. *Associated Newspapers Ltd.*, 1979 J.C. 1 (see Angela M. MacLean, "Contempt in Criminal Process," 1978 S.L.T. (News) 257) that the court's jurisdiction in contempt begins when the accused is arrested or when a warrant for his arrest is granted, or (in summary proceedings) from the service of the complaint, whichever is earliest. The statement in *Stirling* v. *Associated Newspapers Ltd.* that jurisdiction arises the moment a crime is committed was rejected by the court in *Hall*. They held, however, that it was not a defence that the offenders were unaware that there had been an arrest or that an arrest warrant had been issued, but that statement must now be read subject to the Contempt of Court Act 1981; see *infra*, para. 51–14a.

Where the statement complained of is made with the intention of creating prejudice it may, of course, be punishable as a contempt or as an attempt to pervert the course of justice, at whatever stage of the investigation it is made, or even if it is made before any investigation has begun: *supra*, para. 48–40; *Hall, supra*, L.J.-G. at 15; *Skeen* v. *Farmer*, 1980 S.L.T. (Sh.Ct.) 133; Contempt of Court Act 1981, s.6(*c*).

51–14   The need for the contempt to be deliberate was stressed in a number of recent cases involving the failure of solicitors to appear timeously in court: *Macara* v. *MacFarlane*, 1980 S.L.T. (Notes) 26; *McKinnon* v. *Douglas*, 1982 S.C.C.R. 80. Where the solicitor arranges his affairs so as deliberately to take the risk of delaying proceedings by being late, he may be guilty of contempt: *Muirhead* v. *Douglas*, 1979 S.L.T. (Notes) 17.

Add new paragraphs **51–14a** to **15–14e**:

51–14a   CONTEMPT OF COURT ACT 1981. Sections 1 to 6 of this Act limit the application of the rule that *mens rea* is unnecessary in relation to conduct which constitutes contempt as tending to interfere with the course of justice in particular legal proceedings, which the Act calls "the strict liability rule."

Section 2, as amended by the Broadcasting Act 1990, Sched. 20, provides:

> "(1) The strict liability rule applies only in relation to publications, and for this purpose 'publication' includes any speech, writing, programme included in a programme service or other communication in whatever form, which is addressed to the public at large or any section of the public.
>
> (2) The strict liability rule applies only to a publication which creates a substantial risk that the course of justice in the proceedings in question will be seriously impeded or prejudiced.
>
> (3) The strict liability rule applies to a publication only if the proceedings in question are active within the meaning of this section at the time of the publication.
>
> (4) Schedule 1 applies for determining the times at which proceedings are to be treated as active within the meaning of this section.
>
> (5) In this section 'programme service' has the same meaning as in the Broadcasting Act 1990."

"Proceedings" include proceedings in any tribunal or body exercising the judicial power of the State; proceedings before United Kingdom courts sitting in Scotland, as well as before the House of Lords in appeals from any court sitting in Scotland are treated as Scottish proceedings: s.19.

Criminal proceedings (*i.e.* proceedings against a person in respect of an offence, other than appellate proceedings) are active from the stage of arrest or the grant of a warrant of arrest, or from the grant of a warrant to cite, or from the service of an indictment or other document specifying a charge, whichever is the earliest, until they are concluded by acquittal or sentence, or by any other order putting an end to the proceedings, or by discontinuance or operation of law: Sched. 1, paras. 3 to 5. "Sentence" includes a deferred

51–14a   sentence under sections 219 or 432 of the 1975 Act, so that the strict liability rule may cease to apply before the accused is actually disposed of: Sched. 1, para. 6. The Act specifically provides that express abandonment or desertion simpliciter constitutes a discontinuance: *ibid.*, para. 7(*b*), so it appears that desertion *pro loco et tempore* does not. A finding of insanity in bar of trial consitutes a discontinuance of the proceedings, but they become active again if they are resumed: *ibid.*, para. 10(*a*).

Where proceedings begin with the grant of an arrest warrant, they cease to be active after twelve months if there has been no arrest, but revive with a subsequent arrest: *ibid.*, para. 11.

Appellate proceedings are active from the time they are begun by notice of appeal or application for a stated case until they are "disposed of or abandoned, discontinued or withdrawn": *ibid.*, para. 15. When the appeal court remits the case to the lower court or grants authority for a retrial, any further or new proceedings become active from the conclusion of the appeal proceedings: *ibid.*, para. 16.

51–14b   Section 3 of the Contempt of Court Act 1981 provides a specific defence of reasonable care which limits the application of the strict liability rule even in those cases where it applies by reason of section 2 of the Act. It provides:

> "(1) A person is not guilty of contempt of court under the strict liability rule as the publisher of any matter to which that rule applies if at the time of publication (having taken all reasonable care) he does not know and has no reason to suspect that relevant proceedings are active.
> (2) A person is not guilty of contempt of court under the strict liability rule as the distributor of a publication containing any such matter if at the time of distribution (having taken all reasonable care) he does not know that it contains such matter and has no reason to suspect that it is likely to do so.
> (3) The burden of proof of any fact tending to establish a defence afforded by this section to any person lies upon that person."

51–14c   The strict liability rule does not apply to publication as part of a bona fide discussion of matters of public interest if the risk of prejudice is merely incidental: Contempt of Court Act 1981, s.5; see *supra*, para. 51–11.

51–14d   Section 6 of the Contempt of Court Act 1981 specifically provides that the preceding sections of the Act will not (*a*) prejudice any common law defence to strict liability contempt, (*b*) make any publication a contempt which would not otherwise have been so, or (*c*) restrict liability for contempt in respect of conduct intended to impede or prejudice the administration of justice.

51–14e   The maximum penalty for contempt is now two years' imprisonment and a fine where the contempt relates to proceedings on indictment. In relation to summary proceedings it is three months' imprisonment and a fine of level 4 in the sheriff court and sixty days and a fine of level 4 in the district court: Contempt of Court Act 1981, s.15(2); Criminal Justice Act 1982, Sched. 7. It is no longer competent to order a person to be detained until he purges his contempt, but the court may discharge the offender before the conclusion of the fixed term of imprisonment imposed: *ibid.*, s.15(1).

51–15 Section 9 of the Contempt of Court Act 1981 prohibits the use of sound recording devices in court without leave, except for the purpose of official transcripts. There is apparently no prohibition on making silent films. Section 9 provides:

> "(1) Subject to subsection (4) below, it is a contempt of court—
> (*a*) to use in court, or bring into court for use, any tape recorder or other instrument for recording sound, except with the leave of the court;
> (*b*) to publish a recording of legal proceedings made by means of any such instrument, or any recording derived directly or indirectly from it, by playing it in the hearing of the public or any section of the public, or to dispose of it or any recording so derived, with a view to such publication;
> (*c*) to use any such recording in contravention of any conditions of leave granted under paragraph (*a*).
> (2) Leave under paragraph (*a*) of subsection (1) may be granted or refused at the discretion of the court, and if granted may be granted subject to such conditions as the court thinks proper with respect to the use of any recording made pursuant to the leave; and where leave has been granted the court may at the like discretion withdraw or amend it either generally or in relation to any particular of the proceedings.
> (3) Without prejudice to any other power to deal with an act of contempt under paragraph (*a*) of subsection (1), the court may order the instrument, or any recording made with it, or both, to be forfeited; and any object so forfeited shall (unless the court otherwise determines on application by a person appearing to be the owner) be sold or otherwise disposed of in such manner as the court may direct.
> (4) This section does not apply to the making or use of sound recordings for purposes of official transcripts of proceedings."

Add new paragraphs **51–15a** to **51–15c**:

51–15a CONTEMPT OF COURT ACT 1981. The common law rule is preserved by section 4(1) of the Contempt of Court Act 1981, which provides:

> "(1) Subject to this section a person is not guilty of contempt of court under the strict liability rule in respect of a fair and accurate report of legal proceedings held in public, published contemporaneously and in good faith."

Publication may, however, be restricted by the court in terms of section 4(2) which provides:

> "(2) In any such proceedings the court may, where it appears to be necessary for avoiding a substantial risk of prejudice to the administration of justice in those proceedings, or in any other proceedings pending or imminent, order that the publication of any report of the proceedings, or any part of the proceedings, be postponed for such period as the court thinks necessary for that purpose."

(See *R.* v. *Horsham JJ., ex p. Farquharson* [1982] Q.B. 762; *Keane* v. *H.M.A.*, 1987 S.L.T. 220).

51–15a   Publication of a report which is postponed by an order under s.4(2) is contemporaneous if it is published as soon as practicable after the expiry of the order: s.4(3)(*a*).

51–15b   Where a court allows a name or other matter to be withheld from the public in court proceedings it may give such directions prohibiting its publication in connection with the proceedings as appear necessary for the purpose for which it was withheld: Contempt of Court Act 1981, s.11.

51–15c   Section 8 of the Act renders jury deliberations confidential. It provides:

> "(1) Subject to subsection (2) below, it is a contempt of court to obtain, disclose or solicit any particulars of statements made, opinions expressed, arguments advanced or votes cast by members of a jury in the course of their deliberations in any legal proceedings.
> (2) This section does not apply to any disclosure of any particulars—
> (*a*) in the proceedings in question for the purpose of enabling the jury to arrive at their verdict, or in connection with the delivery of that verdict, or
> (*b*) in evidence in any subsequent proceedings for an offence alleged to have been committed in relation to the jury in the first mentioned proceedings,
> or to the publication of any particulars so disclosed."

It may also not apply to inquiries conducted on behalf of the Criminal Appeal Court under section 252(*d*) of the Criminal Procedure (Scotland) Act 1975: *McCadden* v. *H.M.A.*, 1985 J.C. 98.

51–17   Section 169 is rewritten by section 22 of the Criminal Justice (Scotland) Act 1980, and now reads as follows:

> "(1) No newspaper report of any proceedings in a court shall reveal the name, address or school, or include any particulars calculated to lead to the identification, of any person under the age of 16 years concerned in the proceedings, either—
> (*a*) as being a person against or in respect of whom the proceedings are taken; or
> (*b*) as being a witness therein;
> nor shall any picture which is, or includes, a picture of a person under the age of 16 years so concerned in the proceedings be published in any newspaper in a context relevant to the proceedings:
> Provided that, in any case—
> (i) where the person is concerned in the proceedings as a witness only and no one against whom the proceedings are taken is under the age of 16 years, the foregoing provisions of this subsection shall not apply unless the court so directs;
> (ii) the court may at any stage of the proceedings if satisfied that it is in the public interest so to do, direct that the requirements of this section (including such requirements as applied by a direction under paragraph (i) above) shall be dispensed with to such extent as the court may specify;
> (iii) the Secretary of State may, after completion of the proceedings, if so satisfied by order dispense with the said requirements to such extent as may be specified in the order.
> (2) This section shall, with the necessary modifications, apply in relation to sound and television broadcasts as it applies in relation to newspapers.

(3) A person who publishes matter in contravention of this section shall be guilty of an offence and liable on summary conviction to a fine not exceeding [level 4 on the standard scale].

(4) In this section, references to a court shall not include a court in England, Wales or Northern Ireland."

Section 365 of the 1975 Act is repealed by Sched. 8 to the Criminal Justice (Scotland) Act 1980.

Footnote 61. The sections are applied by Sched. 20 to the Broadcasting Act 1990 to any programme included in a programme service as defined by that Act.

51–18 Section 374 is rewritten by s.22 of the Criminal Justice (Scotland) Act 1980, and is now in the same terms as s.169 of the 1975 Act; *supra*, para. 51–17.

51–19 Section 58 is applied by Schedule 20 to the Broadcasting Act 1990 to any programme included in a programme service as defined by that Act.

Add new paragraphs **51–20** and **51–21**:

51–20 *Fatal Accident Inquiries.* Section 4(4) of the Fatal Accidents and Sudden Deaths Inquiry (Scotland) Act 1976 empowers the sheriff to make an order prohibiting the publication of details leading to the identification of persons under the age of seventeen. Breach of such a prohibition is a summary offence: maximum penalty a fine of level 4: s.4(5).

51–21 *Committal Proceedings.* It is an offence to publish anywhere in Britain any details of committal proceedings in England and Wales which result in the committal of anyone for trial until after the trial unless the magistrates' court on application by an accused permits publication: Magistrates' Courts Act 1980, s.8; maximum penalty a fine of level 3. This prohibition does not extend to the limited information as to the names of those concerned, the place of committal and the charges involved set out in s.8(4) of the Magistrates' Courts Act.

CHAPTER 52

GAME LAWS

(For detailed discussions of game laws see Stanley Scott Robinson, *The Law of Game, Salmon and Freshwater Fishing in Scotland* (Edinburgh, 1990) and the article on "Game" in the *Stair Memorial Encyclopaedia*.)

52–04 Section 43(1) of the Agriculture (Scotland) Act 1948 is repealed by the Deer (Amendment) (Scotland) Act 1982, and is replaced by s.33(3) to (4E) of the Deer (Scotland) Act 1959 as substituted by s.13 of the said Act of 1982.

52–10   "Game" does not include deer: *Ferguson* v. *MacPhail*, 1987 S.C.C.R. 52.

52–18   The provision quoted is now section 22(1), and it applies also to intentionally injuring deer: Deer (Amendment) (Scotland) Act 1982, s.6.

Section 22(2) makes it an offence, subject to section 33, for any person without legal right to take or kill deer on any land, or without permission from someone having such right, to remove any deer carcass from that land: Deer (Amendment) (Scotland) Act 1982, s.6(*c*). This provision follows on the decision in *Miln* v. *Maher*, 1979 J.C. 58 that "takes" in section 22(1) refers to the capture of a live deer and does not extend to the removal of a deer one has killed: the maximum penalty for contravening any provision of section 22 is now a fine of level 4 per deer or carcass and three months' imprisonment and forfeiture of the deer or carcass: Deer (Amendment) (Scotland) Act 1982, s.6(3)(*c*); Sched. 1. The court may also cancel any firearm or shotgun certificate held by the offender: Deer (Scotland) Act 1959, s.28A, as inserted by Deer (Amendment) (Scotland) Act 1982, Sched. 2.

Max. pen. under s.24 is now a fine of level 5 per deer and six months' imprisonment, and forfeiture of the deer: Deer (Amendment) (Scotland) Act 1982, Sched. 1. Max. pen. for preparatory acts is now a fine of level 4 and three months' imprisonment: Deer (Amendment) (Scotland) Act 1982, Sched. 1.

52–25   Footnote 79. The Protection of Birds Act 1954 is now replaced by the Wildlife and Countryside Act 1981, of which see Sched. 1.

52–26   Section 21 now applies to wilful injuring as well as to taking or killing: Deer (Amendment) (Scotland) Act 1982, s.6(*a*).

Section 21 does not apply to the killing of deer by or on behalf of any person who keeps those deer by way of business on land enclosed by a deer-proof barrier for the production of meat or skins or other by-products, or as breeding stock, provided the deer are clearly marked to show that they are so kept: s.21(5A) as inserted by Deer (Amendment) (Scotland) Act 1982, s.7.

Max. pen. as for contraventions of s.22: *supra*, para. 52–18.

52–29   For maximum penalty for preparatory acts, see *supra*, para. 52–18.

52–32   Section 23(2A) to (2C) of the Deer (Scotland) Act 1959, as inserted by section 8(1) of the Deer (Amendment) (Scotland) Act 1982 provides:

> "Subject to subsection (2B) below and section 33(1) of this Act, if any person—
> (*a*) discharges any firearm, or discharges or projects any missile, from any aircraft at any deer; or
> (*b*) notwithstanding the provisions of section 23(5) of this Act uses any aircraft for the purpose of transporting any live deer other than in the interior of the aircraft,
> he shall be guilty of an offence.

(2B) Nothing in subsection (2A)(*b*) above shall make unlawful anything done by, or under the supervision of, a veterinary surgeon or practitioner.

(2C) In subsection (2B) above 'veterinary practitioner' means a person who is for the time being registered in the supplementary register, and 'veterinary surgeon' means a person who is for the time being registered in the register of veterinary surgeons."

For s.33(1) see para. 52–18 in the main work.

Section 23A of the Deer (Scotland) Act 1959, as inserted by section 10 of the Deer (Amendment) (Scotland) Act 1982, empowers the Secretary of State to make orders regarding the classes of firearms, ammunition, sights and other equipment which may lawfully be used to kill deer and the circumstances in which they may be so used. Breach of such an order is punishable by a fine of level 4 for each deer taken or killed and three months' imprisonment: s.23A(3). The court may also cancel any firearm or shotgun certificate held by the offender: Deer (Scotland) Act 1959, s.28A, as inserted by Deer (Amendment) (Scotland) Act 1982, Sched. 2.

Section 23A(5) makes it a summary offence to use any firearm or ammunition for the purpose of wilfully injuring deer: maximum penalty as above.

Add new paragraph **52–32a**:

52–32a   *Use of Vehicle to Drive Deer.* Section 23(3A) of the Deer (Scotland) Act 1959, as inserted by section 9 of the Deer (Amendment) (Scotland) Act 1982, makes it an offence to use a vehicle to drive deer on unenclosed land with intent to take, kill or injure them: max. pen. a fine of level 4 per deer and three months' imprisonment.

52–33   The Protection of Wild Birds Act 1954 is replaced by the Wildlife and Countryside Act 1981, and section 5(1)(*d*) of the 1954 Act is now section 5(1)(*c*) of that Act: *infra*, para. 52–36.

52–36   The Protection of Wild Birds Act 1954 is repealed by the Wildlife and Countryside Act 1981 and section 5(1) of the 1954 Act is substantially re-enacted by section 5 of that Act which , as amended by the Wildlife and Countryside (Amendment) Act 1991 provides:

"(1) Subject to the provisions of this Part, if any person—
(*a*) sets in position any of the following articles, being an article which is of such a nature and is so placed as to be calculated to cause bodily injury to any wild bird coming into contact therewith, that is to say, any springe, trap, gin, snare, hook and line, any electrical device for killing, stunning or frightening or any poisonous, poisoned or stupefying substance;
(*b*) uses for the purpose of killing or taking any wild bird any such article as aforesaid, whether or not of such a nature and so placed as aforesaid, or any net, baited board, bird-lime or substance of a like nature to bird-lime;
(*c*) uses for the purpose of killing or taking any wild bird—
   (i) any bow or crossbow;
   (ii) any explosive other than ammunition for a firearm;

       (iii) any automatic or semi-automatic weapon;
       (iv) any shot-gun of which the barrel has an internal diameter at the muzzle of more than one and three-quarter inches;
       (v) any device for illuminating a target or any sighting device for night shooting;
       (vi) any form of artificial lighting or any mirror or other dazzling device;
       (vii) any gas or smoke not falling within paragraphs (*a*) and (*b*); or
       (viii) any chemical wetting agent;
  (*d*) uses as a decoy, for the purpose of killing or taking any wild bird, any sound recording or any live bird or other animal whatever which is tethered, or which is secured by means of braces or other similar appliances, or which is blind, maimed or injured; or
  (*e*) uses any mechanically propelled vehicle in immediate pursuit of a wild bird for the purpose of killing or taking that bird; or
  (*f*) knowingly causes or permits to be done an act which is mentioned in the foregoing provisions of this subsection and which is not unlawful under subsection (5),
he shall be guilty of an offence and be liable to a special penalty."

The remainder of section 5 of the Wildlife and Countryside Act 1981 is as follows:

"(2) Subject to subsection (3), the Secretary of State may by order, either generally or in relation to any kind of wild bird specified in the order, amend subsection (1) by adding any method of killing or taking wild birds or by omitting any such method which is mentioned in that subsection.

(3) The power conferred by subsection (2) shall not be exerciseable, except for the purpose of complying with an international obligation, in relation to any method of killing or taking wild birds which involves the use of a firearm.

(4) In any proceedings under subsection (1)(*a*) it shall be a defence to show that the article was set in position for the purpose of killing or taking, in the interests of public health, agriculture, forestry, fisheries or nature conservation, any wild animals which could be lawfully killed or taken by those means and that he took all reasonable precautions to prevent injury thereby to wild birds.

(4A) In any proceedings under subsection (1)(*f*) relating to an act which is mentioned in subsection (1)(*a*) it shall be a defence to show that the article was set in position for the purpose of killing or taking, in the interests of public health, agriculture, forestry, fisheries or nature conservation, any wild animals which could be lawfully killed or taken by those means and that he took or caused to be taken all reasonable precautions to prevent injury thereby to wild birds.

(5) Nothing in subsection (1) shall make unlawful—

  (*a*) the use of a cage-trap or net by an authorised person for the purpose of taking a bird included in Part II of Schedule 2;
  (*b*) the use of nets for the purpose of taking wild duck in a duck decoy which is shown to have been in use immediately before the passing of the Protection of Birds Act 1954; or
  (*c*) the use of a cage-trap or net for the purpose of taking any game bird if it is shown that the taking of the bird is solely for the purpose of breeding;

but nothing in this subsection shall make lawful the use of any net for taking birds in flight or the use for taking birds on the ground of any net which is projected or propelled otherwise than by hand."

52–36   Footnotes 9, 10. Max. pen. now a fine of level 4: Criminal Justice
52–37   Act 1982, Sched. 6.

52–39   Section 5(1)(*a*) of the Protection of Wild Birds Act 1954 is now
section 5(1)(*a*) of the Wildlife and Countryside Act 1981: *supra*,
para. 52–36.

52–40   Section 5(1)(*a*) is now section 5(1)(*a*) of the Wildlife and Countryside Act 1981, and section 5(3) of the 1954 Act is now section
5(1)(*e*) of the Act: see *supra*, para. 52–36.

52–42   Footnote 27. Add *Wyper* v. *O'Brien*, 1990 J.C. 23.

CHAPTER 53

FISHING LAWS

(For detailed discussions of fishing laws see Stanley Scott Robin-
son, *The Law of Game, Salmon and Freshwater Fishing in Scotland*
(Edinburgh, 1990) and the article on "Fisheries" in the *Stair
Memorial Encyclopaedia*).

53–02   Footnote 2. The 1862 Act was repealed by the Salmon Act 1986.

53–05   Although the Schedules to the 1868 Act containing the byelaws
to   were repealed by the Salmon Act 1986, the byelaws which were
53–19   made under section 6(6) of the repealed Salmon Fisheries (Scotland) Act 1862 and which relate to close times and methods of
fishing are kept in force by section 3 of the Salmon Act 1986 so far
as not inconsistent with any Regulations made under that section.

53–07   "Low water mark" is replaced by "mean low water springs":
Salmon Act 1986, Sched. 4.

53–08   The Salmon Fisheries (Scotland) Act 1828 was repealed by the
Statute Law (Repeals) Act 1977.
    The taking of trout by set lines was prohibited by the Trout
(Scotland) Act 1860, and is therefore illegal under sections 2(2) and
24(2) of the Salmon and Freshwater Fisheries (Scotland) Act 1951
which repealed the 1860 Act. Rods which are left lying on the
ground with lines trailing in the water are set lines even though they
are not secured to the ground in any way: *Lockhart* v. *Cowan and
Anr.*, 1980 S.L.T. (Sh.Ct.) 91.
    Section 21 of the Salmon Act 1986 inserts a new subsection 2(1A)
into the 1951 Act, which prohibits the fishing for or taking of salmon
in any waters in a salmon fishery district other than inland waters,
except by rod and line, net and coble or bag net, fly net or other
stake net. The 1986 Act also inserts a new section 2(2A) into the
1951 Act, which empowers the Secretary of State to define net and
coble, bag net, fly net or other stake net.

53–11   Section 22 of the Salmon Act 1986 inserts the following additional
section 7A in the 1951 Act:

"(1) A person who—

(*a*) is in possession of salmon and believes; or

(*b*) is in possession of salmon in circumstances in which it would be reasonable for him to suspect

that a relevant offence has at any time been committed in relation to the salmon shall be guilty of an offence and liable—

(i) on summary conviction to imprisonment for a term not exceeding three months, or to a fine not exceeding the statutory maximum or both;

(ii) on conviction on indictment to imprisonment for a term not exceeding two years, or to a fine or both.

(2) It shall be a defence in proceedings for an offence under this section to show that no relevant offence had in fact been committed in relation to the salmon.

(3) It shall be lawful to convict a person charged under this section on the evidence of one witness.

(4) For the purposes of this section an offence is a relevant offence in relation to a salmon if—

(*a*) it is committed by taking, killing or landing that salmon, either in Scotland or in England and Wales; or

(*b*) that salmon is taken, killed or landed, either in Scotland or in England and Wales in the course of the commission of the offence.

(5) In subsection (4) above, 'offence,' in relation to the taking, killing or landing of salmon either in Scotland or in England or Wales, means an offence under the law applicable to the place where the salmon is taken, killed or landed.

(6) A person shall not be guilty of an offence under this section in respect of conduct which constitutes a relevant offence in relation to any salmon or in respect of anything done in good faith for purposes connected with the prevention or detection of crime or the investigation or treatment of disease.

(7) Where an offence under this Act committed by a body corporate is proved to have been committed with the consent or connivance of, or to be attributable to any neglect on the part of, any director, manager, secretary or other similar officer of the body corporate, or any person who was purporting to act in any such capacity, he as well as the body corporate shall be guilty of the offence and shall be liable to be proceeded against and punished accordingly.

(8) Where the affairs of a body corporate are managed by its members, subsection (7) above shall apply in relation to the acts and defaults of a member in connection with his functions of management as if he were a director of the body corporate."

A person charged with an offence under section 7 or 7A may be convicted of either offence, or of a contravention of section 21 of the Salmon Fisheries (Scotland) Act 1868 or section 10 of the Tweed Fisheries Amendment Act 1859 or of reset: Salmon Act 1986, s.23.

A person convicted of unlawful fishing under section 1 or 2 of the Act cannot also be convicted under section 7 of unlawful possession of the fish so caught or the instruments used to catch them: *Wyper* v. *O'Brien*, 1990 J.C. 23.

Footnote 30. See also *Corbett* v. *MacNaughton*, 1985 J.C. 8.

53–13 Section 9 does not now apply to salmon: Salmon Act 1986, Sched. 4. Section 28(1) of the 1986 Act exempts from conviction acts or omissions relating to salmon or salmon roe or eggs done for scientific purposes, or for the purpose of developing stocks of fish or conserving any creature or other living thing, if done with the permission of the Secretary of State or a district board.

Section 27(1) of the 1986 Act gives the Secretary of State a general power to exempt from conviction any act or omission relating to fishing for or taking salmon, if local fishery owners and the district board have consented to it.

53–14 Section 15(7) was repealed by section 5(1) of the Salmon Act 1986.

The Salmon Act 1696 was repealed by the Salmon Act 1986.

Footnote 33. The forfeiture provisions of the 1951 Act are applied to offences under s.15 of the 1868 Act by s.5(1) of the Salmon Act 1986.

53–15 The Secretary of State has power to amend section 13 by Regulations, but not to reduce the periods specified in the section: Salmon Act 1986, s.3(3). Section 13(2) has been amended by inserting "Friday" before "Saturday," and section 13(3) has been amended so as to make the weekly close time run from 6 p.m. on Friday to 6 a.m. on Monday: Salmon (Weekly Close Time) (Scotland) Regulations 1988.

53–16 The Secretary of State has power to make regulations regarding the observance of the weekly close time, the construction of cruives, etc., and the size of nets: Salmon Act 1986, s.3.

Footnote 41. Add: *Cf. Fishmongers' Company* v. *Bruce*, 1980 S.L.T. (Notes) 35.

53–17 The annual close time can now be set by designation order by the Secretary of State, but must still be a continuous period of not less than 168 days: Salmon Act 1986, s.6.

53–18 A person charged with a contravention of section 21 of the 1868 Act may be convicted of contravening sections 7, 7A or 10 of the Salmon Act 1986: Salmon Act 1986, s.23.

53–21 The last phrase, from "or to any person" onwards, was deleted by Schedule 4 to the Salmon Act 1986.

53–22 The words from "uses" to "purpose or" were deleted by Schedule 4 to the Salmon Act 1986.

53–23 The words from "for the purpose of artificial" to "purpose or," were deleted by Schedule 4 to the Salmon Act 1986.

53–24 The Salmon Acts Amendment Act 1863 was repealed by the Salmon Act 1986.

53–26 The use of fixed engines in the Solway is prohibited by section 7B of the Salmon and Freshwater Fisheries (Protection) (Scotland) Act 1951, as inserted by section 25 of the Salmon Act 1986.

53–26   Section 1 of the Salmon and Freshwater Fisheries (Protection) (Scotland) Act 1951 (and sections 3 and 18 to 20 so far as relating to offences under section 1) apply to the Esk: Salmon Act 1986, s.26.

53–27   Footnote 73. The Fisheries (Scotland) Act 1756 was repealed by the Statute Law (Repeals) Act 1978.
Footnote 74. The Sea Fish Industry Act 1970 was substantially repealed and replaced by the Fisheries Act 1981.

53–28   The prohibition imposed by s.2(2)(*b*) of the Fishery Limits Act 1976 on fishing by foreign boats applies only to boats which have entered British waters for a recognised purpose; boats which have entered in order to fish illegally should be charged with illegal entry under section 2(2)(*a*): *Mackenzie* v. *Uribe*, 1983 J.C. 39.
In the last paragraph, for "poinding," read "arrestment": Debtors (Scotland) Act 1987, Sched. 6.

53–29   The Herring Fisheries (Scotland) Act 1867 was repealed by the Inshore Fishing (Scotland) Act 1984, which gives the Secretary of State power to prohibit all fishing, or fishing of a specified kind, in a specified sea area, and also to prohibit the carriage of specified nets. Section 4 of the Act makes it an offence to contravene any order made under the Act: max. pen. a fine on indictment, £5,000 on summary conviction and forfeiture. For the European dimension, so to speak, see *Walkingshaw* v. *Marshall*, 1991 S.C.C.R. 397. Section 1(3) of the Act requires any prohibited fish which are caught during lawful fishing operations but which are of a prohibited kind or are caught by a prohibited method to be returned to the sea: max. pen. as above.
Section 3 of the Inshore Fishing (Scotland) Act 1984 makes it an offence to fish by means of a trawl, seine or other fishing gear from a moving vessel within half of a mile of any fixed salmon net: max. pen. as above.

53–30   Section 4 of the Sea Fisheries (Scotland) Amendment Act 1885 was repealed by the Inshore Fishing (Scotland) Act 1984.

Footnote 77. Max. pen. now three months and a fine of level 5, and forfeiture: Criminal Justice Act 1982, Sched. 6.

53–31   Section 6 of the Sea Fish (Conservation) Act 1967 was amended by section 23 of the Fisheries Act 1981, and section 6(1A) gives power to prohibit the transhipment within British fishery limits of sea fish or any particular description of sea fish, being fish caught in any waters specified by order.
Section 1 of the Sea Fish (Conservation) Act 1967 is now as substituted by s.19 of the Fisheries Act 1981.

Footnote 79. Max. pen. on summary conviction under section 6 of the Sea Fish (Conservation) Act is now £50,000: Fisheries Act 1981, s.24.

53–32   The Sea Fish Industry Act 1970 is replaced by the Fisheries Act 1981 which empowers the Government to prohibit the landing or sale of fish of a smaller size than that prescribed: s.1. The 1981 Act also deals with the licensing of fishing boats, mainly by inserting additional provisions in the Sea Fish (Conservation) Act 1967.

53–33 to 53–36   These provisions were all repealed by the Inshore Fishing (Scotland) Act 1984.

53–33   Footnote 91. Maximum penalty six months' imprisonment and a fine of level 5: Criminal Justice Act 1982, Sched. 6.

53–37   The Whale Fisheries (Scotland) Act 1907 was repealed by the Fisheries Act 1981.

Footnotes 5 to 7, 8. Maximum penalty now £50,000 on summary conviction, a fine on indictment: Fisheries Act 1981, s.35(3), (4).

53–38   The Sea Fisheries (Regulation) Scotland Act 1895 was repealed by the Inshore Fishing (Scotland) Act 1984.

Footnote 11. See also Sea Fisheries (Shellfish) Act 1973.